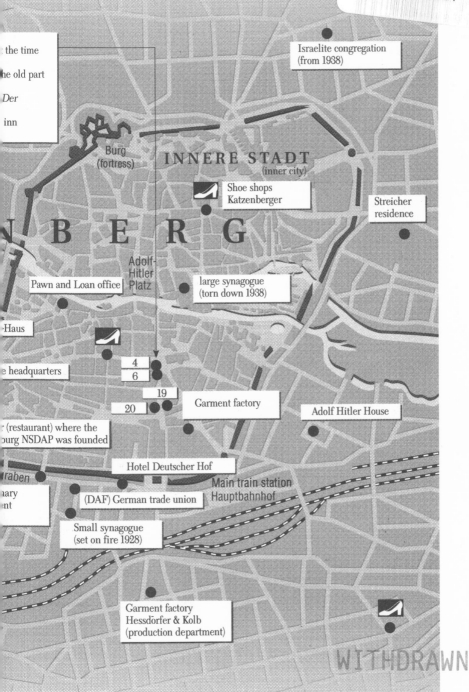

the time

he old part

Der

inn

Burg
(fortress)

INNERE STADT
(inner city)

NBERG

Shoe shops
Katzenberger

Streicher
residence

Pawn and Loan office

Adolf-
Hitler
Platz

large synagogue
(torn down 1938)

-Haus

e headquarters

4
6

19
20

Garment factory

Adolf Hitler House

(restaurant) where the
ourg NSDAP was founded

Hotel Deutscher Hof

raben

Main train station
Hauptbahnhof

aary
ent

(DAF) German trade union

Small synagogue
(set on fire 1928)

Israelite congregation
(from 1938)

Garment factory
Hessdörfer & Kolb
(production department)

THE MAIDEN
AND THE JEW

THE MAIDEN AND THE JEW

THE STORY OF A FATAL FRIENDSHIP IN NAZI GERMANY

CHRISTIANE KOHL

TRANSLATED FROM THE GERMAN
BY JOHN S. BARRETT

STEERFORTH PRESS
HANOVER, NEW HAMPSHIRE

First published in German as *Der Jude und das Mädchen* by Spiegel-Buchverlag
in Hamburg, 1997

The publisher wishes to thank the City of Nuremberg's Office for International
Relations for their support of this project.

For information about permission to reproduce
selections from this book, write to:
Steerforth Press L.C., 25 Lebanon Street
Hanover, New Hampshire 03755

Library of Congress Cataloging-in-Publication Data

Kohl, Christiane, 1954–
[Jude und das Mädchen. English]
The maiden and the jew : the story of a fatal friendship in Nazi Germany /
Christiane Kohl ; translated from the German by John S. Barrett. — 1st ed.
p. cm.
Includes bibliographical references.
ISBN 1-58642-070-4 (alk. paper)
1. Jews — Germany — Nuremberg — History — 20th century.
2. Nuremberg (Germany) — Ethnic relations. 3. Katzenberger, Leo, 1873–1942.
4. Scheffler-Seiler, Irene, 1910–1984. 5. National socialism —
Germany — Nuremberg. I. Title.
DS135.G4N85313 2004
940.53'18'092243324--DC22
2004011818

FIRST EDITION

THIS BOOK IS DEDICATED TO THE MEMORY OF
LEO KATZENBERGER

I

IRENE WAS STRIKINGLY TALL, WITH DARK, WAVY HAIR and slightly slanted
brown eyes. More than one respectable family man living in the apartment
house at 19 Spittlertorgraben stole a look at the young lady of the photography
studio. On an early summer day in 1932 she had carried her suitcases and boxes
up to the second floor and opened up her business. Her somewhat impertinent
sounding Brandenburg accent and the cheeky hats she wore imparted an excit-
ing, exotic flair to the community of Franconian apartment dwellers. A fresh
breeze had swirled up the stairwell that constantly smelled of floor wax.

Johann Mäsel, a man in his late twenties, was one of the first to subject his
new neighbor to closer scrutiny. Not that Mäsel would have been considered
a ladies' man — the skilled toolmaker, whose broad face was framed by hair
neatly parted on the side, lived with his wife and mother in an adjoining
building that opened onto the courtyard. When he was free on a Saturday,
Mäsel often looked out their kitchen window, presumably from sheer bore-
dom, and occasionally observed Irene as she walked diagonally across the
cobblestoned courtyard to the rear building that housed D. & M.
Katzenberger's Wholesale Shoe Company warehouse.

"A good-looking woman," stated the man in his testimony thirty years later, when the war was long over and the Spittlertorgraben property, including its side tract and rear building, lay in ruins. By then, no one but a few lawyers wanted to know the details of the terrible events that had led Irene to prison and Leo Katzenberger — also no stranger to Mäsel — to the guillotine. When members of the Nuremberg Department of Justice asked him about Irene in 1962, Mäsel, then in his late fifties, still clearly recalled the vivacious person with all those hats who "in my judgment as a man, was not disinclined to enjoy life."

Paul Kleylein also showed interest in the pert young lady whose uninhibited laughter echoed clear as a bell through the hallway, even during the gloomy days of the Nazi regime. Kleylein moved into the building in 1938. With his wife and three children, he lived in a three-room apartment on the first floor, in the front building, to the right. The prosthetheses maker, at that point in his late thirties, was a hard-working man, and he could generally be found at his shop, a few street corners away, producing artificial legs, back braces, and elastic stockings. But no matter how tired the family man Kleylein might be, if he met Irene in the stairwell on his way home in the evening, he enjoyed chatting with his attractive neighbor.

"Tall and pretty" is how she remained in his memory. "You just couldn't be mad at her," he stated to investigators in 1962. But she was also a woman who, according to Kleylein, "appeared available with regard to sex." His wife, Betty, a resolute hausfrau with fiery red hair, had her own opinion of the attractive neighbor. She looked upon Irene as "a little tramp."

Johann Heilmann lived on the attic floor with his wife and two daughters. A family photo shows him to be a man of rather small stature with strikingly large ears. Trained as a carpenter, he was employed as a jack-of-all-trades in the shoe warehouses behind the apartment building. Heilmann stacked shoe cartons, parked the firm's Hanomag truck in the courtyard, and delivered stock to the shoe stores in the vicinity. To his neighbors, he bragged that he knew everything that went on around the courtyard, and Irene, the single woman living in the front building, was considered an especially interesting subject for gossip.

Soon after Irene moved in, Heilmann announced to his curious fellow tenants that the young woman frequently received male visitors. Heilmann even claimed to have seen the owner of the property and of the wholesale shoe business based there, Leo Katzenberger, elegantly dressed as usual in one of his dark wool suits, in front of Irene's apartment door. This observation was deemed as particularly important in this gossipy community because Katzenberger was a Jew. Heilmann wasn't inclined to believe that the Jewish businessman was merely collecting the rent from the pretty Aryan photographer; many years later he said, "They certainly weren't just playing *Mensch ärgere Dich nicht!*"*

*Mensch ärgere Dich nicht!: a board game similar to Parcheesi. —Trans.

2

WHEN IRENE FIRST MET LEO KATZENBERGER, in 1928, she was a young thing of eighteen. She lived in Guben, east of Berlin, but was visiting her older sister Hertha, who had started a photography studio in Nuremberg, in the apartment house owned by Katzenberger. Hertha was an aquantaince of Katzenberger's, but that didn't interest the curious neighbours. The times were different and the two sisters could scarcely have resembled each other less: Hertha was short, not particularly pretty, and industrious as a bee. Irene — tall, slender, and attractive — liked to behave extravagantly and had her eyes on things more fun than school or a job. "You sort of had the feeling," said a former neighbor from Guben, "that she'd do well with men."

Katzenberger had soon created a friendship with the girls' father, Oskar Scheffler. On a business trip in 1932 he visited the Scheffler's handsome brick villa on the bank of the Neisse River. The family led a happy life in a house that was always open. "Everyone was welcome there," said the former neighbor, recalling her childhood days. "Mother Scheffler took us all under her wing." Father Scheffler, a retired accountant, was active in one of the Freemasons' lodges that were soon to be banned by the Nazis. According to rumors that made the rounds later, the mother, whose family name was Friedländer, was of Jewish descent.

Presumably it was during that visit to Guben in 1932 that Herr Scheffler took the businessman Katzenberger aside, sat down, lit up a big cigar, and steered the conversation toward his daughter Irene. Little I, as he called his favorite daughter, hadn't accomplished very much — she'd left high school before graduating and after barely a year had broken off the study of professional photography that she'd begun at the Leipzig Academy of Graphic Arts.

Little I had since turned twenty-two and was at the point where she had to think about earning a living. Father Scheffler had arranged for Hertha to give Irene her Nuremberg studio so that the younger sister would finally get some work experience. But leaving Irene, the apple of his eye, to her own devices in far away Nuremberg did not sit well with the accountant, and so he asked his friend, the shoe magnate Katzenberger, if he would keep a fatherly eye on the high-spirited young woman.

At the time, Katzenberger was a staid gentleman of nearly fifty-nine years. As a young man, he'd lived in Paris, which accounted for a certain cosmopolitan aura that surrounded him, even in Nuremberg. He wore custom tailored three-piece suits, and on his rotund abdomen gleamed the gold chain of a heavy pocket watch. When he went on business trips, Katzenberger was driven around in a luxurious Chrysler Model 66 limousine, the sight of which was sure to incite envy among the auto enthusiasts of those days. He always stayed at the best hotels and enjoyed the best food. And he liked to play the cavalier when it came to pretty women.

"He was a bit of a *bon vivant*," says Marga Weglein, a niece by marriage who later emigrated to America. Her husband, Sally Weglein, often went on business trips with "Uncle Leo," as Lehmann Katzenberger was known in his rather extensive family. "Uncle Leo was something of a model for my husband," Marga observed. "Sally always said his uncle taught him how to live."

In 1929 there were still 10,200 Jews living in the Franconian metropolis of Nuremberg. The Nuremberg Jewish community was the largest in the Reich after Berlin, Frankfurt, and Leipzig, and the city was home to one of the richest of the German congregations, the Israelitische Kultusgemeinde, hereafter referred to as the congregations. In the congregations' administration building the officers took their places in heavy, leather-upholstered chairs. The walls were covered with silk paper, and the library contained costly volumes of Hebraica.

Leo Katzenberger had served on the congregational council since 1925, and in April 1932 the members once again unanimously elected him deputy vice chairman. When Chaim Weizman, then chairman of the World Zionist Organization and later the first president of Israel, visited Nuremberg, the congregation asked Leo to hold the reception at his mansion on Praterstrasse.

Katzenberger was a devout man, an Orthodox Jew who held strictly to the old religious traditions and attended a smaller synagogue on Essenwein-strasse in Nuremberg. He had made a name for himself as an effective nego-tiator in the early 1920s when, after two years of difficult deliberations, the more conservative organization Adas Israel — of which Katzenberger was also a member — was induced to merge with the congregations, which had a more liberal theological orientation. With his open, cosmopolitan ways, Katzenberger proved a skilled mediator between the disparate factions. He also had good connections in political circles; indeed, according to the recol-lections of his daughter Lilo, he even maintained friendly contact with Benno Martin, who became Nuremberg's police commissioner. The leader of Franconian's malicious anti-Semitic campaign, the Gauleiter Julius Streicher, was his bitter enemy.

Leo Katzenberger also held the reins of the D. & M. Katzenberger Wholesale Shoe Company, which was headquartered behind the Spittlertorgraben apartments. The firm was founded by his two younger brothers, David and Max, but trade began to flourish when Leo, a confident businessman, joined forces with them. Soon the brothers expanded their com-pany, Shoe Sales en Gros, into the retail market and acquired a chain of shoe stores in Bavaria, Hesse, and Thuringia. Toward the end of the 1920s they were running some thirty branches, and their footwear firm was considered one of the largest in southern Germany. In Nuremberg the brothers con-trolled three shoe stores. The one located on Karolinenstrasse, still a fashion-able shopping street today, had seven show windows and numbered among the most beautiful shops in the city. The Nuremberg central office's yearly sales figures amounted to nearly three million Reichsmarks.

The firm's headquarters was directly around the corner from the Plärrer, a spacious, noisy square, which at that time was already a central traffic junc-tion and the entry point to the old section of the city. Every day trolleys bat-tled with constantly increasing automobile traffic. More than a dozen local and longer-distance streetcars ran through the Plärrer, contributing the majority of the noise; the automobiles that threaded their way between them added their low-pitched rumbling. In the middle of the busy crossing a huge automat squeaked as it did its duty: a passerby inserted a few coins, pulled a lever, and out popped a sandwich.

From the apartment house on Spittlertorgraben it was just a few steps to that modern wonder on the Plärrer, and just a few steps to the medieval old city, which began behind the imposing wall on the opposite side of the street. But, from the Katzenbergers' offices in the property's rear building, the warehouse, one looked out over the lower-lying terrain of Rosenau Park, an attractive area with big, old trees framing a small pond. The part of the building that housed storerooms and the shipping department, with a modern freight elevator connecting the various warehousing spaces, opened onto the courtyard.

The brothers had divided the areas of responsibility among themselves. Max and David Katzenberger looked after the technical aspects, the inventory, and the business details. Leo was in charge of finances, kept tabs on the turnover in the outlets, and negotiated purchase prices with shoe manufacturers. The firm had nearly 150 employees, twenty of them at this central office in Nuremberg.

Margarete Hölzel presided over the reception room. A spinsterly woman of thirty-eight who meticulously typed out columns of numbers, Fräulein Hölzel dealt with the bookkeeping and the monthly rental payments, so she knew each of the tenants in the front building. Behind, in the warehousing area, the Jewish worker Otto Feuchtwanger stacked shoe cartons beside the Aryan Johann Heilmann and several other warehouse clerks. The firm employed a number of Jews, tending to prefer those who were Orthodox. Heilmann, the company's jack-of-all-trades, was sometimes a little slow figuring things out. Because of this his Jewish coworkers often had him jumping to their tune. As Feuchtwanger told it, "Sometimes he may have grumbled a little at our orders."

Two nephews of the extensive Katzenberger clan also occupied executive positions in the business. Sally Weglein was constantly on the road visiting the various branch outlets. His brother Leo Weglein was in charge of the bookkeeping and was the only member of the family who eventually occupied an apartment in the building facing Spittlertorgraben.

Toward the end of 1932 Leo Weglein lived with his wife and their son, Walter, in an apartment in the neighborhood behind the main railroad station. In the square in front of their house, the Nazis and the Communists frequently became involved in violent confrontations, even exchanging gunfire. When a stray bullet found its way into two-year-old Walter's room, the

Wegleins finally had enough. "My parents were suddenly confronted by fear," says Walter today, "and they just wanted to get away." And so the Wegleins moved into the *belle etage* of the Katzenberger building.

The five-story building at 19 Spittlertorgraben, built around 1810, had a comparatively plain facade of light-colored stucco. The entry hall, with its beige Solnhofen tiles, was kept sparkling clean by the housewives; the wooden staircase was regularly waxed and polished. On the third floor lived the head of the district court, Dr. Heidner, and one floor above him the salesman Wolfgang Östreicher and his wife, who usually had several lodgers. In the attic, Johann Heilmann had constructed a small apartment, which did not have a private toilet. Now and again, Heilmann could be seen carrying a coal scuttle up to the fifth floor while his little daughter Margarete hopped nimbly down the polished stairs to get away from her stern mother. She would shyly squeeze by the door of the confectionery shop, temporarily housed in rented space in the front of the first floor, or slip across the courtyard to the low side building that was originally a carriage house but which now provided lodgings for the Mäsel family. The tiny kitchen here was presided over by Mother Mäsel, a stout matron with a sour expression.

Irene fluttered into this world, with its ever-present smell of floor polish, like a brightly colored butterfly. The young photographer wanted more out of life than did the women who hung their featherbeds out of the windows to air them out early each morning, then washed dishes, polished stoves, and straightened crocheted doilies in living rooms. Instead of tying on an apron, Irene preferred to wear a striking hat. Instead of spending hours in her studio — which also served as her apartment — waiting for customers, she would rather stroll along the shopping streets in the old city. And when she saw a pretty dress or a blouse that suited her, she was frequently unable to resist and bought whatever it was, on credit if necessary.

Irene occasionally visited the rear building where Katzenberger had his office. In the beginning, she didn't know a soul in the city except for the old friend of her father's. She also had a penchant for chic shoes, so she often returned home carrying a shoe box. The young woman could hardly have imagined the venomous attention that was directed at the progress of those shoe boxes across the courtyard. Without a second thought, Irene would climb into the elegant Chrysler, driven by the Katzenbergers' chauffeur, Wilhelm Fabro. Entranced by everything that seemed modern and hungry for anything that smacked of luxury, she loved to ride along in the classy automobile.

Leo Katzenberger was pleased to have such pretty company. On his business trips the aging *bon vivant* thoroughly enjoyed looking at women from his car, a fact Fabro had noticed. Katzenberger was flattered by the straightforward affection Irene directed toward him. Whenever he made her a gift of pralines or cigarettes, Irene thanked him effusively. If he invited her along on an afternoon business trip to Frankfurt or Regensburg, she joyfully threw her arms around his neck.

In those early days, Irene's business was not going well and it is totally feasible that Katzenberger wanted to help her find work during these trips. But there was just not enough money to be earned from photos of the Katzenberger stores or views of other cities. In Nuremberg there was demand for wedding, event, and portrait photographers, but there was also a lot of competition. A photo shop opened right around the corner on the Plärrer and, in addition, several shops could be found in the nearby streets of the old city. Irene had the disadvantage of being on the second floor, and so had few walk-in customers. As if that weren't enough, her studio and apartment, with its six spacious rooms, was much too large; she felt lost in them and could barely scrape together the monthly rent of two hundred Reichsmarks.

Getting by with little money was something the pampered favorite of Oskar Scheffler had never learned to do. Soon Irene was slipping out of one tight spot and into another. On occasion, an expensive dress she just had to have was repossessed, or she had to pawn her camera.

One of her main problems was the rent, so Katzenberger found her cheaper quarters. On the ground floor to the left, a three-room apartment, exactly the right size, had just been vacated. That the Mäsels could look directly into her future living room from the small side building did not disturb Irene, and after living in the upstairs apartment for only a few months, she moved downstairs. The apartment on the second floor was taken over by Katzenberger's nephew Leo Weglein, so the shoe dealer's family derived some benefit from Irene's move. Her financial distress, however, was not completely alleviated by the lower rent of around sixty-three marks. For that reason, Katzenberger sometimes slipped her small sums of money. He also gave Irene twenty marks to redeem a camera she had pawned. In order to bring customers to the young photographer, Leo encouraged his two married daughters, Käthe and Lilo, to have portraits made with their children. And one day, decked out in pin-striped suit as befit his station, he sat for a photograph himself.

3

THE PHOTOGRAPH IRENE TOOK REVEALS A DIGNIFIED, older gentleman with a goatee and a pocket handkerchief. Obviously a prosperous entrepreneur who appears happy with himself and the world, he holds a big cigar in his right hand. The picture was made nearly seventy years ago; a scrawled signature on the lower right-hand border identifies the photographer as Scheffler. The photo has become somewhat faded after many years in Lilo's home in Israel. She and her older sister Käthe had emigrated from Germany a few years after Hitler came to power. Yellowed editions of Zuckmayer's works, *Knaur's Encyclopedia,* and a few photos that she keeps in her old-fashioned secretary are about all she'd been able to carry to safety. "Father was a smart man," she says, "but he didn't believe things would turn out the way they did."

In Nuremberg, Lilo had known Irene only slightly. They'd once met in the street when a troop of SA rabble-rousers marched through the old city bellowing "Heil Hitler!" at all passersby and shouting anti-Semitic slogans. Fearing that she would be accosted, Lilo took refuge in an entryway until the Brownshirts had tramped by. As she reemerged onto the street, she noticed that Irene, too, had made herself inconspicuous by slipping into a corner. The two women, nearly the same age, exchanged knowing glances. "From then on I was sympathetic toward her," says Lilo.

Long before 1933, gangs of Brownshirts could be extremely unpleasant to Jewish citizens in Nuremberg. They harassed nurses for wearing a Jewish charity organization pin on their blouses, accosted Jewish worshipers in front of the large synagogue on Hans Sachs Platz, and attacked individuals at night. Marching Nazi mobs crisscrossed the countryside. "In Nuremberg and Franconia," noted the congregations' secretary, Bernhard Kolb, "conditions had gotten so bad that they were hardly equaled in any other district of the German Reich." Germany stood on the threshold of Nazi dictatorship. Nuremberg, the home of gingerbread bakers and pencil makers, marched in the front ranks.

When it lay in ruins in 1945, American newspapers called the city on the Pegnitz River "the sacred shrine of Nazism." Indeed, high-level Nazis had always favored the old mercantile center, and its inhabitants flocked to the National Socialists in droves. Long before coming to power, Adolf Hitler was a frequent guest in the city. In the fall of 1923 he and his comrade-in-arms, Julius Streicher, celebrated Deutschen Tag (German Day) in Nuremberg's market square amid nationalistic brouhaha, with war veterans and party sympathizers filing by the self-proclaimed Führer for hours on end. In 1927 the Nazis held their first Reichsparteitag (Party Rally) in Nuremberg. Hitler's headquarters were next to the opera house, in the Hotel Deutscher Hof. When he looked out of his suite's windows the old city lay at his feet — a German idyll straight out of a National Socialist picturebook.

The medieval city walls, with their stout towers of sandstone blocks, enclosed a cityscape of sway-backed red tile roofs that looked as if they had been created by a master confectioner. Along the crooked, cobblestoned alleys the steep-gabled, half-timbered houses leaned against each other like close friends; right next to them the pastel-colored sandstone facades of early patrician houses stood out proudly with their decorative oriel windows, artistically carved stone garlands, heavy oak portals, and daringly constructed roof lines. And over all of that, delicate as spun sugar, floated a white veil of smoke from the tiny chimney pots.

The Nazis considered Nuremberg the "Reich's treasure chest," the "original German city." Many of its citizens, however, felt torn between the new age and tradition. The rapidly growing industrial zones, ever larger and constantly more extensively mechanized, signified a threat to many. The new department stores that were going up generated not only the wish to buy, but envy and fear for one's existence as well. Around the picturesque old city, a broad belt of factories and smoke stacks had long been established. The workers' neighborhoods were in front of the gates of heavy-equipment firms, including MAN, Siemens, and AEG. Nearly a third of these inhabitants were out of work in 1932; many of the artisans and small shopkeepers in the narrow streets of the old city had lost their businesses to the winds of inflation. The Franconian capital offered fertile ground for anti-Semitic rabble-rousing.

In earlier centuries, Nuremberg had been a proud mercantile center and a Freie Reichsstadt (Free Imperial City). The city and its leading patrician families were not forced to pay tribute to some provincial princeling, but were subjects of the emperor alone. Famous artists, such as Albrecht Dürer, and the troubadour poet Hans Sachs had been active in Nuremberg. But the golden age was long gone. Toward the end of the nineteenth century the city had rapidly developed into an industrial center where machinery, vehicles, and tin toys were produced. The hop trade also flourished. But no noteworthy cultural or political impulse originated in Nuremberg — proud independence had turned into stuffy provincialism. Even before World War I, Nuremberg was considered a bastion of anti-Semitism. In the spring of 1923 the atmosphere was so poisoned that during Passover, members of the Israelite congregations stood guard in the larger synagogue night after night for an entire week, fearing attack.

The Ludwigstorzwinger was a tavern known for its hearty fare. Tucked away behind the thick walls of an old tower, it was right around the corner from 19 Spittlertorgraben. On October 20, 1922, a coterie of older party members and determined young men from the murky regions of the nationalist far-right came together to found the Nuremberg Regional Group of the National Socialist Party. Julius Streicher, a 37-year-old teacher, was elected chairman of the organization. A year later, Streicher, a bald-headed gnome in black boots, was marching in the front line next to Adolf Hitler when he attempted the Munich Putsch of 1923.

The small group from the Ludwigstorzwinger quickly won new recruits and by 1924 the Streicher Panel was elected to the Nuremberg city council, filling six of the fifty seats. By the end of the 1920s, the number of votes cast in the province for the Nazi Party was always several percentage points higher than in the rest of the Reich. The Social Democrats still maintained their majority in the industrial center, however, and the Communists were strong as well. There were often violent political confrontations: during party meetings brawls were not out of the ordinary, and there was even the occasional exchange of gunfire in the streets. In the propaganda tract titled *Der Stürmer* (The Storm Trooper), which Streicher began publishing in 1923, he pounded anti-Semitic views into the heads of his readers week after week. When the election campaign got underway in 1932, he had posters made up with one simple, venomous assertion: DIE JUDEN SIND UNSER UNGLÜCK (The Jews Are Our Misfortune).

On January, 30, 1933, Hitler assumed power in the chancellery in Berlin. Streicher's followers in Nuremberg decided that they were in control as well. The elections for the Reichstag followed on March 5, and the Nazis gained the majority. Bavaria was forced to toe the party line, a victory that the Nuremberg Nazis celebrated on March 9, 1933. Activists and sympathizers alike assembled on the Deutschherrenwiese, the German Lords' Field. People in street clothes could be seen next to SA men in their light brown uniforms, Hitler Youth in their dark blue shorts, members of the National Socialist Girls' Organization in their flowing skirts, and then of course, flag after flag.

Toward three o'clock, the procession began to move; the Nazi motorcycle cavalcade was followed by the SA band. "These are the days when German history is being made," Streicher roared at the crowd. The church bells rang at St. Sebald and St. Lorenz, the two splendid Protestant houses of worship in the old city; three swastika flags were raised, and the crowd sang the Horst Wessel song. The same ceremony was repeated shortly afterward at the Kaiserburg, the old imperial castle. The Nazis had come to power in Nuremberg.

"From that time on," wrote Bernard Kolb in his memoirs, "the Jews in Nuremberg and Franconia literally feared for their lives. They were outlawed, at anyone's mercy." In the succeeding years Kolb was summoned to Gestapo headquarters almost daily; the Nazis chose him to carry their orders to the congregations.

Many rabbis and leaders of the congregations were unable to recognize the approaching danger. Even Katzenberger, whose political attitude tended to be conservative, was among those who believed in the beginning that the Nazis would "be out in just a few weeks," his daughter Lilo remembers. He felt, as did many of his Jewish contemporaries, that he was a German citizen of the Jewish faith — Franconia was his home. Many underestimated the potential of the new rulers. The left-liberal mayor of Nuremberg, Hermann Luppe, was said to have remarked condescendingly in February 1933, "We worked under the red flag for several weeks in 1918, so now we'll just have to work under the swastika flag for a few weeks until the scare is over." A month later, Luppe had to leave the city hurriedly in order to avoid arrest — the "scare" was just getting started.

At Nuremberg's city hall the new age began with shuffling chairs. By the time of the city council's first meeting following its Gleichschaltung, or Coordination — a euphemism for being forced into line — the Social Democratic members were no longer allowed into the venerable, wood-paneled council chamber. Streicher threatened to use his whip to keep them out of the building if they tried to enter. His vassal, Willy Liebel, the thirty-five-year-old son of a printing company owner, was named mayor. He immediately set out to purge the city administration of Jews and people of undesirable political leanings. Whether schoolteacher or streetcar conductor, hospital physician or official at the property tax office, Jewish municipal employees had to leave their posts immediately. By August, 108 had been dismissed; the legal basis was provided by the federal Law Governing the Reconfiguration of the Civil Service passed by the Nazis in April 1933.

In the schools, where there were a good many Nazi supporters among the teaching personnel, the change was also immediately noticeable. Fritz Söltner, later the son-in-law of the storeroom clerk Heilmann, recalls that when he was in first grade he had to yell "Heil Hitler!" before the class began. Instead of the customary textbooks, some of Söltner's teachers were now pulling copies of *Der Stürmer* out of their pockets. In gym class, Herbert Kolb, son of Bernard, spent most of the time marching. Herbert was an athletic young boy, but during those new drills he always had to bring up the rear. "The one who gave the commands was never Jewish." He left school a few years later. The Aryan Fritz Söltner, six years younger than Kolb, later joined the Hitler Youth.

Soon Jews were being marginalized throughout Nuremberg, and always a little more thoroughly than anywhere else. The city decreed that Jews would no longer be admitted to the swimming pools in the municipal bath houses. Those who had no facilities at home would only be permitted to use the "tub and shower baths in municipal bath houses" — if they could stand the insults from the other users. Jewish artisans who had rented space from the city were forced out between one day and the next. Jewish physicians were no longer permitted to perform surgery in municipal clinics. Leading public organizations and clubs forced their Jewish members out. For instance, in March 1933, the Jewish members on the board of directors of the Chamber of Commerce and Industry had to leave office, as did those in the management of Nuremberg Emergency Aid, a local charity; even among the directors of the Natural History Society the order was "Out with the Jews!" The chairmen of Nuremberg industrial and cultural organizations who were Jewish had to resign. The director of the art museum was suspended; the dance and gymnastics club Rot-Weiss got rid of its Jewish dancers. Approximately half of Nuremberg's lawyers were Jews, but from that point on, the only ones permitted to practice were those who had served in the First World War or who had opened their offices before 1914. The Nazi bureaucrats cooked up a similarly absurd ruling for Jewish physicians: only those who served as front line physicians or in military hospitals could continue to see patients on health insurance plans; other doctors had to withdraw.

The Nazis could rather quickly force Jewish civil servants, lawyers, and physicians from their professions by either dismissing them directly or by withholding their licenses. It was somewhat more difficult to restrict the Jewish business community. The Nuremberg Nazis therefore depended on the two instruments they knew how to use best: mobilization of the masses and violence.

On the evening of March 31, 1933, Nuremberg's marketplace, soon to be renamed Adolf Hitler Platz, saw the usual crowd assembling to hear the proclamations — brown- and black-uniformed men, Hitler Youth, members of the veterans' organizations, girls and boys from the gymnastics and sports clubs, and thousands of other "compatriots" who had joined the marching order. On the following day, a Saturday, at ten o'clock in the morning, thousands of SA and SS men posted themselves in front of Jewish businesses. Their message was simple: No one should buy from Jews. "Throngs of curiosity seekers made their way through the city," reads one report of that day, "coming to a halt and forming large crowds in front of the department stores." If individuals dared to enter a store they faced loud boos and verbal insults as they left. SA men had taken up their spread-legged stance in front of the Katzenberger's shoe stores on Karolinenstrasse, Theresienplatz, and Wölkernstrasse. Several placards featured Streicher's favorite slogan: The Jews Are Our Misfortune.

Boycotts had been organized throughout the entire Reich; responsibility lay with Julius Streicher, whom Hitler had named Leiter des Zentralkomitees zur Abwehr der jüdischen Greuel- und Boykotthetze.* It was a frontal assault on the Jewish business community, but again the congregations only timidly set about to protect themselves. A conciliatory article appeared in the newsletter of the Nuremberg-Fürth congregations in which the writer referred to Jewish blood shed for Germany in the First World War and reported on the efforts of Jews abroad to tone down international criticism of the Hitler regime, nominally the cause for the boycotts. Streicher, however, thought up another special slap in the face for his Franconian dominions: after the boycott was over, he demanded that the congregations in Nuremberg and Fürth repay the cost of feeding the SA men and other expenses incurred during the boycott.

For several weeks Streicher focused directly on the Katzenbergers' shoe business. In February 1933 *Der Stürmer* came out with an article urging people not to buy anything from the "Katzenberger Shoe-Jews." In its overheated report, the periodical "revealed" that behind the Aryan-sounding Springmann's Shoe Stores were, in fact, "the Jews Max, David, and Leo Katzenberger." Those three businessmen, *Der Stürmer* continued, deliberately stirring up the envy of its readers, "are making buckets of money. Each one of them has a lordly apartment in a palatial villa." They only looked in on their stores "now and then"; the real work was done "by German sales ladies." However, when it came to destroying non-Jewish competition, "no method was too base" for putting their unwanted rivals out of business. Then the Streicher paper made an unconcealed threat: "The days of supremacy" were numbered; "housecleaning on a large scale" was going to start any moment. The businessman Leo Katzenberger, in particular, would "receive the special attentions of the Nuremberg National Socialists." *Der Stürmer* itself would "deal with him, in short order."

At that point, *DerStürmer* had a circulation of over one hundred thousand copies, and it could be found anywhere in the Reich. The article had the potential to do severe damage to the Katzenbergers' business. What *Der Stürmer* did not know, or bother to investigate or disclose, was that Springmann, from whom Leo Katzenberger had purchased the chain, was herself a Jew.

---

*This committee's title is very difficult to translate. Its purpose, however, was clear: To organize and justify actions taken against Jewish businesses. It was a firmly held Nazi belief that international criticism against the regime was propagated by German Jewish businesses through their international business contacts. —Trans.

The article had been instigated by the business manager of a competing shoe store who had presumably, as was so often the case, turned to *Der Stürmer* for help. Streicher's paper had become a mouthpiece for social envy and a bulletin board for informants. The rival manager-owner had been an employee of the Katzenberger firm who had purchased a branch store in the center of Nuremberg, but apparently had not been very successful. The Katzenbergers, well aware of modern advertising methods, had made it clear through mass mailings that the store no longer belonged to the Springmann Group — which didn't sit well with the new owner of the business, who wanted to profit from the company's good reputation.

Leo Katzenberger must have been enraged when he read the article. He usually thought things over carefully before acting, but in this case he immediately instigated a lawsuit for slander. One evening a short time later, the old gentleman came home beaming with delight. "Guess what, Lilo? I won the suit against Streicher," he told his favorite daughter.

"Cold shivers ran down my back," recalls the old woman now, and she unconsciously hunches her shoulders together as if she still feels a chill.

In Nuremberg, Jewish citizens were being arrested more and more frequently and taken to the newly constructed concentration camp at Dachau, one of the first that the Nazis built in the Reich. Sometimes relatives received an inmate's bloody clothing for cleaning and more often than not, Kolb, in his role as business manager of the congregations, would have to send a hearse to the camp. Kolb always had the coffins opened when they arrived in Nuremberg. When he received the body of twenty-one-year-old student Arthur Kahn, a distant relative of his, he commissioned a Jewish physician to perform a postmortem. Kolb committed the findings to his computerlike memory: "Penetrating gunshot wound to the head with destruction of portions of the base of the brain and adjacent medulla, grazing bullet wounds of the right upper arm and right side of the chest, penetrating soft-tissue gunshot wound of the upper right thigh." The death certificate of Arthur Kahn, issued on April 14, 1933, mentions paralysis of the brain caused by penetrating gunshot wound to the head.

4

THE SA MEN TOOK KATZENBERGER AWAY early on the morning of July 20, 1933. In his pajamas, unwashed and uncombed, he was pushed down the stairs and forced into a delivery truck already tightly packed with other older gentlemen. Many were members of the international lodge B'nai B'rith, to which the Katzenberger brothers belonged. Only the most reputable and well-off men belonged to the lodge, among them respected lawyers, professors, and industrialists. In accordance with its precepts, they had all pledged themselves to be "unconditionally honorable in their professional dealings and private lives" and "true sons and citizens of their fatherland."

Nearly three hundred leading figures of the Nuremberg Jewish community were driven out of their houses that day by Brownshirts under the command of an SA squad leader and loaded in delivery vans like cattle. They were driven to a remote stadium to the south of the city, where they were given senseless tasks, such as loading and unloading bricks. They were forced to tear out tufts of grass with their teeth and lick dog feces lying on the ground. Those who could not bring themselves to be humiliated were beaten bloody by club-swinging Nazi tormentors.

It was a beastly hot day. Toward evening, after hours of degradation and mistreatment, the men were released on the condition that they keep quiet about their terrible ordeal. Leo Katzenberger returned home panting and sweating. Surviving the day must have seemed like a miracle to him, since he had suffered from a heart condition for years. "He never breathed a word to his family," reported Marga Weglein about "the affair of the grass stains." And little about the other horrible events currently taking place in the streets was allowed into the beautiful sandstone villa on Praterstrasse where he lived with his family. Perhaps Katzenberger still hoped the terror would soon be over; perhaps he wanted to keep the anxiety-inducing news far away from his loved ones. "There was little talk," says his daughter Lilo, "about politics at home."

In the bay window of the dining room stood a sturdy club chair where Katzenberger habitually took his midday rest with coffee and the newspaper. Absolute quiet was observed in the house; the grandchildren had to sneak across the parquet floors on tiptoe. Katzenberger had suffered a severe heart attack when he was fifty, and everyone was concerned about his health. Because of his heart trouble, he was forced to observe a strict diet; but he refused to give up his cigars.

In the summer, he liked to have his coffee served in the garden, where a pretty fountain babbled soothingly, and his favorite reclining chair sat beneath a sun umbrella. "I always got the sugar cube that came with the coffee," remembers Lilo. But for some time now, the yelling of the SA men who occupied a property in the neighborhood had been intermittently carrying over into the Katzenbergers' garden. The merchant and his family could even see the back of Nuremberg's SA headquarters.

Praterstrasse, scarcely three hundred yards from the Katzenbergers' offices, was located in one of the distinguished districts of the city, where one splendid villa stood next to another. Their family home, Lilo says ecstatically, "was far and away the most beautiful house." A lively ensemble of little neo-Baroque towers and bay windows flanked by columns adorned the sandstone facade, which also featured pointed neo-Gothic windows with artistically decorated sills. The interior of the building was so spacious that it had previously housed a private women's clinic. Max and Leo Katzenberger purchased the house in the spring of 1918 for 115,000 Reichsmarks.

Max lived on the first floor with his wife and daughter; Leo occupied the second and third floors with his family. The apartments were comfortably furnished. In Max's there was a Moorish-style living room and two kitchens — kosher cooking requires strict separation of meat and milk products. Leo's extensive apartment included guest rooms and maids' quarters, bedrooms for the family members, a large entry hall with reception room, and living and dining rooms. Claire Katzenberger, Leo's wife, was a good-looking though rather imposing woman who had a reputation for being strict and meticulous. When she scolded someone, her voice would occasionally carry down to the first floor. Max's wife, also named Claire, was petite and timid in comparison and was hence known within the family as "little Claire."

The floors in the living areas in Leo's apartment were covered with expensive rugs; in the hall stood a beautiful old secretary. There was a piano, and a library with valuable historical tomes, encyclopedias, and volumes of art history. The showpiece, however, was the dining salon. From the ceiling of the large room, which was accented by attractive bay windows and niches, hung a gigantic chandelier and beneath it a long table with fifteen chairs. Valuable oil paintings adorned the walls and there was always a bouquet of fresh flowers on the buffet; Leo frequently brought flowers home with him.

A central steam-heating system warmed the building during the winter; the furnace in the basement was stoked twice daily by Heilmann, who came over from the factory warehouse. Heilmann knew the housemaid Elise quite well — she'd gotten him the job at Katzenbergers'. One day at the end of the 1920s, recalls Lilo, Elise had complained to Leo Katzenberger that a relative of hers had lost his job. "So, of course, he hired the man," says Lilo, "even though he was illiterate and not the smartest person in the world." Since the man didn't have a decent place to live, Katzenberger offered him attic space and so, sometime in 1929, Johann Heilmann moved into the apartment house on Spittlertorgraben.

Katzenberger donated considerable sums to social agencies and supported families in financial distress. "Whenever someone got into trouble," reports Lilo, "it was natural for him to help." His involvement in charitable activities reflected the rules and obligations of the B'nai B'rith lodge. Founded by a German immigrant in New York in 1843, the declared purpose of the lodge was to promulgate humane activities. In order to spread their ideas further, the American lodge brothers built schools and libraries. In Europe, other organizations soon merged with B'nai B'rith. In Nuremberg these were the Maimonides and Jacob Hertz lodges. Their members had taken vows to maintain "propriety in outward appearance" and "modesty in actions." They swore to be "ready to support institutions and charitable activities for the common good," and to "hold in esteem laws and activities reflecting a genuinely patriotic attitude."

The lodge brothers of B'nai B'rith, in keeping with their principles, opposed the growing hostility toward Jews and worked to "secure recognition for Jews in the community at large." For that reason, all hostility was discouraged during lodge meetings, and political debates or "partisan religious discussions" were not permitted. Instead, the members wished to present "a phalanx of honorable, intelligent, and cultured Jews" who would commit themselves to uphold the ideals of humanity, brotherly love, and justice. Following the humiliation of July 1933, the lodge brothers themselves were not, of course, the recipients of any such justice. The Jewish community did indeed lodge legal complaints concerning the "grass stain" incident; however the proceedings were canceled since the new Bavarian regime led by Hitler had at that very time declared an amnesty for offenses with a political basis.

Now denunciations against the Jews were occurring daily in Nuremberg and elsewhere. Employees with National Socialist sympathies who worked for Jewish businesses wrote out page-long reports and sent them, labeled "strictly personal," to Gauleiter Streicher.* At the Gundelfinger iron and steel firm, informers smeared their foreman because he had not shown sufficient favoritism toward Nazis working for the firm and had failed to sign his business letters "Heil Hitler." The Jewish factory owner Kurt Aufochs was taken to Adolf Hitler House on Marienplatz by SA men because of reports that he had improperly hung portraits of Hitler that had been recently ordered displayed in all places of business. Instead of putting them up in the firm's offices or on the factory floor, Aufochs had taken the liberty of using them to decorate the bathrooms. Thanks to a bit of luck, he was allowed to go free, according to his report, after he'd sat in Hitler House's cellar for several hours. When he walked into his business office again, he found his bookkeeper making herself comfortable in his easy chair.

In the cellar of "Brown House," as the Nuremberg Nazi headquarters on Marienplatz was colloquially known, there was a windowless room. It was there that Justin Hessdörfer, co-owner of the Nuremberg men's clothing factory Hessdörfer & Kolb and relative of Bernhard Kolb, was incarcerated

---

*Gauleiter: the head of an administrative party district during the Nazi regime. —Trans.

during the summer of 1933. The factory produced upscale men's suits of dark fabrics, in pinstripe or in the muted glen plaids that were all the rage at that time. Since this was Bavaria, jackets and knickers in the various peasant styles were also produced. For the trousers, the firm had a supply of special yellowish brown fabric stored in large bales.

That fabric was the *corpus delecti*. An apprentice reported to Adolf Hitler House that Hessdörfer & Kolb had huge quantities of the brown cloth that could be used to produce SA uniforms, but instead they were using it to make peasant costumes. After the Nazis ascended to power, droves of sympathizers joined the party. And the paramilitary wing, the SA, had an even larger enrollment after the National Socialists declared a temporary suspension of registration on May 1, 1933. From January 1933 to June 1934, the ranks of SA members swelled from six hundred thousand to 4.5 million. Clothing factories were under tremendous pressure to turn out brown uniforms and were bound to experience shortages of supplies. Following Hessdörfer's denunciation, SA men showed up in the assembly rooms of Hessdörfer & Kolb and confiscated the cloth.

Hessdörfer was ordered to appear at the Brown House, where he was so abused and beaten that he decided to emigrate immediately. Several of the older men who, like Leo Katzenberger, had been subjected to the humiliations of July 1933 also emigrated. Katzenberger, however, acted as if nothing had happened — and stayed.

In the fall of 1933, a procession reminiscent of those held during the medieval inquisitions moved through the romantic, cobblestoned streets of Nuremberg. Strange-looking figures with shaved heads were pulled along by ropes like circus animals; from their necks dangled crude placards with big letters. On closer inspection passersby were able to recognize that the fearfully mistreated creatures were girls and young women whose "Aryan-ness" was questioned by the insanely racist Streicher, who was punishing them because they had allegedly had relationships with Jewish men. Information about such relationships could only have come from informants. The head of the Franconian Nazis had declared an open spying season on Nuremberg's lovers' lanes and other cozy places.

In the apartment house at Spittlertorgraben, things seemed to be continuing as usual. The housewives waxed and polished the steps, and Heilmann carried up his coal. His little daughter Marga now had a playmate with whom she could run around in the courtyard — little Walter Weglein from the second floor, a tyke of three years. The elder Wegleins were friendly with the Heilmann family as well. When there was some little thing to repair in the Wegleins' apartment, it was likely to be Heilmann who lent a hand. Since the stockroom clerk had trained as a carpenter, he "was always ready to help," as his daughter tells it. The Wegleins reciprocated with a gift that was more than just polite: in 1933, when the Heilmanns had a second daughter, christened Betty, Frau Weglein brought the young mother a baptism present. "It was an unusually beautiful child's dress," recalls Marga Heilmann Söltner.

Johann Heilmann did not occupy himself solely with household repairs and his job in the rear building. He was now a Nazi sympathizer and liked to go out into the streets to the big rallies. Even his neighbor, Mäsel from the side building, was impressed by the fresh wind that blew through Nuremberg with the beginning of the Nazi dictatorship. To be sure, Mäsel was not particularly interested in politics. A toolmaker by training, he was employed as a supervisor in the brush factory that was located on Praterstrasse just a few hundred yards from Spittlertorgraben. After work he coached the women's team at the gymnastics club, sometimes took his wife to the theater, and enjoyed socializing with his friends.

And yet Mäsel was clearly moved by all those flags, the bands, and the marching men who occasionally passed by the building on Spittlertorgraben. In fact, it seemed as if things were getting better in Nuremberg. The number of people out of work and on welfare in the city had dropped by four thousand since February 1933. The mayor was announcing further measures to create jobs: numerous historic structures, such as the old city walls, were to be restored, a new streetcar line was being planned, and a private housing development received strong injections of funds. The political situation in Nuremberg promised to become settled and orderly once again. Mäsel was certainly in favor of that. He didn't like change; he needed the stability of his home, where his wife, compulsively neat, was always polishing something.

Exactly when the first rumors began to circulate among the tenants of 19 Spittlertorgraben can no longer be determined. The record of the investigation, a yellowed copy of which miraculously survived, makes it clear that Mäsel and Heilmann claimed to have noticed the friendly relationship between Katzenberger and Irene as early as 1933. Back then the neighbor ladies in the front building gossiped about this and that; in the shoe warehouse, the Aryan workers made remarks. And Heilmann, who worked in both buildings, carried the newest rumors from one to the other. There was a good deal of talk about "something shady" going on between Katzenberger and Irene.

In his own home Heilmann didn't have much to say. He was, as Marga and his son-in-law, Fritz Söltner, both report, "completely under his wife's thumb." And she was clearly a dragon. Little Marga was frequently spanked and spent many hours locked in the bathroom. "I wouldn't like to go through my childhood again," says the retiree today. Her father didn't have an easy time with his wife either, since she was constantly complaining. Old photographs reveal her to be prematurely aged, with a hardened expression. "And there wasn't much going on sexually," relates Marga's husband. So it may well have been that Heilmann occasionally turned a wistful eye on pretty Irene when she made her way across the courtyard in high-heeled shoes.

Heilmann had a lot to do at the factory. He not only stacked shoe boxes in the storeroom, he loaded and unloaded the firm's truck in the courtyard; and then there was the automobile to be washed and the courtyard to be swept — all of which sometimes took part of the evening. So he couldn't fail to notice that Irene often went to Katzenberger's office after business hours. What "got talked about and done there," Heilmann of course didn't know, as he later indicated to the Gestapo. According to his testimony, however, it certainly wasn't anything proper. Johann Mäsel had also been struck by Irene's visits to the rear building. From his kitchen window, Mäsel observed the young woman disappearing into the office at the rear of the courtyard "for a half an hour or an hour at a time." That she was frequently carrying a shoe box under her arm on the way back seemed particularly suspicious to the proper toolmaker.

The shoes couldn't really all have been gifts, argued Mäsel, and it never entered the modest machinist's head that they could have been purchased. Who needs that many shoes anyway? The only thing he could imagine was that Irene was carrying the shoe boxes across the courtyard "for appearances' sake," as a sort of alibi for her extended visits. Heilmann was likewise of the opinion that the shoe boxes were intended to camouflage the immoral activities he suspected were going on in the firm's office. Thus the shoe boxes were always noted with suspicion and, in the eyes of the neighbors, eventually taken as proof of the forbidden activities they imagined were taking place behind the door of the rear building.

Even today Marga Heilmann Söltner, who as a child frequently heard adults talking about the presumed relationship, always sees the businessman with a shoe box in her mind's eye. She believes it "probably comes from all the talk about it." That Irene perhaps really did have a penchant for beautiful shoes and that the old gent was a soft touch and gave her a few pairs or sold them to her cheaply —without "something in return" — was not even considered by the building's inhabitants. Yet they themselves had purchased Katzenberger shoes at give-away prices. For example, once when Mäsel's relatives were visiting, he took his niece to the firm's office. The little girl had caught sight of a pair of red patent-leather shoes that, given Mäsel's circumstances, were much too expensive. She begged and begged for the shoes, but her uncle wouldn't buy them. Katzenberger reduced the price to the point that Mäsel couldn't go on saying no. The little girl, today an old woman who lives near Nuremberg, has had a soft spot in her heart for the businessman ever since.

But perhaps what Irene was actually carrying across the courtyard were just a few empty shoe boxes that she'd asked Katzenberger for. She needed a lot of storage space for her pictures and shoe boxes made ideal containers for her photographic equipment. So the idea is not far-fetched that those were empty shoe boxes finding their way across the courtyard, totally without immoral context. No one seems to have taken the trouble to investigate, and whatever was or wasn't in those shoe boxes will remain a secret. The judges and prosecutors of the Nazi era, as well as afterward, were only interested in the same question that preoccupied the curious neighbors as early as 1933: What was going on between Katzenberger and Irene? Were the aging Jew and the pretty young woman hugging and kissing each other like father and daughter, or were the two of them lovers?

5

THE OCCUPANTS OF THE FRONT BUILDING on Spittlertorgraben could not look directly into Katzenbergers' offices. All that they could see was Heilmann or his Jewish colleague, Otto Feuchtwanger, on the ramp, loading or unloading shoes. The Katzenbergers rarely showed themselves in the storage area. Their offices were in the rear of the building, their windows facing the park. Leo Katzenberger managed the Spittlertorgraben property, so the renters had met him at least once when they'd moved in.

Rent collection, however, was left to the office secretary, Margarete Hölzel. Each tenant brought her the rent on a monthly basis, generally in cash. Mäsel, for instance, showed up on the first of the month with 28.40 Reichsmarks. The salesman Östreicher from the fourth floor, whose wife always sublet a few rooms, paid 119.60 Reichsmarks. Heilmann only had to come up with 9.60 marks for his attic apartment. When she received the money, Margarete Hölzel always conscientiously signed the little payment book that each renter kept. Katzenberger could not get involved with such details. He had numerous obligations with the Jewish congregations; had Adas Israel meetings; and attended the weekly sessions of the B'nai B'rith lodge, which continued to take place on Tuesdays for a considerable time, even after the frightful "grass-stain" incident. Only on the weekends did Katzenberger have a little more time. Though the merchant counted himself among the Orthodox who lived according to the traditional tenets of their belief, he did allow himself to go to his office on the Sabbath, perhaps to get the mail or to take care of some of the paperwork. Then the short, corpulent man would occasionally trudge over to the front building and climb up to the second floor to visit his nephew or look in on Irene; as he did, there were often one or two pairs of eyes intently following him.

Thus far, however, no one had seen the two of them standing too close together — with the exception, perhaps, of Mother Mäsel. The old lady, short and rather heavyset, was seventy-nine years old in 1933. She spent her days at home for the most part, and if she had nothing to do, she prowled around the apartment to help pass the time. From the carriage house where the Mäsel family lived there was a direct line of sight into the photographer's first-floor apartment, and Mother Mäsel very likely looked over to the front building on occasion. The photographer occupied three rooms and a small kitchen, which was connected to a wooden veranda on which the toilet and a sink had been installed. The bedroom was tiny on the street side; there was barely room for the narrow couch that Irene used as a bed. In a window of her studio, which likewise faced the street, she'd put a large advertisement, which was always covered with particularly good photographs; for the longest time, a portrait of a pretty blonde hung there. The third, somewhat smaller room facing the courtyard had been set up as her living room. This room was in full view of the Mäsels. Their small dwelling stood on slightly lower ground than the front building. The entire area along Spittlertorgraben dropped off toward the low point of the Rosenau Park. For that reason, the courtyard, side tracts, and rear building of the property at number 19 were a good half-story lower than the street side of the front building. The Mäsels' house had low and somewhat slanting roofs, and was built so close to the front building that one could almost reach from one building to the other.

On the ground floor, the Mäsels had a small kitchen with windows facing the courtyard; their bathroom was in the basement of the front building. Climbing a narrow, steep staircase would bring one to the attic floor of the coach house, where a small bedroom was located, together with the living room where the Mäsels enjoyed coffee with their friends. This room was a little above Irene's first-floor apartment. Mother Mäsel, who was a little senile and not very mobile, could stand there as if she were on the bridge of a ship and look down into the photographer's living room. In addition, there was a large wall mirror in the Mäsels' living room. Hung on two brass hooks, the mirror had been mounted at just the right angle to the windows so as to allow an undetected view of Irene's studio apartment, even into corners that could not be seen straight on. By means of that mirror, Mother Mäsel could look down into the photographer's studio. One day she made an observation that was considered extremely significant to the building's gossips: Katzenberger had gone into Irene's apartment, old Mrs. Mäsel related excitedly, and had "hugged and kissed" the photographer.

Mother Mäsel's news spread to the front building and up the stairwell like wildfire; what the old woman claimed to have seen took on more importance as the news spread to a higher floor. Had the Jew and the young woman embraced by way of greeting, or kissed, or even fondled each other? Soon the facts became distorted like the image in a fun-house mirror; what Mother Mäsel had actually seen had long since receded into the background. The old woman died later that year, but her observation lived on, amplified by talk within the building, and quickly assumed the level of confirmed fact: it was said that the businessman and the photographer had "always embraced" and also "kissed each other repeatedly."

The happy-go-lucky photographer, with her audacious hats, fashionable shoes, and tendency to shower people with kisses when she was happy, seemed, in that community of straight-laced apartment dwellers, to be from another planet. The news that the Jew and the girl had been observed secretly caressing one another incited the curiosity of the other tenants. Some of them made it a point to watch the pair more carefully. The toolmaker started to look down into Irene's living room, without being noticed, and later shame-facedly confessed to using the mirror to see into the concealed corners of her studio. Heilmann did not stop at merely observing the photographer from the courtyard as she went to Katzenberger's office; he even began spying on the businessman from the stairwell of the front building. The two men's obser-vations were mulled over by the apartment dwellers, turned into firm testi-mony, and then spread throughout the neighborhood. Almost imperceptibly, those who lived on Spittlertorgraben turned into informers — a little more with each passing year.

Katzenberger was totally unaware. But even if any of the nasty chatter in the building had reached his ears, it is unlikely that he would have attached any significance to it. In Nuremberg, Streicher's home territory, there was already a long tradition of anti-Semitism. On almost every street corner stood large glass cases displaying the latest edition of *Der Stürmer*. On white wooden frames Streicher's men painted the famous quotation in thick Gothic letters: "The Jews Are Our Misfortune." To avoid public hostility, many Jewish families lived quite retiring lives even before 1933; social gatherings took place in the homes of friends and relatives. When Nuremberg Jews were confronted by political agitators of the Nazi Party in a theater or restaurant, they took as little notice of the Brownshirts as possible. A process of accommodating the anti-Jewish smear campaign began; Jews segregated themselves.

"For me, Nuremberg was a city with a lot of walls," says Marga Weglein, "even in people's heads." As a young woman of twenty-five who'd grown up in Hamburg, she came to Nuremberg in 1930 after she had married Katzenberger's nephew Sally. To the new bride, the climate of the city was oppressive; the curious coexistence with the Brownshirts scared her. Once, before 1933, Marga was sitting at the opera with her husband when Hitler, Streicher, and their bodyguards came clomping in with their heavy boots and sat down in the best seats, in front of the orchestra pit, just two rows ahead of them. Marga wanted to leave right away, but her husband saw no reason to. "Why should we?" he asked. "We're staying right here."

Old, established families such as the Katzenbergers presumably had long considered the Nazi yelling and carrying on part of the usual background noise. The marching, the flags, and the torchlight processions were familiar to them from Party Rally Days, held since 1927 — long before the official beginning of the Nazi era. The Katzenbergers usually went off to the spa at Karlsbad when the brown mob showed up in Nuremberg. And thus it may be that many Jewish businessmen did not notice the new self-confidence and more strident tone displayed by the representatives of the Nazi community, from smallest sympathizer right up to the Führer himself.

For Marga, by contrast, the moment of change was almost palpable. When she came to Nuremberg in 1930, there was an extreme housing shortage. Even for well-off renters like the Wegleins, it was hard to find a place to live. Finally, a Nuremberg family came forward and offered to make room for the young couple in their apartment on Johannisstrasse. "The people had a very large apartment," recalls Marga, "but not that much money." So they divided the space in return for a generous financial contribution. In the beginning they all got along very well. They sat together in the little garden house; "We became real friends." When the two families had children, the women pressed their diapers on the same mangle. After 1933, however, "it was all off," says Marga. The family broke off contact immediately and from then on, only Aryan diapers were good enough for the ironing machine.

But this was a time of mixed messages, and for that reason it may have been difficult for many Jews to discern the danger signals. Things were not going downhill in every respect. During the Party Rally in the fall of 1934, Nazi gangs did climb over the fence surrounding the large synagogue on Hans Sachs Platz, put up *Stürmer* handbills, and attacked worshipers. However, business was going extremely well for many Jews: the building boom brought about by state contracts and the reduction in unemployment even seemed to have an invigorating effect on the economy. There were isolated examples of athletic clubs in Nuremberg where Jews and non-Jews still played soccer together. And in the courtyard behind the Spittlertorgraben, Marga Heilmann, now seven years old, ran around with little Walter Weglein just as she always did, while her father sniffed around behind his boss. Walter can still remember how every Friday morning, even in later years, he would take the fresh dough for the Sabbath to a non-Jewish baker and pick up the finished baked goods in the afternoon.

Nevertheless, in mid-1933 the Nuremberg Jewish congregations opened an office to provide advice to those wishing to emigrate, and there were discussions of the subject even in the imposing villa on Praterstrasse. Leo's oldest daughter, twenty-seven-year-old Käthe, wanted to leave and settle in Palestine with her husband and children. One night in September 1934, the loyal chauffeur Fabro drove the young family to Marseille, and the ship to Palastine. The Katzenberger brothers, however, could not imagine leaving Germany. "They were all such good patriots," says Marga Weglein.

Nor could Leo see any reason to change the way he lived. Toward evening, if he had no obligations, the old gentleman picked up his hat and strolled from the office over to Café Gisela, which was located at the end of the street. It was a plush coffeehouse with velvet sofas and white, frilly curtains. Most of the time there were a few older Jewish men sitting around one of the elegant tables playing Tarock, a card game popular in Bavaria at that time. "My father was a passionate card player," Lilo Katzenberger says.

Likewise, in the old-fashioned taproom of the Blaue Traube, located a few hundred yards from Café Gisela in the old city, another group of men frequently sat over cards after business hours. The inn on Pfannenschmiedgasse,

THE MAIDEN AND THE JEW

where they served bratwurst with sauerkraut and pork with dumplings, was well known as a meeting place for local Nazi bigwigs. The bar and dining room, as well as the small hotel in the same building, were run by the party member Georg Haberkern, who soon advanced to the position of Nazi District Inspector for Franconia and who, when the war was over in 1945, lay down in a wheat field and bit open his cyanide capsule. Even he loved to bet on cards.

In the Blaue Traube the guests did not just play cards, however. Sometimes fates were decided, too. Futures were forged, but some promising professional careers came to an abrupt end after a confidential conversation in the taproom. The Blaue Traube was a sort of unofficial Nazi headquarters in Nuremberg. "That's where anyone who had a name or rank showed up," reports Erna Gügel, who occasionally accompanied her father, a fairly high-ranking SA functionary, to the inn. "All the bigwigs would be sitting there."

On occasion, even Gauleiter Julius Streicher turned up at the tradition-rich pub in the shadow of St. Lorenz Church. The one-time public school teacher now called himself the "Führer of Franconia" and carried in his belt a riding crop with a silver knob that had been given to him by Hitler. A more frequent visitor was Streicher's loyal henchman, thirty-nine-year-old Deputy Gauleiter Karl Holz. The Nazis' local leader, graduate engineer Hans Zimmermann, was likewise frequently seen at the Blaue Traube. Two men from the feared Security Services of the SS were steady customers, as was Nuremberg's police commissioner, Benno Martin. The police chief, a strapping six-footer of forty-one with a distinctive saber scar on his cheek, was to become one of the most enigmatic figures of the Nuremberg Nazi organization. The career policeman had won the trust of Streicher several years earlier, when he had a blanket taken to the cold cell in the Nuremberg prison where Streicher was held following his arrest on November 10, 1923, in connection with the Munich Putsch. The shivering Streicher was grateful for the favor. With Hitler, whom he knew from the organizational sessions for the early Party Rally Days, Martin liked to talk about operettas and architectural matters. He likewise maintained excellent relations with the Reichsführer of the SS, Heinrich Himmler. The impressive-looking policeman was even successful with Nazi society ladies. Frequently seen in his black SS uniform, he was known as the Black Knight of Nuremberg.

Martin was not a Jew-hater from conviction; the son of a civil servant, he had attached himself to the Nazis for the sake of his career, but also kept contacts to the Jewish community in town. He held negotiations with Walter

Berlin, the chairman of the Centralverein, an organization established to protect against anti-Jewish actions, as well as with Ludwig Rosenzweig, the head of the Jewish congregations, whose office Leo Katzenberger later assumed. The good relations with the chief of police, reports Lilo Katzenberger, was "something we looked upon as sort of insurance for father." Martin had another face, however: he was responsible for signing the orders when the Nuremberg Gestapo assembled the first deportation train to Riga in 1941.

There were also a few lawyers from Nuremberg's Palace of Justice who were regulars at the Blaue Traube — public prosecutor Oswald Rothaug, for instance, a man of short stature with coarse facial features and strikingly bad teeth. Innkeeper Haberkern had known Rothaug since the 1920s, when the jurist was his tenant and the two men and their wives often went on outings to the hop farms in Hallertau. In the noisy circle of men who met at the Blaue Traube in 1934, the inconspicuous, thirty-seven-year-old Rothaug attracted little attention at first. Several years later, however, after he had been appointed presiding judge of the Nuremberg Special Court, even tough Nazis pulled in their necks when he entered the pub. Rothaug became known at the Blaue Traube simply as the "executioner," reports the eyewitness Erna Gügel: "Even his buddies said he was not a guy to fool around with." Rothaug was the judge who would later sentence Leo Katzenberger to death.

6

MARGA WEGLEIN WAS CONFINED TO BED; she'd given birth to a son. That was on a Monday in February 1935. Outside, the first gentle spring breeze was blowing. A few days later, still a little tired, Sally's wife leaned against her pillows and thought about the preparations for the ritual circumcision of her little boy. The ceremony was to take place on the eighth day after birth, and if possible, ten Jewish men were to be present to say the prayer together. Usually the parents served a banquet afterward to express their joy over the fact that their child had been taken into the community of Jewish believers.

It was customary among the Nuremberg Jews for the young family to give a small reception on the Friday evening preceding the day of the circumcision, and Marga wanted to observe that custom. When she discussed the details of the planned festivities with the rabbi, however, he strongly advised against any sort of celebration that might attract attention, given the anti-Semitic climate of Nuremberg. Instead, the religious ceremony would be better observed in some small, less noticeable way. "Ten Jewish men in one home," reports Marga, "was already considered too dangerous in Nuremberg by then."

The rabbi's caution was well-founded. To be sure, neither in the written memoirs of former Nurembergers nor in the old municipal records is there any mention of an explicit ban on Jewish family celebrations from early 1935 on. But for months, *Der Stürmer* had been agitating in ever-sharper tones against Jewish citizens. Likewise, at the entrances to the surrounding Franconian towns and at the doors of restaurants and cafés, placards with the inscription JEWS NOT WELCOME began to appear more and more frequently.

Like a ship plowing through the sea, making the smooth surface of the water curl into waves, reaction to the Nazis' propaganda had fluctuated since their ascendancy in 1933. After the initial boycotts and violence against Nuremberg businessmen, civil servants, and other respected Jews, a certain sobering was noted in 1934 in Franconia and elsewhere. Many of the inhabitants, probably including some seasoned Nazis, were shocked at the wave of violence that had flooded the land since the Nazi takeover. In addition, the ruling Nazis, weakened by internal conflicts, such as the Röhm affair in the summer of 1934, turned their attentions from the "race question" to economic consolidation. Streicher and his Nuremberg henchmen, nonetheless, had only one motto: "The Jews Are Our Misfortune."

Disappointed by what he considered a lax attitude on the part of the Nazi leadership in Berlin, *Der Stürmer's* publisher ratcheted up his hysterical propaganda campaign with each week's issue. There were new horror stories about Jewish citizens, dealing for the most part with sex — a reflection of Streicher's interests. In all possible variations, the paper portrayed the alleged sexual lust of Jewish men for "German women." In his speeches, Streicher himself espoused the most incredible theories about a sort of racial blood poisoning: Women who had gone to bed with Jews, the Franconian Führer exclaimed in front of thousands of listeners, would later bear nothing but children with "typical Jewish features," because their blood had been infected forever.

Soon, Nazi party officials were pressuring clerks in city halls throughout Germany to refuse to process applications for marriage licenses from Jewish–Aryan couples. From mid-1935 on, justices of the peace increasingly refused, on their own initiative, to conduct mixed marriages. In a later essay about those times, Bernhard Lösener, then minister in charge of racial problems in the Reich's Ministry of the Interior, complained: "As regards marriage between Jews and Aryans, there was in several districts a complete cessation of adherence to the laws of the land" — which Lösener would soon help to overcome. He was one of the authors of the Blutschutz- and Reichsbürgergesetze passed at the Nuremberg Party Rally in 1935 — laws concerning racial purity and citizenship in the Reich, which not only became a legal cornerstone for the Holocaust, but also a murderous instrument in the hands of Nazi jurists such as Judge Oswald Rothaug.

When the party rally opened on Tuesday, September 10, 1935, Nuremberg was a giant sea of flags. The angular, gabled buildings of the old city had been decorated with swastika flags, green leafy boughs, and fronds of evergreens; in the narrow alleyways, the cobblestones trembled beneath the heavy, booted tread of SA and SS men. Even the church bells rang out on command. The prelude to the rally, as always, was Hitler, standing in his gleaming black Mercedes convertible, proceeding through the streets on the way to his suite in the Hotel Deutscher Hof, where he greeted Nuremberg from a bay window. Several thousand citizens joyously welcomed him.

The party rally had long been an important factor in the city's economy, a conjunction of superlatives that provided work for every sort of tradesman in Nuremberg. Business geared up for several weeks prior to Hitler's opening spectacle. Flags had to be sewn and wooden bleachers for prominent party members constructed. On the rally grounds to the south of the city, loudspeakers had to be installed and portable kitchens set up. Construction firms dug trenches for new power cables, plumbers laid water lines, transportation companies arranged for vehicles. For the party rally in the fall of 1935, the Reichsbahn put on 532 special trains, and postal employees added thirty-five hundred miles of telephone line to the Nuremberg network. When the close to one million rally attendees finally showed up, the butchers, bakers, and gingerbread makers got their chance. According to an old listing, during the rally of 1935 meat deliveries alone increased threefold.

In Nuremberg, the party rally not only stimulated the local economy; it stimulated the inhabitants' proper Nazi inclinations as well. From the flag decorations to the torchlight processions to the huge fireworks display, from the colossal military parades with their modern equipment to the march of fifty thousand shovel-carrying men from the Work Brigades, right up to the boys and girls of the gymnastics and costume groups who skipped across the Nuremberg marketplace in endless columns — everything was overwhelming and impressive. The SA and various bands drummed marching songs into people's heads. It was a huge, monumental spectacle in a historic setting that was county fair, shooters' festival, *Christkindlmarkt,* and Oktoberfest all rolled into one. And the inhabitants of Spittlertorgraben, along which the marchers passed now and again on their way from the Plärrer, had what amounted to ringside seats.

After the massive anti-Semitic propaganda campaign at the beginning of 1935, it was only a question of time before some sort of law against relations between Jews and non-Jews was passed. But the Law Concerning Protection of the Blood, or Racial Purity Law, found its way onto that fall's rally program only by chance. Originally Hitler had intended to use the yearly spectacle to introduce a foreign policy statement in which he would demonstrate reinvigorated German self-confidence and make new demands for revisions in treaties with neighboring countries. As an accompaniment, the Flag Law, making the swastika flag the German national flag, was to be passed at a session of the Reichstag specially convened in Nuremberg. Hitler's chief diplomats, however, had advised against such a broad presentation, keeping only the portions that dealt with the flag. But that seemed a bit too threadbare to Hitler, given the tense mood in the country. And so, on Friday evening, September 13, 1935, he ordered his Minister of the Interior, Wilhelm Frick, to present in the course of the party rally a law forbidding marriage between Jews and Aryans.

That same evening, the phone rang in the Berlin home of an interior ministry officer named Lösener: it was Frick, requesting that the racial specialist of his department appear in Nuremberg by nine o'clock the next morning. In Nuremberg, Lösener met with the secretaries of the Ministry of the Interior, Wilhelm Stuckart and Hans Pfundtner, with whom he was to work out the "Jewish paragraphs." Toward midnight, they presented four versions of a so-called Racial Purity Law. But that did not satisfy the Führer; he now demanded a pair of basic rules regarding the citizenship of Jews "to round out the lawmaking program." It was 12:30 when the exhausted ministry officers set about drafting a "basic law" for the Thousand Year Reich. On the following evening, September 15, the Reichstag met in Nuremberg for a special, supplementary session in order to pass the new laws. Red gladiolas decorated the corners of the hall, garlands threaded with gold hung from the walls. At around 9 P.M., Hitler convened the session with a speech against "smears by the foreign Jewish press." Reichstag President Hermann Göring then read the drafts of the new laws, which were unanimously accepted.

The Citizenship Law of the Reich consisted of only three paragraphs, yet it was to become the pseudo-legal basis for the planned persecution and annihilation of Jews in Germany. The law differentiated between nationality and a newly created citizenship within the Reich — and with that the long-practiced marginalization of Jews was legally confirmed. Anchored within the Citizenship Law was a type of legalized denial of rights for Jews. All else was to be governed according to procedural details yet to be finalized. In fact, thirteen regulations were later issued on the basis of this law, ranging from the prohibition of Jews from public-service positions in 1935 to the "coordi-nation" of Jewish congregations in 1939 to the eleventh, twelfth, and thir-teenth regulations of 1941 and 1943 that ordered the confiscation of Jewish property and the final withdrawal of their German citizenship. With these regulations, the last legal hurdles blocking the orchestration of the mass destruction of Jews had been surmounted.

The Law Concerning Protection of German Blood and German Honor was seven paragraphs long. They were to insure "the purity of German blood," which, according to Nazi ideology, was seen as a "prerequisite for the continued existence of the German people." According to this regulation, marriages between Jews and Aryans were forbidden and even "extramarital relationships" were to be punished. Beyond that, "women and girls of German blood" less than forty-five years of age could no longer be employed in Jewish households. Violations would be punishable by fines or prison sen-tences. In cases of so-called "racial disgrace" without a marriage license, the man alone would be subject to punishment, because according to the rigid, masculine ideas of the Nazis, women never initiated sexual encounters.

With a great deal of public fanfare, the legislation was announced throughout the Reich. In front of the Hotel Deutscher Hof, Julius Streicher accepted congratulations from thousands of jubilant bystanders. There were newspaper reports and radio broadcasts and, of course, all across the country *Der Stürmer* cases were covered with the news. On Nuremberg's Plärrer a wooden showcase displayed, behind glass, that week's edition. Irene Scheffler and the other tenants from the apartment house on Spittlertorgraben walked by it daily. There is no record of whether the photographer ever glanced at the issue with the Reichstag proceedings on it; in any case, she "never both-ered about those laws back then," as she testified before an American military tribunal after the war.

At that time, she was a vivacious person, living just for the moment, and she cared little for the rest of the world. She was twenty-five and enjoying life to the fullest, playing the role of the urbane artist in the modest apartment

house. Her sister's plain business sign with the words PHOTOGRAPHIC
WORKSHOP was exchanged for one with a presumably more ambitious message: eventually, a metal plaque was displayed to the right of the entrance
with SCHEFFLER STUDIO — PHOTOGRAPHIC ART in large letters.

Not far from the apartment house was a popular nightclub called Müller's
Musicals. It may have been that the photographer occasionally went there to
dance. In her happy-go-lucky way Irene took her amusement where she
found it, meeting up with one beau, then another, sometimes providing an
admirer with lodgings for the night. If it happened that the following morning a freshly awakened young man walked out of the door, there was an
immediate buzz in the building. Many of the men in the apartment house
probably wished they could risk a dance with their pretty fellow-renter.

Irene seemed to spend less time maintaining her photography studio. By
the end of 1935 her business was going from bad to worse, but she had long
since given up worrying about that. What could happen to her? Basically, she
had a double safety net. She looked upon Katzenberger as her "Daddy in
Nuremberg," the man who would take care of the demands of the world.
And, in fact, the harried businessman, who had so many obligations he hardly
had time for his own firm, let himself be persuaded to take care of those both-
ersome bills in the studio and even filled out Irene's tax forms. Katzenberger
also deferred the social butterfly's rent for ever-increasing intervals. Should
the pile of debt ever get too high, Father Scheffler in Guben would, of course,
settle everything.

Katzenberger enjoyed the game. At home in his handsome villa, the old
man was sometimes overcome by a strange sense of emptiness after Lilo emigrated to Palestine in January 1936. Katzenberger had taken her to the railroad station, where she, her husband, and their son, nearly three, caught the
night train to Genoa to board the ship *Tel Aviv*; in her coat pocket was Käthe's
address. Since then, the Nuremberg villa was quiet. None of the grandchildren went sneaking across the parquet floor when the old gentleman was
having his coffee in the spacious dining room; their voices no longer echoed
from the garden house near the fountain to the rear of the building, formerly
a favorite place for the little ones to play. All that could be heard now was the
muted yelling of orders from the nearby SA quarters.

In the huge two-floor apartment, with its high, stuccoed ceilings and
creaking stairs, Katzenberger and his wife must have felt a bit lost. It is true
that both daughters had left home years before they emigrated; Lilo had even

lived in Dortmund for a few years while her husband was in charge of one of
the Katzenbergers' shoe stores there. But one or another of the grandchildren
or nieces or nephews were constantly in the villa, be it Käthe's two sons dashing madly through the rooms or dainty little Hilde from the first-floor apartment, a thirteen-year-old whirlwind, the only daughter of Leo's brother Max.
Something was always going on. Not long before, the Katzenbergers gave
dinners and evening receptions in their splendid home. They held the seder
for a large family circle. On those ceremonial evenings, Leo Katzenberger, as
the elder of the family, read aloud from the Haggadah and hid the unleav-
ened bread. Thereafter the Christian maid, Elise, probably served hardboiled eggs, bitter herbs, horseradish and gefilte fish. After the Racial Purity
Laws were passed, Elise had to find a new position. Now Jewish businessmen
and factory owners gathered around the large dining room table to play
Tarock. They were no longer being served in the city's cafés and inns.

Leo and Claire Katzenberger had a good marriage. However, Lilo admits
it wasn't "a love marriage," pointing out that her parents had been of very different character. Claire had been brought up within strict, middle-class,
small-town constraints; Leo, on the other hand, was more of a worldly hedo-
nist, basically God-fearing, but at the same time very liberal. Admittedly, he
came from an even smaller town in lower Franconia, where his parents had
run secondhand stores and groceries. Leo was the oldest of twelve children.
The time in Paris, however, where he'd gone after his thirteenth school year,
seemed to have permanently marked him. When he returned to Germany
several years later, his parents had arranged for him to marry Claire, who was
half a head taller. "People just made a match," says Lilo with a touch of indif-
ference in her voice, "and they got used to each other instead of being in love."

Katzenberger was a religious man, and extremely aware of his responsi-
bilities. He would never have disclosed that his marriage wasn't exactly bub-
bling over with passion. And when he went on business trips, who was to
know what went on? His chauffeur, himself a strikingly handsome young
man who drove a Harley-Davidson during off-hours, may have observed the
occasional flirtation back then. But at no time did Fabro ever make mention
of it. Only when he was interrogated after the war did the chauffeur report
with rather noble reserve that it was his impression that Katzenberger was
certainly "interested in pretty women."

The businessman was very close to Lilo. "I was cut from the same cloth as
he was," she says. So it pained her father all the more when she emigrated in

1936. It may well be that he sought to compensate for the loss by redirecting his paternal solicitude toward the young photographer. In fact, Irene did have a certain resemblance to Lilo: both women were approximately the same age, tall, dark-haired, and high-spirited. But Leo may have harbored more than fatherly feelings toward the pretty photographer. Irene liked to flirt, and she clearly enjoyed the small attentions he paid her. Sometimes, under the careful watch of the Spittlertorgraben neighbors, he threw little boxes of pralines into his favorite's kitchen window; the next time it might be a pack of cigarettes. Occasionally the young woman would look happily out of the window and give a few waves in Katzenberger's direction. The two of them did not try to hide their relationship. Katzenberger took to disappearing into Irene's studio for an occasional coffee but, at the same time, he was likely to be carrying film from his daughters in Palestine in order to have prints made. It's probable that Irene often got right to work developing a few photos, since Katzenberger was eager to see the new pictures from his far-off loved ones. Afterward, the improbable couple would stroll through Rosenau Park.

The two "courted" so openly and unconcernedly, relates Marga Weglein, that even Katzenberger's brothers got wind of it. One day Max and David appeared in Leo's office and warned their older brother not to be so frivolous, in view of the strict racial laws. But Leo merely laughed at them. "What's going to happen?" he countered cheerfully. "I'm just an old man."

7

WHAT A PRETTY LITTLE KITTEN SLINKING ACROSS the sidewalk over there! Herbert Kolb was quite taken. A man was trying to catch it with a sack as Herbert bicycled past, but the agile cat always hopped away, and the boy could not take his eyes off it. In a flash he climbed off his bicycle and stood there in the middle of the heavily traveled Gostenhofer Hauptstrasse, a main street leading to a city district in the west of Nuremberg. At that moment three huge limousines rounded a blind curve at high speed, but Herbert had the presence of mind to jump back just as the black Mercedes roared by, a hair's breadth away. It was Adolf Hitler and his cohort. The Nazi procession had almost run down the Jewish boy.

This event took place in the spring of 1937, some time after Herbert had left public school. From the very beginning, the Nazis had been intent on excluding Jews from the school system. On April 8, 1936, Councilman Fink, who was responsible for educational affairs, had announced before the city council that the "public high schools in the city of the party rallies would be free of Jews" before the start of the next school year. And the "de-Jewification" of the grade schools would soon be concluded as well. The declaration, noted the minutes, was accepted "amid great applause."

Herbert was doing a business apprenticeship. The Jewish congregations, and particularly its business manager — Herbert's father, Bernhard — had worked hard to promptly set up their own Jewish school. As early as 1934, teaching started in the rooms of a former factory on upper Kanalstrasse, in the same building where the Adas Israel had its meeting rooms. But Jewish boys were not likely to occupy their school benches for very long. Their parents were insistent that the children learn something practical, a trade that could help them to live abroad. For that reason, the fourteen-year-old Herbert had begun an apprenticeship in his uncle's clothing factory — the company where the Nazis had in 1933 confiscated brown-yellow cloth for SA trousers.

At noon, the boy rode his bicycle from the firm's office on Luitpoldstrasse to his home on Knauerstrasse for lunch. He always passed the Hotel Deutscher Hof. On the day that Herbert watched the agile cat, he'd noticed that a rather large crowd of people had formed in front of the hotel. When he asked what was going on, someone whispered from the crowd, "The Führer's here!"

The dictator visited his showpiece town often. Not just for Rally Day — other occasions as well drew him back again and again to the "Treasure Chest of the Reich." More often than not he dined at the Deutscher Hof with his Nuremberg trusties. Julius Streicher would be seated at the table, frequently his henchman Karl Holz as well, and Mayor Willy Liebel, and sometimes even Chief of Police Benno Martin would be invited. The latter enjoyed Hitler's particular sympathies. Once, when the chancellor of the Reich arrived at the railroad station, he made a beeline over to Martin, who was standing in the third or fourth row, and greeted the head policeman with special enthusiasm. Of course it was hard to overlook the chief of police, with his Aryan guardsman's appearance at well over six feet.

The dictator also appreciated the cultural offerings in the "City of the Party Rally." Thus, for example, he allowed himself a visit to the Nuremberg Opera on March 21, 1937. As documented by Streicher's appointment calendar, *Die Fledermaus* was performed. This time, Hitler and his Nuremberg viceroy, Streicher, did not sit in the orchestra section as they had in 1932. The Nazi leadership now had their own, reserved "Führer loge" in the very best position. No doubt about it: with the passage of time, the ruling Nazi clique had not merely established themselves firmly in the country; they were living quite well in their positions of power. But the seating arrangements at the

Nuremberg Opera House were a comparatively modest indicator of their spreading self-indulgence.

Within very few years the corrupt city dictatorship Streicher and his people had established gave the impression that Ali Baba had declared himself the Sun King and the forty thieves his courtiers. The false prince put on orgies with his female playmates, and his hangers-on kept pace. And while the Nazi headman snapped up the biggest share of the booty, his henchmen made the smaller coins clink. Meanwhile, the ordinary citizenry were provided with bread and spectacles so they wouldn't make demands.

In addition to the rally days there were constant parades and public festivals to keep the people in a good mood and to simultaneously subject them to mass indoctrination. Even Fasching, the pre-Lenten carnival, was now a National Socialist celebration for the people's amusement: traveling in the carnival procession of 1936 was a wagon with the inscription AB NACH DACHAU, OFF TO DACHAU. On it, penned in behind the rails, stood masked figures easily recognizable as Jews, racial offenders, or troublemakers. To the public's enjoyment, men dressed as police officers ran around the wagon, herding the unregenerate delinquents toward Dachau. Once, at the time of winter solstice in December 1936, SA men piled cord wood in the moat along the old city walls; at the signal, a ring of flames shot up all around the old city. For anyone standing at a window of the building on Spittlertorgraben, directly opposite the city wall, the flickering spectacle must have had an overwhelming effect.

As soon as the Nazis assumed power in the spring of 1933, Streicher started to look for new quarters in keeping with his position, and the town palace of the industrialist Baron von Cramer-Klett seemed just right. Surrounded by an attractive park, the imposing building with a view of the old city lay a bit beyond the railroad station. The municipality bought the palace and, at considerable cost, remodeled it for the Führer of Franconia, who then enjoyed it without paying rent or utilities.

In the first years of the Nazi era, Streicher was the uncontested ruler of Nuremberg. Police Chief Martin, the second most prominent figure in the Nuremberg Nazi scene, quickly realized this and the ambitious civil servant did his utmost to be of service. Each month the two men set aside a special day when Martin provided a situation report. Martin also appeared frequently at the numerous banquets at Palais Cramer-Klett, during which Streicher enjoyed the company of the whoever happened to be the leading lady at the municipal theater. Indeed, the police chief himself found the lady of his heart at the theater, but of course the beauty played a supporting role at the theater.

Streicher's leadership style was absolutist, brutal, and extravagant — sometimes even perverse. For example, with sums of money so enormous that some asked where they came from, the head Nazi expanded his estate, Pleikershof, located near Nuremberg, pouring 1.3 million Reichsmarks into it by 1938. The stall for the pigs cost more than a single-family home, or so went the grumbling amongst the people. At the same time, he was systematically embezzling funds from various party organs accessible to him, as an internal investigation later established. The finances of the *Franconian Daily News* are but one example. The paper, originally founded by Streicher and eventually taken over by the party, paid for all sorts of things, including a five-thousand-mark car for Streicher's son Lothar and other vehicles for friends and relatives. In addition, Lothar drew a monthly salary of 110 marks from the paper, without seeming to perform any services in return; his brother Elmar received an allowance of twenty marks a month, which in those days was not an insubstantial sum.

For several years Streicher had carried on a liaison with Anni Seitz, an actress and dancer who always played leading roles at the Nuremberg Theater. The prima donna's father, however, a metalworker, was unemployed and traveled around the countryside with his cart peddling soap. Streicher had the *Franconian Daily News* employ the man at a salary of 420 marks per month, provide him with a car, and even pay his personal telephone bill. The paper also had to pay for a typing and stenography course, because Seitz was hardly qualified to be of any use to a newspaper. A monthly wage of 420 marks was a considerable amount of money at that time; a skilled metalworker earned between forty and fifty marks per week.

But the newspaper paid for even more. Streicher got the paper's publisher, Councilman Max Fink, to build a country house, which included a special room where Streicher could enjoy himself with the actress Seitz undisturbed. The Nazi newspaper even had to help finance this rural setting for Streicher's dalliances: the Gauleiter advanced Fink twelve thousand marks from the paper's account to cover the building costs.

There were various other actresses who now and again enjoyed largess from the newspaper's purse, depending on how high the ladies stood in the Gauleiter's favor at the moment. Anni Seitz, however, received yet another, quite special, gift from her lover. For some time, Streicher had been collecting wedding rings from his underlings, all of whom had had absolute obedience drilled into them. "Real men don't wear wedding rings," Streicher pronounced to Fink, and with that simply took the piece of jewelry, as he did from anyone in his circle. The number of rings collected is unknown; in any event, after they had been melted down, there was enough material to make a gilded jewelry box, which Streicher presented to his lover.

All in all, ladies of the stage played supporting roles that were by no means insignificant in Nuremberg's Nazi society. Anyone who wanted to be a member of the Streicher clan took up with a starlet. Accordingly, not only had Police Chief Martin established an intimate relationship with the actress Lola Grahl, but Streicher's adjutant, Hanns König, was soon billing and cooing with a soubrette. Hanns König's real name was Johann Karl Aron König, but he didn't like the Jewish-sounding first name, so he changed it to the staunchly Aryan Hanns. He began his career as a bank employee, then became a deliveryman for a cheese company. He landed a job as Streicher's chauffeur in 1928 and, with cunning and viciousness, worked his way up in the Nazi district leadership to the position of adjutant by 1930. In 1935, as a thirty-one-year-old member of the city council, he was named Overseer of Municipal Theaters, where he promptly took a blond songstress under his wing.

Adjutant König soon acquired the reputation of being the "evil spirit" among the ruling Big Three, as the Nazi trio that included Streicher and Holz were popularly known. Even within the party, König was considered to be an extremely unpleasant customer who, according to a report from an internal investigation, "tyrannized the district leadership, the authorities, and the population in an unheard-of manner." König was often with Streicher when the latter took one of the many opportunities to "strike a blow for liberation" with his riding crop. The two of them beat the Nuremberg SA man Richard Steinruck bloody in the cell where he was being held in conjunction with the Röhm Affair in 1934. Afterward, when Streicher was on his way from the police lock-up to the Deutscher Hof, he was heard to say, "Now I'm relieved. I really needed that again."

Even in Nazi Party circles some members were put off not merely by the brutality of the Nuremberg Nazi bosses but by their pronounced avarice as well.

Over the years, many a member of Streicher's gang came to wealth in strange ways. König, for instance, had so much money by 1937 that he could outbid other potential buyers and pay 150,000 marks for a brick works in Forchheim, located between Nuremberg and Bamberg. Functionaries at all levels in the Nazi hierarchy also had their hands in the till: donations to a certain charity were redirected by Gauleiter Streicher to his personal account, while those in the middle and lower ranks sought to enrich themselves with commensurately smaller sums.

There were even irregularities with the Nuremberg division of the Winter Aid Program, the Nazi charitable organization for which block wardens were always holding out collection boxes. In the mid 1930s, a trial was carried on behind closed doors against eight party members and functionaries who had embezzled considerable sums from Winter Aid.

It was not lost on the populace that many Nazis had sticky fingers. As a result of the complaints, Gauleiter Streicher felt compelled to speak out against "common liars and rumor spreaders" as early as May, 1935. His deputy Karl Holz had not been seen publicly for a long time, which seemed to confirm a rumor that he had fled because he'd embezzled a large sum of money. Streicher had bulletin boards and kiosks covered with red placards titled "To Every Citizen." In the text, the Gauleiter emphatically denied any wrongdoing on Holz's part and openly invited potential informers to "report verbally or in writing to Hitler House those originating or spreading rumors."

In mid-December 1937, using similar posters, Streicher called for what was the longest and last boycott of Jewish businesses before they closed once and for all. His men dragged red, six-foot signboards with the inscription "No German crosses the threshold of a Jewish shop!" up to store entryways. SA men now watched even more carefully to insure that the ordered boycott was obeyed — whoever did business with Jews was branded a "lackey of the Jews" or "traitor to the German people." The goal of the boycott was to thoroughly ruin business for Jewish merchants during the Christmas season. The citizens of Nuremberg apparently cooperated fully. "The measures proposed by the Gauleiter," states the municipal chronicle, "were adopted and carried out with the greatest enthusiasm."

When Aryan businesspeople were requested afterward to donate three percent of the increase in their stores' profits that resulted from the boycott to buy worthy birthday gift "in the name of the small business owners" for Streicher — the person who started it — a certain degree of grumbling was heard. When it involved one's own cash register, the enthusiasm disappeared.

8

SLOWLY THE SHIP PLOWS THROUGH THE ADRIATIC. The *Galilee* is a comfortable ocean liner. Groups of women sit in deck chairs chatting. Several men lean against the railing, absorbed in conversation, among them Leo Katzenberger. Half of Nuremberg, at least the more prosperous part, is on the ship. They are mostly Jewish businesspeople, lawyers, and factory owners — friends among friends. Toward evening the group withdraws to the interior of the ship; later, ladies and gentlemen in evening dress can be seen strolling to the large dining salon, where the ship's orchestra will soon open the festivities organized for the diversion of the guests.

In the harbor of Brindisi, the *Galilee* drops anchor for a few hours; on the following day the ship glides gently past Greek isles to tie up once more at Lanarka, Cyprus. It is Friday evening; the Sabbath is beginning. In the small synagogue on deck Jewish worshipers sing, then they meet at the festive table in the dining room. For the most part, those on board are older ladies and gentlemen. The ship is truly, as one of the travelers writes in an *On the Spot Report* for the newsletter of the Nuremberg-Fürth Jewish congregations, a "ship of parents" — Jewish married couples visiting their émigré children, motivated by worries, hopes, and uncertain prospects for the future.

In March 1937 the ship landed at Haifa. At dawn, the guests crowded to the railing to experience sunrise in the tableau of the ancient harbor city: "A splendid spectacle" reported the congregations' newsletter. But for many of those traveling on the ship, just as for Leo Katzenberger and his wife, Claire, it was to be the last crossing to Palestine: several failed to board for the trip back to Germany; others, including the Katzenbergers, did not get out of Nazi Germany later. In that spring of 1937, the businessman and his wife wanted to celebrate the Jewish Passover with their émigré daughters and, coincidentally, check on the womens' finances and living situations.

It was a warm reunion. Käthe's third child was born during her parents' visit. Recently, Käthe and her husband, Bernhard Freimann, had opened a shoe store in Jerusalem's inner city. Lilo was living with her son in Tel Aviv and having problems with her husband. It seemed divorce was unavoidable. But how would she earn a living? In Palestine she was unable to work as a kindergarten teacher, the profession for which she'd studied, because she didn't speak enough Hebrew. Leo Katzenberger decided he'd probably have to provide a small amount of financial support.

The Freimanns' business was hardly a gold mine. One has to imagine what it was like in Palestine: elegant street shoes, such as those the Katzenbergers sold in Nuremberg, were a sensation, because the only shoes most stores offered were the kind farmers wore to work. However, the number of customers who actually bought chic, European-style shoes — mostly British officers and rich Arab families — was limited. And it generally took time for a new business to get established. Katzenberger took a look at the store and realized that the profits were not going to feed another mouth in the foreseeable future.

And so, Leo Katzenberger had quietly reached his decision when his daughters tried to persuade their parents simply to stay in Palestine and not return to a city ruled by barbarians. "Father didn't want to risk being a burden to us," recalls Lilo. Back then it would still have been possible to get an immigration visa for the Near East region from the Mandate authorities. The British demanded a sort of head-tax of around two thousand pounds per person, certainly a manageable sum for Katzenberger in those days. But he was also thinking about his brothers and sisters in Germany. As the eldest, he felt responsible for them and was unwilling to leave them to fend for themselves.

Leo and Claire returned to Germany in spring 1937. The threats and boycotts against Jewish businesses had been taking their toll for some time, and shoe business sales had dropped considerably by 1937. For several years, Katzenberger had been selling off individual stores, beginning with the large one on Karolinenstrasse in Nuremberg, then a smaller one on Wölckenstrasse. In January 1936, the shop in Fürth was sold as well. Even the three branches in Dortmund, which generated eight hundred thousand Reichsmarks yearly when times were good, now had to be closed. Meanwhile, the Nazis had fixed the prices for Jewish merchandise. "You could hardly earn anything," Otto Feuchtwanger later said, "since the dealers weren't free to calculate their own prices any longer." The new prices, however, frequently did not cover their costs. Leo, David, and Max Katzenberger — who only ever referred to each other by the shorthand LK, DK, and MK, and even used the two initials on their business notes and memorandums — now had to meet more often behind closed doors to go over the situation and decide which branch to shut down next. Meanwhile, Wilhelm Fabro frequently drove the Hanomag truck from store to store, collecting damaged furniture and broken windows. "In 1935, 1936 the reprisals began," recalled Fabro later, "and more and more windows were smashed." Fabro had driven only the noble Chrysler. However, in 1937 he began driving the firm's truck as well, because Johann Heilmann had been fired, an event that had to do with Irene.

For Heilmann, the relationship between the businessman and the photographer had long been a thorn in his side, as he explained to the Gestapo in 1941: "I was angry about the behavior of Scheffler and Katzenberger." For that reason, he made derogatory remarks about the two of them to anyone who would listen. The Nazis had appointed Heilmann building warden in 1936, which gave him even more opportunity to nose around in the apartment house on Spittlertorgraben. And every month he went from door to door with his red tin box, collecting for the National Socialist People's Welfare Fund, one of those mass organizations that the Nazis used as both an instrument of surveillance and a propaganda forum. Heilmann could be seen carrying his collection box from one building to the next along the entire stretch of the street. As he did, he presumably took a quick look around in the respective apartments, asked if there were anything new, and passed on the local gossip as well as the latest Nazi slogans.

Irene Scheffler was the object of Heilmann's special attentions. If she didn't have any money — something that happened rather frequently — he was happy to come by a second time. Once when he returned for her donation, she told him she wouldn't be able to contribute her few pennies until her friend came by. Whereupon Heilmann brazenly hid in the stairwell and kept his eye on Irene's door. The stairway snitch later reported to the Gestapo, "I observed that Katzenberger came to Scheffler's apartment during that interval," and Katzenberger rang Irene's doorbell. When Heilmann called on the photographer again, she was able to make her payment. With that, it was clear to Heilmann that the businessman was supporting the young photographer financially and he could picture precisely what services were provided in exchange — sexual favors, of course. Heilmann spread the gossip throughout the building that Irene was easily able to "work off her debt" to Katzenberger.

His prattling reached Katzenberger, who became extremely angry. He called in the house warden and read him the riot act, but let him off with a warning. However, a short time later Katzenberger caught his clerk spreading false rumors again, and he threw Heilmann out of the firm. With that, Leo Katzenberger made a real enemy out of the Nazi sympathizer, who, thanks to his post as house warden, was able to continue spying in the apartment house.

There could have been a bit of jealousy at work. The pretty photographer had always given Heilmann — wiry, in his mid-forties — the cold shoulder, and her sympathies were obviously reserved for the old businessman. Perhaps the clerk, whom his Jewish coworkers heckled because he was a bit slow on the uptake, also read a bit too much of *Der Stürmer*. His daughter Marga couldn't imagine him really hating Jews. "He never said bad things about Jews," she claims. But the clerk may well have wished to show the influential businessman just who was in charge of the country, including the Nuremberg apartment house: men like Heilmann, who were backed up by the strong arm of the Führer. "He thought that now he could get back at the big shots," recalls Marga Weglein, "and Uncle Leo gave him the chance."

Now Heilmann followed Irene's every move with suspicion. Whenever Katzenberger approached the front building, the unemployed clerk was likely to be at his post — after all, now he had plenty of time to spy. "I often saw that Scheffler and Katzenberger communicated by gestures and signs," Heilmann testified to the police subsequently, "and right afterward they both left." Irene then allegedly came home later, "very often with a package under her arm." Naturally, an expensive gift from Katzenberger was what Heilmann's inflamed imagination led him to picture, perhaps a fur coat, a new dress, or a piece of jewelry. However, in that regard, he never actually saw anything. But his neighbor Mäsel was able to confirm his presumptions:

"Frau Scheffler lived beyond her means," Mäsel later testified to the Gestapo, and — as if it were a crime — "She had two fur coats."

By now, Mäsel was frequently peering in on the photographer's reception room from the lookout post in his living room. There, he "always saw fresh flowers standing in the window," as is recorded in the transcripts of the investigation. To be sure, Mäsel admitted to the police that he had no idea who bought those flowers, but he did once state simply that "most of the flowers might well be from Katzenberger." How could the young photographer afford to buy flowers anyway? Everyone knew that she was in trouble financially. There was clear evidence of that for Mäsel: "I know that the Scheffler woman's gas was turned off," he revealed to the Gestapo, "because she didn't pay her bill."

Eventually the photographer must have noticed that she was being watched from Mäsel's house, because he observed that she now pulled the curtains across the windows facing the rear buildings more often. Mäsel considered the pulled curtains further proof of Irene's immoral life and concluded that she was receiving "other male visitors." There was, it seemed, a highly suspicious noise in the front apartment, which strengthened her neighbor's malicious assumption. "After the male visitors left," Mäsel told the police, the photographer usually went into the small wooden annex of the front building, a sort of add-on veranda in which her bathroom was located. "She was washing herself off," asserted Mäsel confidently. "You could tell by the way the water was running."

A narrow hallway separated the wooden addition from the small carriage house where the Mäsels lived. Through the thin wooden planking, the people in the rear building could literally hear every drop of water that trickled down the drain in the front building. While Mäsel pictured some sort of unsavory activity in the front building, the photographer was just going about her work — washing pictures. The sounds of running water after she'd had a customer in her studio were consistent with that — Irene would develop the film she'd just shot or make enlargements and then wash them. Such a plausible reason for the noise of running water, which Irene pointed out many years later when she was finally asked about it in one of the subsequent trials, never occurred to Mäsel and the other neighbors. But presumably, at that point, they wouldn't have believed such a straightforward explanation anyway.

The image of an unseemly love affair had long since taken hold in the minds of the apartment dwellers on Spittlertorgraben. Now whatever they managed to find out was like a piece in a puzzle — each observation fit into a preconceived, overall picture. For instance, Heilmann spread the story that Irene took some children who were playing in her studio and locked them in another room when Katzenberger paid a visit — for immoral purposes, of course. There were readier explanations, such as the fact that she didn't want to be disturbed while photographing or was afraid that one of the children might trip over one of her expensive floodlights. But such plausible reasons were never considered by the suspicious neighbors whose gossip carried this episode up and down the stairs.

One day Margarete Östreicher, the salesman's wife who lived on the fourth floor, got into a quarrel with Irene. Presumably Irene, a first-floor renter, had failed to sweep the street and the two women started arguing about the building regulations. Frau Östreicher, who never let well enough alone, marched right over to Katzenberger. As the indignant woman later reported to the police, "He turned the thing around so that it looked like I was the guilty party in the argument." Frau Östreicher promptly leaped to the conclusion that "Katzenberger and the Scheffler woman have to be on very intimate terms."

The apartment dwellers now showed themselves to be increasingly receptive to the pervasive new spirit in Germany. Many of the tenants suddenly recalled all sorts of reasons to be upset with Katzenberger. Didn't he, as a matter of fact, try to hound the Mäsel family out of the building back in 1923 because he wanted to have the cleaning woman move in? And wasn't it the Besolds' apartment— they had moved out years ago — where Katzenberger wouldn't replace the faulty kitchen sink unless the renters paid some of the cost?

In 1937, the neighbors saw a cast-iron bathtub being carried into Fräulein Scheffler's studio apartment. Yet, on the third floor, where an office had recently opened, the bathroom fixtures had become superfluous. The fellow tenants had a new topic of conversation: the photographer who was always behind with her rent, as Heilmann knew, certainly hadn't paid for the tub; instead, she'd once again offered her tender services. In the summer of 1937, the windows of Irene's first floor apartment were made more secure. On the street side, welders fastened iron bars in front of the panes; in the rear, opposite the Mäsels, wooden shutters were installed. The rumor was that Katzenberger was no doubt shielding his love nest from curious onlookers.

In fact, it was for protection against thieves, since Irene's apartment was going to stand empty for several months. Katzenberger had finally succeeded in convincing the young woman that she had to finish the photography training that she'd been neglecting. After five years' business experience it now seemed high time for her to be officially in charge of her sister's studio, which meant that Irene had to pass her master photographer's examination. And so on a business trip to Berlin, Katzenberger paid a visit to Father Scheffler in Guben. The two men must have sat in the Schefflers' beautiful sandstone villa with their big cigars and hashed out how Little I was going to pass the necessary tests as quickly as possible.

The plan was quite simple: in the late summer of 1937, Irene spent time in Guben with her sister, an accomplished master photographer, to prepare for the second-level test and qualify as a journeyman. In October she passed the exam at the board of trade in Cottbus. Immediately afterward she went back to cramming and took a master class in Weimar, where she then passed the master's examination. It is possible that Katzenberger, who also had two shoe stores in Thuringia, used his influence to find a place for Irene in the Weimar school. A surviving letter from Father Scheffler to Katzenberger mentions an earlier visit in Guben, along with effusive thanks for the businessman's help. "If you hadn't encouraged Irene, I don't know what we would have done," he wrote on December 12, 1937, and "Irene has to be very grateful to you that you've gotten her on the right track!" Then the elderly accountant makes mention of the impending examination at Weimar: "Heartiest thanks in advance for that as well." The letter ends "with many fond greetings from the whole family."

In the summer of 1938, Leo's daughter Käthe Freimann arrived from Palestine with her husband and the two older children to convince her parents to emigrate. Opa Leo heaped the boys with bonbons and gifts, such as flashlights, crayons, and new shoes. Whenever the conversation turned to leaving the country, he immediately changed the subject. It was still possible to live quite happily in their beautiful villa in Nuremberg. Every morning Leo opened his egg at the breakfast table on the balcony, "something he couldn't live without," his grandsons later noted in their travel diary. During the day, he often played cards with them — and for money. Whenever the two boys, then six and nine years old, lost, they didn't have to pay; if they won, their grandpa paid double the sum he'd lost. Katzenberger also had his own flexible way of dealing with the rules of the Jewish faith. Every morning he gave the boys a little money for sweets, with the exception of the Sabbath — "Opa never touched money then," the children stated. But if they begged a little, Leo reached for his change purse anyway and produced the wished-for coins.

Fabro drove the children around the city, let them climb on his Harley Davidson, and showed them the glockenspiel at the former marketplace. When they wanted to have a sausage Fabro hesitated; that was something Katzenberger would have to give his permission for, said the driver — the meat certainly wasn't kosher. According to the children's report, their Opa even took them to a photo studio. There they had to hold a kitten on their laps while a lady took their pictures. Afterward she showed them the darkroom, the children later told their parents, who had no idea who the photographer was —Irene, of course .

On the third floor of the building, directly above the Wegleins', the travel agency Braun and Gutmann had its office at the time; it specialized in trips to America. During the summer of 1938, the agency repeatedly advertised crossings with the Red Star Line in the newsletter of the Nuremberg-Fürth Jewish congregations. Ship's passage from Antwerp to New York — "excellent accommodations, comfortable, inexpensive," were available, according to the ad, from 251 Reichsmarks. Leo Katzenberger knew the owners of the agency well, but didn't seem interested in their offering. During their stay in Germany, Käthe and her husband belabored her father constantly about emigrating. But it "was completely impossible" to convince him, reported Bernhard Freimann later. When Käthe and her family left, the old gentleman stood on the platform and waved his big, white handkerchief at them for a long time.

One month later, in October 1938, Katzenberger's nephew Sally Weglein, who had frequently accompanied the older man on business trips, packed his bags. Sally's wife, Marga, born and raised in Hamburg, had finally convinced her husband to leave Germany. Sally had taken an opportunity to fly to Amsterdam; Marga had been with her parents in Hamburg, but followed him by train, with one child on each hand and an insignificant amount of money in her pocketbook. The Weglein family intended to emigrate from Holland to the United States. Uncle Leo once again showed himself ready to help and gave his nephew the address of a rabbi whom he knew in New York.

On the other hand, Marga recalls that Katzenberger didn't understand the Wegleins' actions. When Sally Weglein informed him that he wanted to go to America, Katzenberger just asked uncomprehendingly, "What are you going to do there — be a shoeshine boy?"

9

THE HAPPY GROUP IN HEILMANN'S ATTIC APARTMENT IS preserved in an old photograph. Somewhat squeezed together, they're sitting around a table in the low-ceilinged room. Mäsel, with his broad face and satisfied appearance, has put on a tie. He's leaning back, his broad shoulders almost touching the door. His faultlessly coiffed wife has leaned forward and is smiling. Heilmann's daughter Marga is standing in front of the window and looking at the camera with a serious expression, her thick, dark-blond braids dangling over her shoulders. Marga's little sister Betty is a bit blurred because she couldn't sit still. Heilmann is not in the picture, so presumably he took the photograph.

A coffeepot, a luscious cake, and two potted geraniums are standing on the table. The room seems small but comfortable. White fringed curtains, freshly ironed, hang in front of the window. A framed proverb has been hung above the old-fashioned paneled door. All sorts of pictures compete for space on the wall. Such kaffeeklatsches took place fairly often, since the Mäsels and the Heilmanns enjoyed sitting together in their friendly circle. As they did, they discussed this and that, the newest neighborhood gossip or the price of food. At the time of the photo, the guests gathered around the narrow coffee table were almost certainly talking about the presumed relationship between Katzenberger and Irene. It was the end of March 1941: Marga Heilmann was celebrating her confirmation, and the Gestapo had arrested Katzenberger a few days earlier.

Of course, the intimate circle of coffee-hour guests in the attic apartment were not discussing the alleged love affair for the first time. Actually, says Marga Söltner, "it was talked about all the time." For several years they'd been even better informed about the goings-on in the photo studio, because a married couple moved into the apartment on the first floor, directly opposite Irene's, and they followed the activities in the neighboring apartment with special attentiveness. Paul Kleylein and his wife, Betty, moved in with their three children in September 1938. Kleylein ran an orthopedic appliance shop on Glockendonstrasse. Katzenberger, who was plagued by flat feet, was one of his customers. When Kleylein mentioned that he and his family were urgently in need of an apartment, Katzenberger obviously knew just what to do. He gave us a place, Kleylein later reported, in the building on Spittlertorgraben. If Katzenberger only had known whom he was taking into his house.

At that point, the question of what was going on between the Jew and the young woman had long been discussed throughout the entire district, from the Plärrer to Praterstrasse, from Fürtherstrasse to the Färbertor. The housewives were already going on about it early in the morning at the dairy shop on Dennerstrasse — Katzenberger had been seen on the street with Irene, and according to the gossip among the customers of the flower woman in the neighborhood, he had given Irene tulips. "Just think, now the Jew's given the Jew-lover a bouquet," was the a tobacconist's charged statement.

The owner of the tobacco shop on the Plärrer, Babette Gilger, with whom Katzenberger sometimes chatted when he bought his cigars, could come up with further proof for the presumed affair: she later reported to the police that the shoe dealer always purchased the same cigarettes as the photographer. "Whenever she changes brands, he does too." Even at the Disabled Veterans' Center, which the prosthesis maker often visited in hopes of getting new orders, the employees were now asking him, "Is Katzenberger still going to the Scheffler woman's apartment?" Kleylein had quickly fit right in with the rest of the denizens of Spittlertorgraben and answered, "Even the sparrows are singing it from the rooftops."

From the beginning, Kleylein considered the presumed affair in the photo studio to be a significant scandal. "One can't just sit here with a situation like that in the building," he said to his wife one evening, and it may have been on that day he decided in earnest to do something about Katzenberger and Irene. Almost all of the renters in the building were spreading nasty rumors about the pair and some, such as the unemployed Heilmann, did it with obvious malice. But none of the neighbors in the building at 19 Spittlertorgraben would take up the cause as consistently and successfully as Kleylein. Scarcely had the man moved into the house before he had the effect of multiplying the rumors. Any malevolent talk Kleylein overheard, he made into poisoned arrows that eventually reached the intended recipients. From Heilmann he knew, as he told the Gestapo later, that Katzenberger had bought Irene a car, which she "could work off easily now." His neighbor Mäsel had told him, he said, that she was getting all sorts of presents. A worker from the rear building could testify to the amount of money the businessman had already given to the Jew-lover, as they all called Irene by then. Kleylein sorted and arranged the ingredients of suspicion and hostility and distilled a corrosive, highly effective substance. No doubt about it: The orthopedic technician was a dangerous tenant.

Probably no one sensed that in the year 1938. And even later, Kleylein always took pains to play down his role, saying, "I just wanted to stay out of it." In the days of the Nazi terror, he was afraid the illicit liaison would have repercussions for his prosthesis business. "At that time you had to be careful you didn't get drawn into things." With all the wooden legs, crutches, and braces he built, Kleylein felt dependent on the health insurance and disabled veterans' agencies. "I had state contracts that I didn't want to jeopardize."

Mäsel had similar fears. Once in the spring of 1938, when the German Wehrmacht occupied Austria and even Mäsel was called up for several weeks, he had had Irene photograph him. On that occasion he advised the photographer to put an end to the affair, because "this relationship with the Jew Katzenberger could end in disaster." Of course he was less worried about the pair of presumed lovers than he was that the liaison could hurt him, because the Nazi authorities would expect that as a neighbor he would want to maintain propriety and take steps against such a forbidden relationship. Mäsel believed in all seriousness, as he later testified, "that they could accuse me of not having stepped in earlier to put a stop to the affair."

It is indeed a special paradox of that era that the very people "afraid of being drawn into things" tended to get themselves actively involved as a precaution and so turned themselves into perpetrators. Yet at the same time they went on living without any awareness of having done anything wrong. Presumably their consciences were clear because so many people were acting the same way. On Nuremberg's Spittlertorgraben there was gossip about the suspected love affair not just in the building, but in the streets all around — the milk lady, the tobacconist, and the employees at the Disabled Veteran's Office all contributed malicious chatter. On the other hand, people such as Katzenberger's chauffeur, Wilhelm Fabro, who paid no attention to the talk and preferred to polish his Harley Davidson, were the extremely rare exception. Each one of the tenants on Spittlertorgraben felt personally innocent, but they combined to provide life and strength to a system of murderous injustice.

"You could see something coming," was Mäsel's explanation for his conduct. And Kleylein claimed the relationship between Scheffler and Katzenberger "had to lead to a catastrophe sooner or later." But the Mäsels and the Kleyleins, the Heilmanns and the Östreichers — they themselves were a part of that catastrophe, if not its initiators.

Irene had run afoul of several of the tenants' sacred laws. She interfered with their need for order and unleashed their feelings of envy. The Weimar Republic, with its currency devaluation, its constantly changing regimes and street battles, had left a feeling of hopeless disarray in many people, especially those of the lower middle class. In the years before the Nazi takeover, a climate of fear had arisen, thanks to unemployment, inflation, and the growing displacement of craftsmen and small businesses by larger firms.

People like Mäsel, who'd lived in the same surroundings on Spittlertorgraben since childhood, felt a great longing for order. The pedantic toolmaker hated confusion. After the war, when he and his family were going on a trip to the country, everyone had to be standing in front of the door with their coats and bags an hour ahead of time, or he would go into a terrible rage. Happy-go-lucky Irene, on the other hand, created only confusion: her lack of concern for money and the easy friendliness with which she greeted even unfamiliar men provoked envy and resentment in the scrub-brush-and-wax world of the apartment house, where the most the husbands could risk was a sidelong glance at the photographer.

But it was primarily a certain hatred of Jews lodged in so many minds that made the catastrophe possible. That hate was directed against Katzenberger as a representative of Judaism and had little to do with his person; it could just as easily have happened to any other Jew. For that reason, people failed to feel guilty afterward. They really had nothing against Katzenberger personally. "Herr Katzenberger was always very obliging," neighbor Mäsel reported later. And Betty Kleylein pronounced sweetly, "He was a fine man."

Nevertheless, the testimony of the neighbors to the Gestapo was based on their opinion that even the slightest contact with a Jew was objectionable. If Katzenberger hadn't been Jewish, perhaps there would have been a bit of talk, but nothing more. People complained about Irene, Betty Kleylein pointed out, "because of her carrying on with Katzenberger." The trouble-makers failed to see themselves as active participants; they all looked upon themselves as victims of propaganda. "We were all trained to think of them as subhuman," says Fritz Söltner, Heilmann's son-in-law, in his comfortable row house, shrugging his shoulders. The old man wiggles forward a bit on the patchwork quilt protecting the sofa, stares straight at the person sitting opposite, and adds, "Problem was that it was a Jew, that's what it was."

By 1938, the tenants had long since separated into two camps. The Jewish Weglein family on the second floor withdrew more and more from their neighbors. Walter Weglein, then eight, was no longer allowed to go to Rosenau Park because it was too dangerous. And while the Mäsels and Heilmanns regularly held their get-togethers over coffee, Irene, too, was increasingly isolated. Only the Heilmann's daughter Marga, who always hopped down the steps so nimbly, still rang Irene's doorbell — punctually at noontime every day after school, to take Irene's dachshund, Dommerl, for his walk in Rosenau Park.

Even Irene's relationship with Katzenberger had changed a little. The old gentleman did indeed still come by her studio to have a cup of coffee and smoke a cigarette, and people still saw the two of them strolling through Rosenau Park. Her lighthearted flirt, the Leo Katzenberger who had even irritated his brothers for a while, had disappeared. Instead of the mature cavalier, a role he loved to play with young women, the merchant had now turned into more of a paternal advisor.

The aging *bon vivant* proved himself a dependable helper in affairs of the heart as well as those of business, in a way that her curious fellow renters would not have foreseen. Irene was twenty-eight years old and it was time to think about marriage. There were, of course, plenty of admirers, but which was the right one? Good-natured Uncle Leo took a look at the young gentle-men and inquired about their financial circumstances. "I advised her in mat-ters concerning marriage," he later testified to the court. With that in mind, he'd once even "done some traveling to have a look at the candidate's family."

The photographer did plenty of fluttering around, so the list of hopefuls kept changing.

But then Irene met the love of her life. He was a smart-looking charmer with dark blond hair, an automobile salesman by trade. In the only photo of him that survives, his right eyebrow is raised knowingly and he's wearing a winning smile. Hans Seiler moved into her apartment in October 1938. Irene introduced the young man as her fiancée. From then on, however, it was not just the handsome car salesman who took to boarding in her studio; his identical twin brother, Josef, moved in for several months as well. The neighbors were hardly able to tell one tall blond man from the other. The happy commune on the first floor must have scandalized their straight-laced fellow tenants, and besides, the photographer wasn't even married yet. And so there was yet another opportunity to go on about Irene and her questionable behavior. Katzenberger was probably not pleased by the three-member commune either, and he turned up less frequently at Irene's apartment. "Her fiancée and his brother were frequent guests," was the way he described the situation later, "so that we got together less often, and certainly not alone."

On one of those infrequent visits, Heilmann spied on the businessman. Katzenberger had stood in front of the building and rung one of the apartment bells; Heilmann, who was following him, thought it was Irene's. But then Katzenberger walked up the stairs to the next floor, to the Weglein family. Heilmann decided that it was a ruse, and hid in the Kleyleins' first-floor apartment. Together with Betty Kleylein, he kept Irene's apartment door under surveillance. After a little while, according to Heilmann's version of the story, Katzenberger came back down the stairs and allegedly disappeared into Irene's studio. Playing the stool pigeon wasn't the least bit embarrassing to Heilmann, who told the police what he'd seen. The fired clerk, revenge on his mind, was now tenaciously pursuing the Jewish businessman.

But Leo Katzenberger had other worries. For some time the Jewish congregations in Franconia had been coming under more and more pressure. As smaller organizations, it was particularly difficult for them to stand up against the sanctions and repressions of the Nazis. In 1937 the first started to dissolve. In the summer of 1938 the process accelerated. Katzenberger belonged to a committee formed by the council of Bavarian congregations to oversee closures and was now constantly traveling around the state to help congregations dissolve in an orderly and legal way.

In June 1938, a board member of the Nuremberg congregations was summoned to the city council by phone. Albert Fechheimer, at that time a deputy chairman of the congregations, along with Leo Katzenberger, returned with the city administration's demand that the congregations should immediately and voluntarily agree to the destruction of the large synagogue on Hans Sachs Platz. Katzenberger and his colleagues on the council indignantly rejected the proposal and made it known at city hall that they would "yield only to force," whereupon the city council, at their session of August 3, voted to expropriate the house of worship. Councilman Georg Haberkern, Nazi district inspector and owner of the Blaue Traube, duly expressed his "thanks for this deed" to the mayor, according to the minutes of the meeting. The legal basis was provided by the First Statute for the Reconfiguration of the City of the Reich's Party Rallies, in which the national government decreed that the synagogue should be destroyed, at the request of Nuremberg's mayor.

On the morning of August 10, 1938, SA troops, Hitler Youth, and thousands of spectators streamed into the square in front of the synagogue. "All those who were able to interrupt their day's work did so," reported the *Franconian Daily News.* "Everyone wanted to experience the beginning of the demolition of the synagogue." The columned entrance was hidden behind a wooden grandstand. In great haste, synagogue members had been able to rescue several valuable Torah scrolls and prayer books. Streicher himself initiated the destruction. Assuming a victor's pose, in a white dress uniform, the short, bald-headed man stood on the wooden platform and rhetorically asked the crowd whether the Oriental-style synagogue building belonged in that German city, Nuremberg. "The answer he received," according to the report in the *Franconian Daily News* was "a thousandfold 'No!' " Immediately afterward, Streicher bellowed "We are living in a great time!" The onlookers had greeted him "with cries that built up into a single roar — Heil!" He continued, "The seed that we have sown is now coming up." Then there was a ringing of bells, and with the words "Let us begin," Streicher gave the order to start the demolition.

Troops of laborers from the construction firm Reinforced Concrete Construction Company took care of the rest. The cost of demolition, estimated by the contractor at 550,000 Reichsmarks, was covered by the city from the Account for Special Building Projects. The construction firm later provided the city with a refund in the amount of seventy thousand Reichsmarks for the heavy sandstone blocks that had formed the walls of the synagogue — the stone was sold for use in canal construction.

I O

A CURIOUS VISITOR PRESENTED HIMSELF AT THE OFFICES of the shoe whole-
salers. The man spoke not a word of German, and Margarete Hölzel, the secretary and receptionist, couldn't understand a thing at first. Gesturing
excitedly, the visitor soon made it clear to her that he wanted to see Leo
Katzenberger and so, on that day in the last week of September 1938, Fräulein
Hölzel led him back to the executive offices. The visitor introduced himself as
Octave Gysermanns, a traveling salesman from Belgium. Katzenberger, who
spoke French fluently, knew the man. The Belgian had already appeared at his
home once, perhaps two months previously, about a somewhat delicate matter.

As Katzenberger closed his office door, Gysermanns got right to the point,
saying he was in transit from Vienna to Brussels and wanted to know whether
the businessman might have "money to be taken along." Katzenberger said
no, then explained to the Belgian that he didn't need to send money abroad,
since he was going to stay in Germany. The Belgian countered, "I can get any
amount through; we work in pairs." And didn't the merchant have friends or
acquaintances who perhaps wanted to move some money? Katzenberger put
him off by telling him he couldn't say right then; he'd have to do some asking

around. The Belgian persisted, "Don't you have a few checks I could take?" By then the conversation was becoming too bizarre for Katzenberger and he tried to get rid of the man. No, there were no checks there in the office, only at home. "But my wife is away," lied the businessman, and therefore the Belgian would have to come back at another time. Gysermanns indicated he would come back the following week, then started to leave.

As Katzenberger accompanied him out, the visitor looked around once more, taking in the business activities that were clearly still being carried out as usual in the rear building, then stopped. "How does it happen," he asked, almost in passing, "that you still have your business?" By that time, many Jewish concerns had already been sold or had closed up, so the question didn't strike Katzenberger as particularly unusual. But he did look upon his own business as an exception. "The Germans don't have time for me," was his sarcastic answer to the Belgian. "They leave me in peace."

Barely two weeks later Leo Katzenberger and his wife, Claire, were in the Nuremberg Police Department's jail while an investigation proceeded. The Belgian businessman Gysermanns provided evidence against the couple for alleged money smuggling. Ancient, dusty records of the 1938 investigation, still archived in the basement of Frankfurt's prosecutor's office, reveal what happened.

It had all started with an anonymous mailing. In July 1938, a large registered envelope without a return address and containing a small, brown package had been delivered to the villa on Praterstrasse. The accompanying note bore, in woman's handwriting, "per instruction of Dr. Jessel." In the package were twelve blank checks for a checking account at the Frankfurt Postal Bank, all bearing the signature "Dr. Jessel." The name and signature were well known to the Katzenbergers, because they belonged to the Frankfurt attorney Dr. Alex Jessel, husband of Claire's sister Berte. Several weeks earlier, Claire had received a postcard from her sister, bearing the cancellation stamp of a Belgian seaside resort near Ostende. Her husband, Attorney Jessel, had suffered a nervous collapse, it said, and therefore they had both come to the spa to recover. Out of politeness, the Katzenbergers sent a card to the address indicated with the brief message, "We wish you a speedy recovery."

A few days after the package was delivered, Claire Katzenberger found herself confronted by a strange man standing in front of the door on Praterstrasse —Gysermanns. The man handed her a letter from the Jessels in which the attorney identified Gysermanns as his representative. Claire telephoned her husband, but he was out of the office and did not return home until late that evening. In the meantime, Claire had questioned the Belgian a little and got him to admit that he didn't know the Jessels personally — which struck her as odd. But the envelope, on which a big K had been scribbled, contained unambiguous instructions in her brother-in-law's handwriting. Katzenberger was to give most of the checks to the visitor and keep a few for himself.

Arriving home late, Leo Katzenberger reached into the drawer of the beautiful old secretary standing in the hallway and pulled out the small brown packet. He counted the checks carefully and placed a number of them in an envelope. He then enclosed a handwritten note indicating the number of checks and scribbled "Greetings to you!" underneath, so that Jessel would have a way of checking on the courier. Whereupon the Belgian departed. A short time later the Katzenbergers received another postcard from Jessel's wife, confirming, in a circumspect way, that the checks had been cashed. The Katzenbergers heard nothing more about the matter.

In the meantime, Gysermanns' travel habits took an unusual turn. During the following weeks, the Belgian appeared in Frankfurt six times, always staying at the Excelsior, a luxury hotel, for one or two days. During his first visit, Gysermanns went immediately to the postal bank located on a side street around the corner from the main railroad station. Then he looked for an address, 17 Unterlindau. A friend of Jessel's lived there — the Jewish businessman Max Gross. The Belgian had an envelope with instructions for him, too. In the following weeks, Gross accompanied his foreign visitor to the postal bank several times; the two of them withdrew sums of money on each occasion: eight hundred, three thousand, and even five thousand Reichsmarks. Gross kept part of the money to pay obligations that Jessel had left behind in Germany. The remainder was spirited across the German-Belgian border by Gysermanns.

On August 25, 1938, however, problems arose at the postal bank when Gysermanns tried to cash a check for eleven hundred Reichsmarks. The teller had reservations about the signature; a second check for the same amount, which the Belgian submitted several hours later, also failed to go through. This time he was told that the account was overdrawn. The truth was probably that the teller had gotten suspicious. In any case, "a person designated by the bank" presented himself to the investigations division of the Frankfurt Customs Office and described what had gone on. Gysermanns had no idea that this had happened and unsuspectingly traveled to Germany for a sixth time on September 19.

When Gysermanns walked over to the teller's window and again produced a check for eleven hundred marks, the bank employee called the customs investigators directly. The Belgian was arrested. For the Frankfurt Public Prosecutor's office that was not an unusual occurrence; they had a whole series of pending cases involving money smuggling. "According to recent evidence from the Customs Investigation Division," stated in Gysermanns' arrest warrant, "Belgian citizens are making a business of withdrawing funds in Germany for Jews wishing to emigrate and smuggling the money across the border." It was not at all surprising that currency smuggling was flourishing. As a rule, Jewish citizens leaving the country were permitted to take very little money with them; however, if their citizenship were revoked first, the state claimed all of their funds. It seems that the policy of the Nazi state with regard to the Jews was, from the very beginning, directed toward confiscating all their possessions. The better-off families did everything possible to shift their money abroad.

In Brussels there were certain cafés and meeting places where one could find people willing to help in that regard. One such address was that of a German, Arnold Oberschmuckler, on Boulevard St. Michel. Gysermanns, who sometimes listed his profession as secretary, sometimes as detective, had met him through an intermediary. In July 1938, Oberschmuckler engaged the Belgian for the first time, asking him to go to Germany "to look after Dr. Jessel's affairs." By the time of his arrest in September, Gysermanns had taken approximately twenty thousand Reichsmarks out of the country for the Frankfurt lawyer.

In the course of the very first hearing, the Belgian was promised by the customs investigators that he'd get a lighter sentence if he would name his collaborators. And so, in September 1938, Gysermanns led the agents to Katzenberger's company. While, inside, the money smuggler was being taken to the director's office by the secretary, Hölzel, the two customs investigators were waiting in the street, hoping to catch Katzenberger red-handed. The plan failed, however, because Katzenberger became suspicious and showed Gysermanns the door. The investigators left. Gysermanns wracked his brain to see what else he could bring up against "that dirty Jew," because the investigators, so he wrote to his wife from prison, had promised "that I might be free by Friday if they manage to arrest that Jew in Nuremberg."

The following day, Wednesday, October 5, 1938, the police rang the doorbell at the Katzenbergers' home in Nuremberg. They interrogated the merchant's wife in her own apartment. It was Yom Kippur, and the devout Claire had been fasting for twenty-six hours. In answer to the investigators' questions, she managed to stammer that neither she nor her husband had "done anything involving business" for Jessel and certainly not anything involving money. Elegantly clad in a blue suit and matching blue hat, she was taken to a detention cell at the police station. The agents arrested Leo Katzenberger at Spittlertorgraben; that was done so discreetly that not even the nosy neighbors got wind of it. During his interrogation, Katzenberger admitted receiving the checks, but claimed he'd believed that they were going to be used to pay smaller debts owed by Dr. Jessel. Said the businessman, "It never entered my mind that someone might withdraw larger sums as well and take them abroad."

The investigating judge was unwilling to attribute that much naiveté to Katzenberger. "There is no doubt," he wrote in his indictment, "that, given the mysterious circumstances, an experienced businessman such as Leo Katzenberger must have known that he was actively cooperating with a money-smuggling operation." But perhaps Katzenberger really had been too trusting to imagine that Attorney Jessel would knowingly involve him in such an questionable affair. When, at 10:50 in the morning on October 7 the arrest warrant was read, Leo Katzenberger said for the record, "I have done nothing wrong. I was not even aware that my brother-in-law had not returned to Germany."

Leo and Claire Katzenberger were detained for three weeks at the prison on Bärenschanzstrasse in Nuremberg; then they were transferred to Frankfurt. The reason the two of them were incarcerated was probably because Gysermanns was lying. In order to better his own position, the Belgian had attempted to pin as many illegal actions on Leo Katzenberger as he could. Thus — so claimed the Belgian — the businessman had met his train in Frankfurt in August 1938, accompanied him to the postal bank, and accepted a check. That was vehemently denied by Leo Katzenberger.

By the middle of November, the investigating authorities finally saw the affair in the proper light. It had become clear even to the state's attorney that he was not holding two practiced currency smugglers, but a Jewish couple who'd gotten themselves involved in the affair out of kindness and ignorance. On receipt of a payment of 2,618 Reichsmarks plus an additional 428.50 for court costs, Leo and Claire Katzenberger were released on November 17 — they'd come through relatively unscathed.

I I

IT LOOKED LIKE IT WAS GOING TO TURN OUT TO BE THE USUAL sort of morning for Walter Weglein. The boy crawled out of bed, ate his breakfast, and slipped his arms into the straps of his backpack. Still a little sleepy, he picked his way carefully — he wore thick glasses — along Spittlertorgraben and over to the Plärrer. From there he would take the streetcar to Fürth, where he attended the Jewish school. He had just gotten to the stop when Richard Erle, a friend of the family, came toward him. "Do you mean to tell me you're going to school?" asked Erle with an expression of horror on his face that remains in Walter Weglein's memory to this day. "Go home, boy, there's no school today!"

There was no school for an entire week. And, for the time being, Walter was sent to stay with his Uncle David, Leo Katzenberger's brother. The move to the spacious apartment on Frommannstrasse seemed a little strange to the eight-year-old boy — David's home looked like it had been through an air raid. The sofa had been broken in two, the cabinets overturned, and broken glass and porcelain were lying around everywhere. "They told me there'd been an explosion in Uncle David's apartment," relates Walter Weglein, who is now in his seventies. "Why was I supposed to be staying in that apartment, then?"

The morning on which Walter unexpectedly had no school was November 10, 1938, the day after Reichskristallnacht. And it was for safety's sake that the elder Wegleins had sent their son to his Uncle David, a widower living alone. In the apartment house on Spittlertorgraben, where the Wegleins were the only Jewish tenants, it had remained quiet overnight and there had been no damage at all to the shoe business in the rear building. But it stood to reason that the gangs might show up one of the following nights and so it seemed to the Wegleins that their son would be safest at David's already totally wrecked apartment.

Richard Erle, who sent the young boy home from the Plärrer, had presumably just come from his father-in-law's apartment on Hochstrasse, which lay behind Rosenau Park. What he'd learned there was shocking. During the night Jakob Speth, Erle's father-in-law and a hop dealer, had been thrown down the stairs. The old man died instantly. Erle himself ran a large business that sold radios, lamps, and other electrical appliances. His store was on Karolinenstrasse, not far from the Katzenbergers' shoe business; on that morning, however, it looked like a pile of rubble.

During the nights around November 9, 1938, synagogues all over Germany were set on fire and Jewish homes and businesses were destroyed by Nazi vandals. At least ninety-one people lost their lives; property damages reached several hundred million Reichsmarks. More than thirty-thousand Jews were interned in concentration camps. In Nuremberg, the Nazis acted with unusual brutality.

Around midnight, SA men assembled in the Nuremberg's marketplace, by then renamed Adolf Hitler Platz; some had been driven in from the surrounding areas in trucks. They were carrying crowbars, hammers, and axes; several even had daggers and pistols. In addition, "every SA man had a knapsack fastened to his belt," reported Bernhard Kolb, "to carry money, jewelry, photographs, and any other valuables they had seized." How they went about their work of destruction was described as follows decades later by an eyewitness who lived on Kaulbachplatz: "Window panes cracked, fragments of glass fell to the ground, men yelled, someone cried out. Terse commands could be heard above the splintering of wood and glass. . . . Furniture flew out onto the street and was hacked into kindling. Mattresses were slit open, feathers whirled around. . . . The scene was illuminated by something burning."

In fact, the synagogue on Essenweinstrasse was blazing brightly. Originally the house of worship was used only by the Adas Israel, but since August, when the larger synagogue had been torn down, other believers were going there as well. The building had been set on fire professionally, by none other than the city's fire department, as Police Chief Martin reported when he arrived later in the evening.

While the synagogue was in flames, Nazi thugs, according to reports of eyewitnesses, drove Jewish families who lived nearby out of their homes and over to the front of their burning synagogue. They must have feared for their lives, because from the crowd of Aryan onlookers around the fire a hysterical voice suddenly demanded that the Jews be driven into the flames — which did not happen.

All the while, SA gangs were creating havoc in Jewish homes, behaving with undescribable brutality. At least nine people were murdered in Nuremberg that night; another twelve killed themselves, or at least suicide was certified as the cause of death. According to later reports by the city authorities, there were twenty-six deaths in all. Bernhard Kolb recorded most of them by name. Paul Lebrecht of 20 Pirckheimerstrasse was beaten to death in his apartment and his body thrown out of the window by SA men. "However, his clothing caught on the iron grillwork of the balcony and he was found hanging there dead," reported Kolb. Nathan Langstadt of 47 Rankestrasse was found by his relatives "in the bathroom of his apartment with his throat cut." Sigmund Oppenheimer, an old man of eighty years, was met in prison by Kolb. He was "completely covered with blood," noted the bookkeeper; "The skin of his head was split open."

On the day following Kristallnacht, Nuremberg's old city was a picture of widespread destruction. Almost all of the businesses still in Jewish hands on the big shopping streets of Königstrasse, Karolinenstrasse, and Breite Gasse had their windows smashed, furniture broken, and stock ruined or looted. The stores of the Katzenberger–Springmann chain were not spared. In Würzburg, where the brothers had a shoe store near the marketplace, there had been an outbreak of vandalism on November 8. All seven show windows had been smashed, after which the crowd poured in, pulled shoes out of their boxes, and threw them on the floor. Someone hacked off a faucet, so that the shop was soon under water. David Katzenberger found that the shoes in the window displays had been "partly stolen, partly slashed to ribbons."

In Straubing, likewise, Nazi gangs had already struck on the night of the

November 8 as well. Show windows, outdoor display cases, louvered shutters, even the cash register of the Katzenbergers' store were totally demolished.

The Katzenberger brothers had to clean up glass fragments everywhere after November 9. The brown-shirted vandals had stormed through almost all of their stores, no matter where they were located — in Fulda, Hanau, Aschaffenburg, or Bad Mergentheim. Their showcases and show windows were destroyed. All together, as David Katzenberger later recalled, the glass damage alone amounted to some seven thousand Reichsmarks. The owners had to pay for it out-of-pocket, since the insurance company refused to cover the damages.

Business owners lodged protests at the office of the insurance commissioner in Berlin to no effect. On November 12, the national government had hastily passed the Statute Concerning Proper Maintenance of Jewish Places of Business, according to which businesspeople like the Katzenbergers had to pay for damages themselves, because they resulted "from the indignation of the people over the provocations of international Jewry."

12

IN CRAMER-KLETT PALACE'S SMOKING ROOM JULIUS STREICHER was sitting at his heavy mahogany desk deep in thought, his arm propped on the olive-green leather surface. The Gauleiter had called the nucleus of his followers together, including his adjutant, Hanns König, and Deputy Gauleiter Karl Holz. Probably also sitting in one of the horsehair-upholstered chairs on that occasion was the district economic advisor, Otto Strobl, who at the same time was president of the Nuremberg Chamber of Commerce and Industry and also chief of AEG, Germany's equivalent of General Electric. The group met at about noon on November 10, 1938, to discuss the events of the previous night. "Each one of us was convinced," reported Holz afterward, "that we were facing an entirely new set of circumstances concerning the Jewish question." The circle of men also seemed unanimous in their estimation that the time had come for "independent action in Franconia."

Holz seemed worked up by the bloodthirsty excesses of the night; from his viewpoint, a new revolution was in progress. He excitedly proposed to the Gauleiter that all Jews should immediately be put in " a sort of internment camp" where they would be kept "under surveillance and control." Holz argued further that "the housing shortage would then be at least partially relieved." But Streicher toned things down, saying it was "not feasible" at the time. Holz, who generally carried out Streicher's orders without grumbling, would not let up. A new, massive wave of Aryanization, argued Holz, could proceed "just as legally" as the transfer of Jewish businesses to Aryan hands that had already been going on in Nuremberg under greater or lesser degrees of pressure. Finally, Holz played his trump card: it would raise several million marks, which would flow into the Nazi district treasury. And with that, Streicher was convinced. "If you think you can carry it out, then do it," he said, then gave Holz a formal order and decreed, "The sums made available are then to be used for the construction of a district party school."

The same afternoon Holz called in the necessary aides to prepare for the real estate theft. In Nuremberg he brought in Johann Heinrich Schätzler, known in the city as a real estate agent and someone experienced in a variety of professions. Schätzler, sixty-one years old, had originally been a gilder, but his business had gone bankrupt twice, and late in the 1920s he moved into real estate. Since May 1933, he'd belonged to the Nazi Party and soon was functioning in the Deutsche Arbeits Front (German Workers' Front, abbreviated as DAF) as a section chief in charge of real estate in the House and Home Department.

The Fürth District was to be the responsibility of city councillor Hans Sandreuther, an unscrupulous party follower who, as it would soon be revealed, had an absolutely insatiable desire to make himself rich. Additionally, Holz requested SA leader Fritz Hutzler to arrange for the necessary patrol squads, because it was doubtless clear to Streicher's deputy from the beginning that the bargains he envisioned were not going to be offered voluntarily in every case. Sandreuther went right to work in Fürth: he requested a trusted notary at city hall to draw up the necessary documents. By the evening of November 11, the first contracts with Jewish building owners were already concluded; the notary processed agreements in assembly-line fashion until five in the morning. At nine, things started up again.

In Nuremberg, Deputy Holz's henchmen were soon disposing of building after building — by February 1939, 596 properties had changed hands. The pattern was straightforward: First, the party took over the piece of real estate; then, upon receipt of a "donation," it would be sold to one of the buyers chosen by the Nazis. Soon it was as if money were pouring into the Franconian party's coffers through a wide-open floodgate; in just a few weeks Holz and his men took in more than 1.5 million Reichsmarks. At the same time, several of them, including König, ended up owning valuable property themselves; others, such as Schätzler, pocketed hefty commissions and private "donations."

While Holz and his buddies were still drawing up plans to get hold of the property of Franconian Jews, representatives of the Nuremberg trade guilds were sitting in Hotel Deutscher Hof discussing the takeover of the businesses of Jewish tradesmen and artisans, those that had not already been destroyed in the nightly forays. Wholesale and retail business came under increased pressure: a separate commission, headed by the Gau inspector Georg Haberkern, was in charge of seeing that these businesses' registration would be canceled with the Board of Trade. According to the division of labor, the person in charge of the confiscation of Jewish industrial buildings was Strobl, the president of the Chamber of Commerce and Industry. The building sales were processed by Holz's assistants, for the most part in the offices of the Deutsche Arbeits Front (DAF) on Essenweinstrasse, just a stone's throw from the burned-out synagogue. Jewish property owners had to appear there when summoned or they would be forcibly brought in. Obviously, the news of impending building takeovers had spread through the populace, because the DAF received scores of telephone calls from people "wanting to know if they'd have a chance to buy a building cheaply."

In order to process the sales as quickly as possible, the notaries had developed an easily workable scheme: the Jewish building owners were forced to sign a standardized sales agreement in which practically all the contractual details were already filled in, including selling price, assumption of mortgage, and date of settlement; all that was missing was the buyer's name. Inserted instead was the notation "Purchaser to be named by the representative of the Franconian Nazi Party Administration." The building owner transferred all of his property rights, and the procedure was "basically simplified," in the words of the broker Schätzler, "since the Jew himself . . . is no longer needed for the sale to take place."

Even the sales prices were firmly stated ahead of time: "Ten percent of the assessed value, providing that the property is not encumbered," was the principle Schätzler settled on; if there was an outstanding mortgage, the property was "taken over for the amount of residual mortgage debt." The Jewish owner either received ten percent or nothing at all.

Ernst Lebrecht was one of the first Jews to be put through the wringer. What Lebrecht experienced is well documented, because a short while later, in January 1939, he testified to the Nuremberg Gestapo about his treatment.

It should be pointed out that, at the time, there was a great deal of talk about the brutal treatment of Jewish building owners at the DAF offices; it even reached the ears of Police Chief Martin. Martin maintained his contacts with several representatives of the Nuremberg Jewish community, and he was becoming more and more of a rival to the Streicher clique, whose moronic brutality offended the ambitious bureaucrat. In strict secrecy, Martin ordered the interrogation of Jewish property owners to find out what was actually going on; of course, the careerist Martin did not do it out of brotherly love — he had begun his battle against Streicher.

The transcript of Ernst Lebrecht's Gestapo interrogation reports several hours of torture. On Saturday, November 12, around 3:30 P.M., agents took him from his apartment to the DAF building, where they led him to a "soundproofed cellar." There he was made to fear for his life — a favorite method of the Nuremberg Nazis. He had to stand with his face to the wall while one of the guards asked him when he wanted to be shot. Lebrecht reacted with presence of mind and said, "When I've talked to my wife." Then he had to do deep knee bends for hours and, along with the seven other prisoners in the basement, had to sing the refrain of a song over and over. According to his recollection, the song went something like this: "On November 7 a German was murdered in Paris by a Jew and we're members of that murderous race."

After several hours, SA men led Lebrecht up to the third floor, where someone from the Harren photography studio in Nuremberg took pictures of him. First he was photographed clothed; then Lebrecht was told to undress and the photographer shot him again. The nude pictures were made on express order Deputy Gauleiter Holz to "photographically document the racial characteristics of Jews," as Karl Harren later explained. At the time, Harren ran a business on Färberstrasse right around the corner from the DAF building. He claims not to have been paid for the photographs: "We worked on a purely voluntary basis."

Around 9 P.M., after being tormented for hours, SA men took Lebrecht up to the conference room. Schätzler was sitting at a table. Lebrecht was placed in front of two extremely bright floodlights that gave off so much heat that anyone standing under them immediately began to sweat. "The negotiations were generally successful," Schätzler reported later, because the Jews softened up in that manner rather quickly "provided the desired signatures." Lebrecht agreed to the price of 10,560 Reichsmarks, which was supposed to represent ten percent of the assessed value, even though the building had been assessed at 120,000 marks.

On one of the days following Kristallnacht, a Nazi automobile pulled into the courtyard of the Katzenbergers' office. At that point, Leo was still sitting in jail in Frankfurt; only his brothers Max and David were taken away. What the two of them went through at the DAF office can no longer be determined. There were various methods of torturing Jews: some had to lash each other with bundles of twigs, others were ordered to bang their heads against the walls. Max and David Katzenberger, as far as can be determined, never talked about their "treatment" afterward.

It is a matter of record, however, that eight days after Kristallnacht, on Thursday, November 17, two comprehensive sales agreements were put in front of them at the DAF office for their signatures. One contract concerned the sale of the villa on Praterstrasse. The building, for which the Katzenbergers had paid 115,000 Reichsmarks in the spring of 1918, was to go to a "purchaser to be named by a representative of the Franconian Nazi Administration" for 45,730 marks: 40,000 marks were to be taken on as a fixed mortgage, and the buyer had to pay 10 percent of the assessed value, which amounted to 5,730 marks.

The second contract dealt with the property on Spittlertorgraben. Schätzler and his people had painstakingly set the price at 65,234.55 marks, which reflected the transfer of the mortgage for 56,234.55 marks plus 10 percent of assessed value of 90,900 Reichsmarks, rounded down to 9,000. In the year 1919, the Katzenberger brothers had bought the centrally located apartment building together with its side and rear buildings for 185,000 Reichsmarks. The assessed value of properties was established more or less arbitrarily and was considerably less than the value placed on them for insurance purposes. That the district authorities were going to pay only 10 percent of the former was quite a presumption, but there was nothing else Max and David could do but sign the contracts. What they didn't yet know was that even the 10 percent would never arrive.

Ten days later the notary Fritz Hussel recorded an additional contract regarding the Spittlertorgraben property. Geo Müller Sr. and Geo Müller Jr., who ran a stamping and engraving business on nearby Jakobsplatz, had come forward to buy the building. Father and son were both members of the Nazi party, and, probably for that reason, they got first crack at the Spittlertorgraben bargain. Geo Müller Jr., now in his nineties, claims that he paid 200,000 Reichsmarks for the property, but on his purchase contract, today a dusty, yellowed piece of paper, is the sum of 65,000 Reichsmark. As he relates this, the old man holds his white-haired head in his hands — the matter appears to make him rather uncomfortable.

The Katzenberger brothers had to deal with buyers who were even worse, including Carl Scheuermann and his son, businessmen from Fulda. Until November 1938, Scheuermann Sr. was employed as the manager of one of the Katzenbergers' branch stores. After Kristallnacht, he wanted to get his own hands on the cash register and the transfer of ownership couldn't go quickly enough. By Sunday, November 13, he had had a contract to purchase the store drawn up by a local notary and then set out on the road to Nuremberg. According to David Katzenberger's memory of the event, Scheuermann brought along the notary and his secretary, the Fulda Gestapo chief, and someone from the local Nazi administration.

"Under certain threats," Katzenberger reported later, he was forced by the travelers to sell the building in Fulda to Scheuermann "for far less than it was worth." The building with three apartments, retail store, and a small rear building in a top business location was let go for 35,000 Reichsmarks; it had been purchased for 60,000 marks in 1919. The selling price included the assumption of the mortgage of 21,000 marks together with a cash payment of 14,000 at settlement. The Scheuermann family didn't even pay that discount price, as was discovered after the war.

At the time, the Katzenberger brothers still had around a dozen stores in their possession. Shortly before Kristallnacht, Max and David had been negotiating with a Berlin investor who wanted to take over the entire business. Through that sale, at least some money would have gone directly to the Jewish businessmen. Sales of that sort generally required approval by the district economic advisor, in this case Strobl, but he handed many applications on to Streicher's adjutant, König. In the case of the Katzenberger brothers, the Gauleiter himself made the decision, curtly rejecting the sale. As David Katzenberger reported later, "The interested party went to Streicher personally, but did not receive the permit." Most of the stores were subsequently demolished during the orgies of destruction and looting; in many cases their value fell to zero and there was nothing to be done but board them up.

Leo Katzenberger had been incarcerated for six weeks because of the currency affair. Yet within that short time, almost everything that he and his brothers had built up over decades was destroyed. When the businessman went to jail at the beginning of October 1938, he could, despite all the troubles of the times, still think of himself as a fairly prosperous man. When released he returned to total devastation, complete disorder, and he no longer had a business. During the six weeks of incarceration a radical change had taken place outside — and there seemed to be no escape, even for Leo Katzenberger.

Katzenberger was asked to appear at the DAF on Monday, December 5, 1938. He was to produce his notarized agreement for the sale of the villa in Praterstrasse. Holz and his men were now in a hurry to take possesion of the property, because there had been indications that the national government in Berlin wanted to shut down the Fraconia real estate scam. Nearly forty houses were resold in Nuremberg in the weeks following Kristallnacht.

Soon, however, the party brokers discovered that it was even more lucrative to hold on to the houses, especially since suddenly nearly 40,000 Reichsmarks flowed into the party till in monthly rents. From then on the party functionaries retained possession of properties like the Katzenberger villa on Praterstrasse. The party pretended to own the properties, because Holz and his comrades didn't pay a penny for the houses, they only dealt with notarized sales offers.

Now there was the threat of a new regulation. Holz realized that the houses were in an an unlegislated area. To be able to continue to collect the rents, they had to immediately be transferred to party ownership in the land registry. So on Sunday, December 4, Holz rounded up a handful of notaries and land registry officials to undertake the necessary notarizations and entries. A certification marathon of sorts took place; the notary Hussel alone certified the sale of fifty-three houses. The buyer was always the same person: Karl Holz.

Even the court officials didn't find their Sunday occupation scandalous, as file by file they entered the sales in the land registry. They all went compliantly along, with the exception of the land registry judge from Fürth, a man named Leis. He had previously refused to enter a sale in the land registry office in Fürth, even though the buyer was the town itself. Now the judge was put under great political pressure and it was said that the matter would be reported to the leadership of the admistrative district. The president of the district court was after him as well. Leis, however, continued to refuse to take part and, as far as is known, nothing happened to him because of it.

In the meantime, the government in Berlin had already quietly passed an

ordinance on Saturday, December 3, which decreed that the disposal of
Jewish property, houses, and bank accounts could only be carried out by state
officials; local officials could no longer be involved. By the time the regulation
was announced on Monday, Holz already had a great deal — he now owned
properties worth over 2.4 million Reichsmarks. The Franconian party earned
an additional 1.5 million marks through rents and sale fees. The Holz campaign was a gold mine for Streicher's party till.

Leo and his brothers lost practically all of their financial resources. They
could not access the little money that was owed to them from the building
sales, because whatever was transferred to them ended up in a blocked
account, and more and more payments were being demanded of Jewish merchants. Since 1934, the Nazis had imposed an "emigration tax" on Jewish
inhabitants. In order to insure that the Katzenberger brothers paid, the
Nuremberg's Finance Department had a compulsory mortgage in the
amount of forty thousand Reichsmarks taken out on the Spittlertorgraben
property. David had informed the clerk in charge that "we do not have sufficient cash."

After the November rioting, Göring demanded of the Jews an Expiation
Payment that amounted to a billion Reichsmarks. Every Jew was to contribute 20 percent of his or her net worth in four installments. The
Katzenberger brothers had to pay between ten and twenty thousand marks
each; the first installment was due on December 15, 1938. And now their
business was consuming funds, not producing income. Almost all the
branches were closed by the Katzenbergers after November 10. Rents and
wages, however, often had to be paid for months afterward thanks to a Nazi
decree, adherence to which was carefully watched over by Streicher's men. To
top it off, the finance authorities demanded additional income taxes of sixteen
thousand Reichsmarks on the proceeds of the building sales, although the
brothers hadn't received a penny of it.

Beyond that, Leo Katzenberger still had to come up with the lawyer's fees
for the alleged currency smuggling, which amounted to twenty-one hundred
marks. Up until then, Fräulein Hölzel, who kept a sharp eye on everything
that had to do with numbers, considered the businessman "always magnani-
mous, even with people who owed him money." Now she was forced to
realize that even generous Leo Katzenberger was at the end of his tether. "I
regret very much," he dictated in his elaborate German as his secretary typed
the letter to the Frankfurt attorney, Dr. Fritz Gutenstein, "that circumstances

for which I am not responsible but which have caused me to lose all of my financial assets and more force me to inform you that I am unable to meet the original figure requested."

The old man now saw his happy flirtation with pretty, young Irene Scheffler in a different light. It appeared that the atmosphere "between Aryans and Jews had become very inhospitable," as he indicated later during his interrogation. And so, when he visited Irene at the beginning of December 1938, he gave the photographer a little sermon on conduct — it was now too dangerous to enjoy each other's company. He would be more reserved in the future and not visit her any longer. "You have your fiancée now," he added paternally, "and he can stand by you with help and advice."

It was a sort of farewell visit, but not the last one.

13

IN FRONT OF NUREMBERG'S ADOLF HITLER HOUSE, the swastika flags were fluttering at half mast. In the party's *Nuremberg Daily News*, a black-bordered death notice appeared, signed by Gauleiter Julius Streicher — his adjutant, Hanns König, was dead. On Sunday, February 5, 1939, at around two in the afternoon, the high-ranking thirty-four-year-old had taken his own life.

The wildest rumors about his death immediately circulated through Nazi ranks. There were whispers about an abortion and stories about possible fraud. In the hours before König shot himself with a pistol in his apartment, there had been all sorts of hectic discussions among the highest circles of the district administration. On the previous evening, Streicher had appeared at his adjutant's dwelling to appeal to his conscience; the following day, the deputy Holz hurried over to see him, and finally, shortly before König's death, Streicher telephoned him again. But Holz, like Streicher, had not attempted to keep the young adjutant from suicide. On the contrary, they had urged him to do it.

"König, things have gone far enough," Streicher had proclaimed with his unique brand of theatrics, according to the report of one of his retinue, "now you have to confess all!" Holz had convinced the hesitant candidate for suicide that "the pistol bullet was the only honorable way out of the situation." It appeared that König had brought disgrace upon himself — but that alone was probably not what cost the young SA man his life. It had more to do with the comedy thriller that was taking place within Nuremberg Nazi society, one in which the adjutant alternately played the villain and the youthful swain.

That corresponded more or less to his public image. König was considered to be the unscrupled, brutal executor of Gauleiter Streicher's will. Contemporaries, such as Police Chief Martin, despised the one-time cheese-delivery man as a nasty, peasant-sly, servile intriguer. Among lesser officials and the general population in the Franconian District, Streicher's adjutant was hated and feared. But the hardened, crude man had a blond-haired blue-eyed weakness: the operetta singer Else Balster. She was linked with him — city councillor and Overseer of the Municipal Theaters — in a liaison that lasted many years. In 1937, however, a mishap occurred and Else Balster found herself in delicate circumstances. The child was not wanted, König was married, and so the blond soubrette sought out a Nuremberg gynecologist who discretely terminated the pregnancy.

Abortion was held by the Nazis to be a "severe transgression against the national community," and was strictly forbidden. Offenses were punished with prison terms. Just think of the scandal that would have shaken the Nuremberg Nazi ranks if the blond singer's abortion had become known! And of course there were several who did know; even Streicher seems to have been in the picture quite early. When, during one of the social gatherings at Cramer-Klett Palace, the beautiful blond was once again seated next to König at the luxuriously appointed table, those nearby heard the Gauleiter drop the occasional smug remark about the scandalous relationship.

During the party rally in 1938, anonymous handbills titled "The Saint and Her Fool" mentioned the illegal abortion. In addition, König was accused of fraud in connection with the sale of a brickworks in Forchheim, north of Fürth, whereupon the Führer's deputy, Rudolf Hess, inquired about the goings-on. Toward the end of 1938, an internal party investigation was finally initiated. Police Chief Martin tapped several phones and in early January arrested Else Balster's gynecologist. Now the affair was becoming more and more difficult for König, which was exactly what Martin wanted to achieve. He had composed the handbill together with an associate, then had it typed by a secretary at police headquarters, and did everything possible to set an investigation in motion.

To be sure, Martin still sat at the table whenever Streicher invited him to join his soirees with actresses. But he was increasingly offended by the man's unpredictable and corrupt behavior, which went against the grain of whatever trace of the respectable policeman remained in Martin. The Nazi technocrat considered Streicher's arbitrary behavior, which was slowly becoming too much for the populace as well, to be counterproductive: Streicher had to go. Martin was not yet powerful enough to attack the Brownshirts' czar directly and therefore he'd chosen the more convoluted route of intrigue against Streicher's adjutant. The police chief also wanted to begin a high-level investigation into the shady building and property transactions by which Holz and his helpers had been filling the Franconian party's coffers since Kristallnacht.

Field Marshall Göring was informed, by persons unknown, of several alleged remarks made by Streicher that were extremely damaging and offensive to Göring's honor. Streicher was said to have stated about Göring's acquisitiveness, "If Göring can help himself, so can we!" Far worse was a later remark Streicher let fall about Göring's virility. Streicher was reported to have said that Göring was not able to sire a child and therefore his daughter, Edda, was not really his. The poison had its effect. Streicher vehemently disputed the statements, wrote an obsequious letter to Göring, and tried to sweep the disagreeable affair under the rug. All efforts were in vain. Göring had taken an extremely deep dislike to Streicher and had already given orders to investigate the strange events in Franconia.

At the beginning of February 1939, the special commission convened by Martin began its work in Nuremberg. The objects of its investigation were to be the "Aryanizations, together with deletions and obfuscations in the property registry, as well as the notarized renunciations and transfers of their property by Jews " occurring in the District of Franconia since November 9, 1938. Josef Meisinger, a senior government official from Gestapa, the administrative office of the Gestapo, in Berlin, headed the commission. Within the Gestapa, Meisinger was the director of the Department for Oversight of the Nazi Party and Its Agencies. Within his jurisdiction fell the matter of abortions.

Meisinger later summarized the results of his investigations in a comprehensive, top-secret report that went to Göring. After the war's end in 1945, the two blue linen loose-leaf binders containing the report fell into the hands of the Americans, who included them in the documents collected for the Nuremberg War Crimes Trials. This file offers unique insight into the internal life of the Franconian Nazi Party: It was a camarilla of careerists, criminals, and the corrupt who held power in Franconia.

Meisinger was considered a hard-liner who went after things with hammer and tongs; in Nuremberg he did honor to his reputation. His plan was to first interrogate Adjutant König, arrest him, and send him off to Berlin, but certainly not because of the abortion affair, which interested the civil servant only peripherally. Meisinger wanted to squeeze König for information about the business and property transactions. He considered the adjutant a key figure in the Nuremberg property monopoly, and knew König would lead him directly to Streicher. Streicher cold-bloodedly thwarted that plan by pushing König to commit suicide. Then Holz dropped out of circulation temporarily because of illness.

Chief Investigator Meisinger struck quickly and unrelentingly. Around five in the morning, several Franconian Nazis were hauled out of bed and arrested. The commission was going about its business, wrote Holz angrily — having obviously followed events closely from his hospital bed — "as if it were trying to uncover a plot against the state or rooting out a nest of criminals." The zealous Meisinger looked upon the Nuremberg Nazi clique as just that, and Martin seemed to believe the same of Streicher's vassals, or at least wouldn't put much past them.

A few days after Meisinger's forceful appearance, König's funeral took place with the usual pomp. An SA squad marched, Mayor Liebel placed a laurel wreath decorated in red and white, the city's colors, on the grave, and high-ranking party henchmen paid their last respects to their comrade-at-arms. Martin, who towered over the funeral party, was careful to keep his right hand in his coat pocket — where his Browning pistol was concealed.

One of the first to be arrested was Johann Heinrich Schätzler. It was quickly revealed that the real estate broker had been making a handsome living from Aryanization for some time. As early as December 1937, Holz had appointed him to oversee "the ridding of the old city of Jewish stores." After that, no one got by Schätzler. Anybody who wanted to take over Jewish businesses had to deal with him, and he used his party position for private interests. He was tough as nails at demanding commissions from the "Aryanization applicants," even though his contract with the DAF provided a monthly remuneration of 320 Reichsmarks for that very activity.

For example, he threatened to arrest one man interested in an old city photo shop that belonged to a Jew if the man failed to pay him his broker's fee. During the Aryanization of the Jewish Mailänder Brewery, Schätzler took such a large cut that he came into serious conflict with his colleagues. According to Meisinger's investigations, Schätzler pocketed a commission of eighty-thousand Reichsmarks. The extent of Schätzler's thievery can no longer be specifically determined; presumably he took a cut from everything he was involved in.

Meisinger didn't limit his investigation to Schätzler; he also targeted Strobl. A favorite game of the Nazi bigwigs was to connive to get each other appointed to various boards of directors, a discipline in which Strobl excelled. As District Economic Advisor and president of the Chamber of Commerce and Industry he was responsible for issuing formal permission to take over businesses. Now, as Meisinger confirmed, the Nazi functionary often made the issuance of Aryanization permits contingent on his appointment to the board of directors of the company involved. Soon Strobl ruled three other important companies, and Nazi friends received other board jobs. The industrial magnate Strobl was, in the judgment of the Meisinger's commission, "a man without backbone who proved to be an easily manipulated tool in the hands of the SA Official König and others."

"Aryanization was, by its very nature, a source of corruption," writes the historian Helmut Genschel in his analysis of the displacement of Jews from economic life. Corruption was prevalent throughout the Reich. In Streicher's administrative district, everyone helped himself to whatever he wanted. One SS squad leader received a dressage horse named Diamond as compensation for his help in a purchase arrangement; District Inspector Haberkern skimmed nine thousand marks off the sale of a clothing factory. And even Deputy Gauleiter Holz, who was not proven guilty of anything, nonetheless arrived at the point where his yearly income was around seventy-six thousand marks. Rather impressive earnings for a department secretary in municipal employ.

But the wildest dealings were König's, who in the turbulent November days acquired firms as if they were shirts. For example, with the help of a straw man named Schneider, he bought the Magnus Transformer Factory in the days immediately following Kristallnacht. Hans Magnus, the owner of the firm, was not in Nuremberg at that time; it was believed that he had gone to Dachau with approximately two hundred Jews arrested in Nuremberg. In such cases, according to a resolution passed just shortly after November 9 by the Nuremberg Probate Court, a trusteeship was to be set up by the district court, and the trustee could then make determinations concerning the estate of the Jewish owner. In Magnus's case a trustee was appointed, and he immediately sold the business, with total assets of sixty-five thousand Reichsmarks, to Schneider for five thousand marks.

Strobl authorized the contract on the same day. But later, when the trustee went to inspect the already sold firm for the first time, he got cold feet: the inventory alone seemed to be worth twenty-thousand marks. As Schneider made his tour through the factory, his head began to spin too — he was a barber by trade and unable to make even a convincing pretense at such a complicated undertaking. He got in touch with König and they agreed to sell the company again as quickly as possible. That happened a few days later, this time for eleven thousand Reichsmarks. When the Jewish factory owner, who hadn't been in Dachau at all, returned from a business trip in the beginning of December, his firm had been sold twice, a half-dozen people had enriched themselves along the way, and yet he hadn't seen a penny of the proceeds.

Using Schneider as the intermediary once again, König bought the insulating materials factory owned by Stern and Company on Nuremberg's Hochstrasse. The concern's assets totaled 161,250 Reichsmarks; the buyers agreed upon a nominal price of forty thousand marks, against which a deduction was made for social expenses and the considerable outstanding debt of the firm. In the end, Schneider paid only 1,244 marks. A few days later, acting as König's agent, the barber sold the company, for the same price of 1,244 Reichsmarks. However, a consultant's fee was negotiated that provided Schneider with a remuneration of ten thousand Reichsmarks yearly for three years; presumably the money benefited König as well.

König always operated behind the scenes, something he'd learned from his boss, Julius Streicher. The Gauleiter, likewise, took a huge share of the proceeds from the million-mark lottery that started on Kristallnacht, even though he rarely put in an appearance. He let others do that sort of dirty work. Streicher kept his eye out for a "good place to invest capital." He'd told the publisher of the *Franconian Daily News*, Max Fink, who also worked as bookkeeper for *Der Stürmer*, "There's a point to that — you never know how things will turn out in the end." Streicher eventually discovered the Mars Works at Nuremberg, a factory that produced bicycles and machine tools. The respected Jewish bank, Bankhaus Kohn, held 40 percent of the shares in Mars Works, nominally worth 112,500 Reichsmarks. The bank's director, Martin Kohn, had been incarcerated at Dachau since November 9, giving Streicher's agents free rein.

Using funds from *Der Stürmer*, Fink bought the Bankhaus Kohn shares for 5 percent of the nominal cost, some five thousand marks. Then, empowered by Streicher, he retrieved the stock certificates from safe deposit at the Kohn bank and put it into safe deposit at the Dresdener Bank. When that transaction had been concluded, Streicher ordered his stooge to take the remaining 60 percent of the shares, which were in the possession of the Dresdener Bank. Payment was to be another fifty-six hundred Reichsmarks from *Der Stürmer*'s account. Then, in a threatening tone, Streicher instructed Fink never to mention his name in connection with the Mars affair, saying, "You know, it would be a sad thing if someone were to betray me now."

But someone did betray him, and Meisinger got several of Streicher's helpers to talk, including Fink. When finished, the three-hundred-page Meisinger Report was given a top-secret classification and presented to Göring. Meisinger summarized his findings by saying that "The confused legal situation prevailing in Franconia has arisen by virtue of completely illegal Aryanization measures." But that situation would never have come about, in Meisinger's estimation, "if the authorities involved, particularly the judicial authorities and notaries, and, additionally, the political leadership and Chamber of Commerce and Industry, had appropriately opposed the breaches of law being demanded of them."

"The state of the Property Registry," Meisinger indicated, would have to be made to correspond with the "true legal status" again. Then, offering his personal appraisal, the investigator said that the Treasury Department of the Reich "would be forced to renounce all financial benefits" the Franconian Nazis illegally gained. This was not a bad result, in the opinion of the Gestapa official, and in his reasoning a premonition of the "Final Solution" can be heard: "The funds being returned to the Jews would, in the end, benefit the Reich," argued Meisinger, "since, according to existing legal regulations or those expected to be passed shortly, they will be accessible to the Reich or could be utilized in the Reich's interest."

In the days following Meisinger's revelations, Benno Martin's coworkers revoked all of the sales agreements and placed the buildings under the Gestapo's administration so that the properties could once again be offered for sale, street by street, this time free of legal irregularities. Sometime or other, the inspectors got around to the Katzenbergers' buildings. First, the Katzenbergers were reinstated as the owners after several entries in the Property Registry that "suffered from internal inconsistencies" had been rectified "according to special orders of Field Marshall Göring." Then they had to sell their properties again. Of course, the Katzenbergers, like other Jewish building owners whose forced sales had now been "cleaned up," never saw a single Reichmark of the proceeds from the new sales. The money ended up in a special account in Nuremberg that belonged to the Gestapo. The money was later deposited at the City Savings Bank of Nuremberg in an account "at the disposal of Field Marshall Göring."

The other 567 Nuremberg property sales called into question by the investigators were dealt with similarly. In truth the huge reform action was just another huge swindle, but this time the money ended up in different pockets.

I 4

AN AUTOMOBILE! IRENE WAS OVERWHELMED WITH DELIGHT — her dream had come true. How she had loved to climb into the backseat of the gleaming black Chrysler! Katzenberger had enjoyed inviting Irene for a drive through the country when he took day trips for business. Now she could go in her own car! Of course, the vehicle was used and wasn't as high class as the limousine, but the man at the wheel was her fiancée, Hans Seiler, a car salesman, and he drove Irene wherever she wanted to go. "I loved to ride in a car," she admitted later.

Seiler had gotten the automobile late in 1938. At first it looked as if he would need another five hundred marks, which Irene, never one to hold back, had mentioned in passing to her neighbor Betty Kleylein. But then the fast-moving Seiler managed to get hold of a car anyway, despite financial problems— after all, that was his business. It may have been that he got an advance from his employer, but it's more likely he'd bought the car at a discount thanks to the favorable opportunities that were coming along just then. Betty Kleylein, however, had her own theory as to where the money came from. She later told the police, "I think Katzenberger gave it to her." Her husband, Paul, shared her view. And he passed on a rumor that Heilmann was spreading through the building: "Katzenberger bought her the car . . . she can pay it off easily."

Since Kristallnacht, every day was bargain day in Nuremberg. There were plenty of opportunities to get cars, household furnishings, even jewelry. While party bosses helped themselves in the real estate market, many citizens reached for more portable bargains: chests, chairs, and rugs changed owners, as did fur coats and diamond necklaces. Many Jews were so badly off that they could pay their bills only by selling household possessions. Aryan customers took advantage of them shamelessly. The hoarding and panic buying got so out of hand that it even worried Nazi district officials. On November 21, 1938, Economic Advisor Strobl noted irritatedly that household items were being acquired for prices that "hardly appear justified, considering the circumstances." Having reached the decision that "such conduct cannot be condoned under any circumstances," Strobl appointed an expert to oversee pricing. The price supervisor's job, as it turned out, was merely to divert 25 percent of the sales price into the coffers of the district administration.

On December 9, 1938, Police Chief Martin decreed that by year's end all Jews had to turn in their drivers' licenses, vehicle registrations, and license plates. "Jews go on foot!" crowed the *Franconian Daily News*. The editors of that very same Nazi paper soon treated themselves to the most luxurious of the now inexpensive cars. The editor in chief, Heinz Liebscher, found a Wanderer, a car worth 1250 marks, for 120 Reichsmarks; three other journalists helped themselves, as did a colleague from the printing office. At that time there were still some three hundred autos owned by Jews in Nuremberg. The newspaper people got their cars through the Nazi district administration; many Jews, however, sought to sell off their cars on the sly, so that whatever money they got would not immediately disappear into a blocked bank account that they couldn't access. These were distress sales, and the prices reflected that.

Hans Seiler could have participated in this thriving black market. On Spittlertorgraben there was a certain amount of disapproval when Paul Mäsel saw a small used-car business developing in the courtyard. "Seiler often bought and sold used cars," was Mäsel's testimony. Irene and Hans were frequently seen in the courtyard, tinkering around with one of the cars. Sometimes Leo Katzenberger walked over and chatted a bit with the young people. He'd allowed them to use one of the garages that had been built beside the coach house, because the firm no longer needed it.

The shoe concern was being closed down; the rear building looked deserted, though there was still some inventory. A commission headed by District Inspector Haberkern oversaw the liquidation of wholesale businesses in Nuremberg. He assigned an administrator to each firm to gather the balances, the inventory's value, and the outstanding debts. Such people were long on party loyalty but short on business expertise and didn't go about their jobs very intelligently. At Katzenbergers', the commission at first confiscated the entire inventory, as the chauffeur Fabro later reported; subsequently, however, that inventory was released and the owners attempted to sell the shoes on their own, bit by bit. Almost all of the employees were gone, with the exception of Fräulein Hölzel, who sat untiringly in the reception room in the rear building, entering columns of numbers into the ledger. She remained in the employ of the Katzenberger firm until February 1939. The certificate of dismissal for Wilhelm Fabro, Chauffeur, is dated April 14, 1939. But for several months afterward he was still driving for the Katzenberger brothers — as an independent contractor.

Toward the end of 1938, Leo Katzenberger had received a summons concerning the company's automobile and reported to the authorities, accompanied by Fabro. Katzenberger had to sign a prepared sales contract on which only the dates had to be entered. The beautiful Chrysler, worth some thirty-five hundred marks in its day, went to a car rental agency for 350 marks. The delivery truck, a Hanomag valued at three thousand Reichsmarks, was taken by Fabro for two hundred marks. The chauffeur promptly registered himself as the owner of a local delivery company, to put it in its official category. His customers would remain, primarily, the Katzenbergers. Leo had worked it all out with Fabro in advance, in order to be able to move the inventory that had been sold. The warehouse was not yet empty.

Throughout the Reich it was evident that conditions rapidly deteriorated after the violence of November 9. If German Jews had been thwarted, demeaned, robbed of their dignity, and stamped as second class citizens since the beginning of the Hitler regime, they now found themselves helpless victims, brutally tormented and deprived of rights and property. With that November night, the persecution had taken on a new dimension; it was the beginning of total annihilation. Even those who had shut their eyes to the course of events now had to see what was going on around them, because violence reigned as never before. "The pogrom night," writes the U.S. political scientist Daniel Goldhagen, "was the most revealing event of the entire Nazi era."

Irene Scheffler Seiler at age thirty-seven,
when she was living in Guben after the war.

Leo Katzenberger, holding cigar and properly
attired in pin-striped suit. This photograph was
taken in Irene Scheffler's studio during the 1930s.

The shoe store on Karolinenstrasse in Nuremberg. All together, the Katzenberger brothers ran
nearly thirty stores.

Katzenberger's chauffeur, Wilhelm Fabro, with the Model 66 Chrysler.

Leo Katzenberger and his wife, Big Claire, out for a walk during a vacation in Garmisch-Partenkirchen.

The Katzenberger villa on Praterstrasse. Leo lived on the second floor, his brother Max and his family on the first floor — "it was the most beautiful house on the whole street."

A 1930s street scene on Spittlertorgraben, showing the building at number 19 (arrow). Since late 1938, the local Nazi administration occupied the corner building on the left.

A happy coffee hour in the Heilmann's attic apartment. Daughter Marga is standing in front of the window; Mäsel is third from the left. The picture was taken at the time of Marga's confirmation in 1941.

Above: A street scene in the old town during the party rally of 1935.

Middle: The Gauleiter of Franconia, Julius Streicher (left), and his deputy and eventual successor, Karl Holz (right).

Below: A float on parade during a 1936 carnival. The sign reads "Off to Dachau," for the amusement of spectators.

Irene Scheffler with her husband, Hans Seiler. The couple married at the end of July 1939. He was a dashing automobile salesman who later helped her in the studio.

Secretary and eventual chairman of the Nuremberg Jewish congregations, Bernhard Kolb, seen shortly after his return to Nuremberg from the Theresienstadt concentration camp. A short time later, he emigrated to the United States.

Größe: 1, ____ m	Kartei= blatt
Gestalt:	
Gesichtsform:	
Nase:	
Haarfarbe:	
Augen:	
Mundart:	
Besonderheiten:	Mittäter: _Seiler_ _Frona, 26.4.10_	Bes. Bemerk. über Tataausführ.: _R. hat mit S. bis Anfang 1940 verschiedentliche Beziehungen unterhalten._
	Polizeiaufsicht:
Pers.=Akt.: _428981_	Arbeitshaus:
Form. 178. 6. 39. 1000. W.	Ehrenrechtsverlust:

The card from the Nuremberg prison file on Leo Katzenberger, begun shortly after his arrest on March 18, 1941. The photo dates from March 19.

Was ist er
Rassenschänder Katzenberger, Schuhjude und Vorsitzender der Israelitischen Kultus= gemeinde zu Nürnberg

Judge Rothaug
in 1937.

With great fanfare, Der Stürmer reported the death sentence passed against Leo Katzenberger on March 14, 1942. The photo was retouched at the mouth, eyebrows, and ears to show his "typically Jewish" features.

The surviving Nuremberg Jews in 1945. Once numbering ten thousand, only some twenty members of the Nuremberg Jewish community remained, all living in "mixed marriages."

Left: Rothaug as defendant.

Below, left: Irene Scheffler Seiler before the American military tribunal in 1947.

Below: The building at 19 Spittlertorgraben following its destruction in 1945.

Right: Irene Seiler at the state-owned photo studio in Apolda. A portrait of Lenin hangs on the wall.

Below: Leo Katzenberger's last telegram to Palestine, written on the evening prior to his execution. His children mounted copies of the text with copies of his photograph; the display now hangs as a memento in the dwellings of several members of the family.

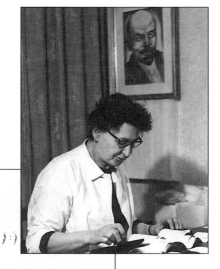

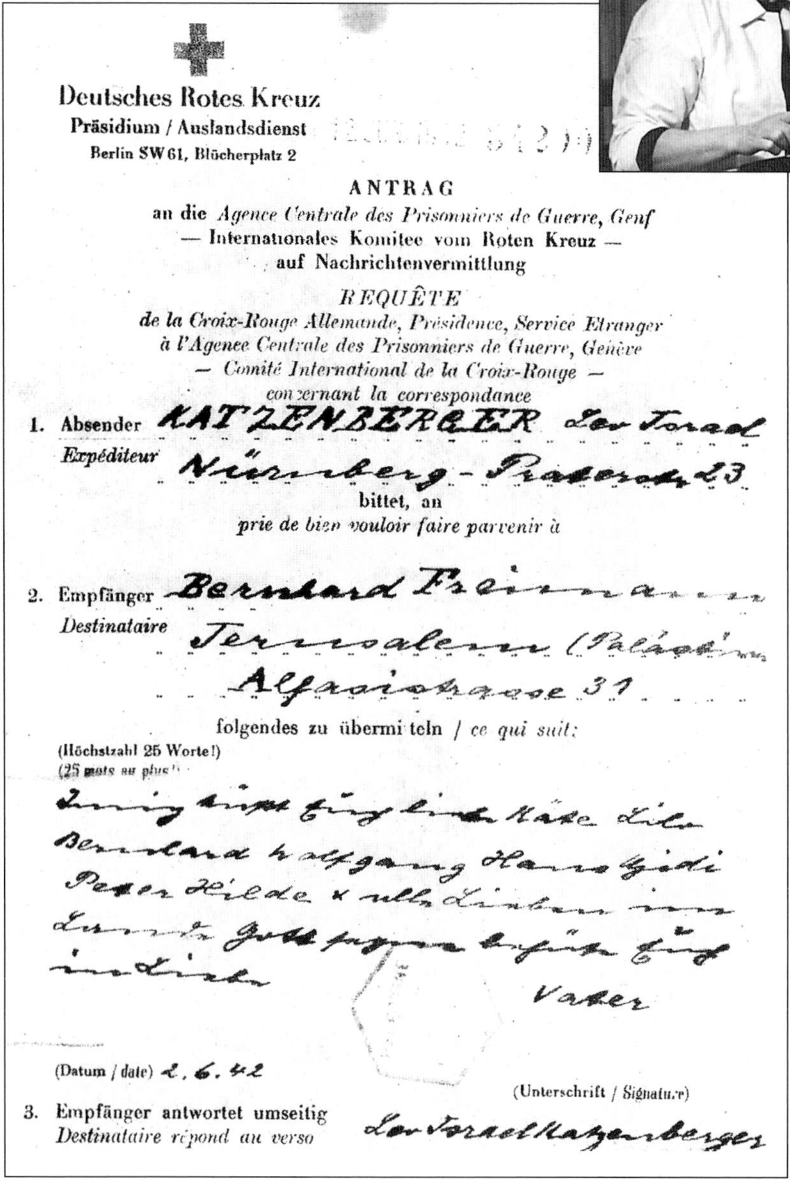

Deutsches Rotes Kreuz
Präsidium / Auslandsdienst
Berlin SW 61, Blücherplatz 2

ANTRAG
an die *Agence Centrale des Prisonniers de Guerre, Genf*
— Internationales Komitee vom Roten Kreuz —
auf Nachrichtenvermittlung

REQUÊTE
de la Croix-Rouge Allemande, Présidence, Service Etranger
à l'Agence Centrale des Prisonniers de Guerre, Genève
— Comité International de la Croix-Rouge —
concernant la correspondance

1. **Absender** KATZENBERGER Leo Israel
Expéditeur Nürnberg - Praterstr. 23

bittet, an
prie de bien vouloir faire parvenir à

2. **Empfänger** Bernhard Freimann
Destinataire Jerusalem (Palästina)
Alfasistrasse 31

folgendes zu übermitteln / *ce qui suit:*
(Höchstzahl 25 Worte!)
(25 mots au plus!)

Innig küsst Euch lieben Käte Lilo
Bernhard Wolfgang Hans Gidi
Peter Hilde & alle Lieben in
Erinnerung Gott segne behüte Euch
im Leben
Vater

(Datum / date) 2.6.42

(Unterschrift / Signature)

3. **Empfänger antwortet umseitig**
Destinataire répond au verso

Leo Israel Katzenberger

But even more revealing was the period directly after the event. In Nuremberg, it had begun on the evening of November 10, with the proclamations at Adolf Hitler Platz and the accompanying demonstrations, during which Streicher, with approximately one hundred thousand people in his retinue, marched diagonally through the old city to the Hotel Deutscher Hof. "The great majority of the men and women of Nuremberg could have stayed away without risk of repression," writes Hermann Glaser, a Nuremberg author and former minister for cultural affairs, but instead "they applauded those who were committing crimes against the state." There then followed the decrees, commands, and contracts that forced Jewish citizens from their homes and robbed them of their automobiles, belongings, real estate, their very basis for existence; all of which was to bring about, at the very least, their total exclusion from the economic life of Germany. German Jews were now forced, under threat of jail sentence, to assume the first name Israel (for men) and Sara (for women) so that, on paper, even their individuality was extinguished.

It may be that many people, as several historians claim, turned away in shock from the Nazi apostles of violence after the bloody night of November 9; not a few, however, now gave their approval to the Nazi regime for the first time. The nightly rampages and the subsequently increasing Aryanization opened floodgates of greed. Hostility toward Jews was suddenly not just a question of conviction and hatred: there were material gains available, both financial and social, that weakened even those who were not hardboiled anti-Semites. Inured by their experience with violence, intolerance toward brutality slackened among the so-called normal citizens, and with that, their morality. If the violence of Kristallnacht was sanctioned by the state, then certainly a modest gesture of extortion toward a Jew trying to sell household property was permissible.

The army of profiteers was recruited from all classes of society. Take, for instance, Dr. Fritz Hussel, a notary with an office right around the corner from city hall. He had come to be well known to the Katzenberger brothers, who saw him at the DAF offices every time a building had to be sold. And even if the businessmen didn't get to see Hussel himself because his assessor happened to be doing the dirty work, they found his statement "for services rendered" discretely appended to the contracts. Hussel had already recorded the first of Deputy Gauleiter Holz's sales contracts for the buildings on Spittlertorgraben and Praterstrasse. Without a second thought, he certified all of the contested entries in the Property Registry in Holz's favor and later drew up the contracts that were supposed to "clean up the mess."

Hussel and two other Nuremberg notaries had desks on the top floor of the DAF building, while in the cellar below the SA man Hutzler was ordering Jewish building owners tortured. Hussel and his fellow notaries alone took in around one hundred thousand Reichsmarks in fees for the legal work necessitated by Holz's building grab at the end of 1938 and beginning of 1939. After Meisinger's investigation, when the contracts were nullified and new ones drawn up, the notaries were back in business and kept every penny of the fees.

Events had even provided a surge in business for Nuremberg's jewelers and goldsmiths. Among them, guild chairman Heinrich Issmayer distinguished himself as a particularly canny businessman. The goldsmith, whose shop was on Adlerstrasse, attracted notice with his huge purchases of jewelry and household silver. Between December 1938 and February 1939, he spent approximately six thousand Reichsmarks on gems, candlesticks, and table silver owned by Jews. In accordance with the local Nazi directives, he withheld a quarter of the sales price from the Jewish sellers to donate to the Franconian branch of the party. But then the jeweler "forgot" to turn the money over to the district administrators, as the records indicate, "remembering" to do so only after an official notice came.

The yellowed papers stored in the Nuremberg archives show how many respected firms turned up among the bargain hunters. The Krefft piano company bought twelve grand pianos at prices ranging from sixty to eight hundred Reichsmarks. The Grand Hotel purchased a valuable carpet for five hundred marks. Leo Katzenberger sold a complete set of furniture to the Östreicher family in the Spittlertorgraben apartment building. The furniture would be mentioned later in the proceedings against him.

Meanwhile, the Katzenberger brothers had closed ranks in the beautiful villa on Praterstrasse. Leo, who had occupied the second and third floors, took in the family of a friend and turned the third floor over to Max and his wife, who had previously lived on the ground floor. David now lived on the third floor as well. Meanwhile, a non-Jewish lawyer moved into the ground floor apartment. Since the ominous sales contract with Deputy Holz, Leo had to pay out 203 marks rent each month; Max paid 178 marks; the money presumably went into the party's till. Those were enormous sums for the previously wealthy merchants, because since November 1938 they no longer had a steady income.

David's move to Praterstrasse was prompted by the Nuremberg Housing and Property Owners' Association, whose chairman, acting jointly with the municipal authorities, had demanded that building owners evict by December 15, 1938, all renters who were considered "full-blooded Jews with German citizenship." This Housing Restructuring had been preceded by a long meeting at which municipal employees, district party leaders, and association representatives had discussed extraordinarily difficult logistical questions. The Nazi bosses wanted to preserve outward appearances. Therefore, as the meeting's minutes reveal, to be avoided at all costs was "a negative effect on our image by the increasing numbers of people moving out toward the end of the month." All agreed that under no circumstances were "pieces of damaged furniture to be taken along" by emigrating Jews — no physical evidence of the Kristallnacht destruction was to go abroad.

Beyond that, however, the Housing Restructuring was to proceed without delay; there were already forty applications from families living in cheaper quarters who wanted to move to a vacated Jewish apartment.

The new era even made its way into the little rental books of the Spittlertorgraben tenants. Until November, Margarete Hölzel had carefully entered the amount of each month's payment, imprinted the firm's stamp over it, and, finally, in her small, precise hand, signed her own name next to the stamp. Now, however, the stamp manufacturer Geo Müller was scribbling his signature across the paper in extravagant loops. Several renters seemed to look forward to meeting their new Aryan owner. On his first visit to the building, they let him in on the hallway gossip about the alleged liaison between the businessman and the photographer. Betty Kleylein, in particular, stood out in that regard. The housewife presented an elaborate complaint about the "unsatisfactory circumstances" in the building. The "relationship between Katzenberger and the Scheffler woman . . . was upsetting the entire building," Müller later quoted her as saying. Then she inquired in a sharp tone whether Fräulein Scheffler was even paying her rent. Apparently the housewife was hoping to get the pretty photographer thrown out, but Müller disappointed her: he answered that she paid by postal bank check, then left.

Irene, however, was considerably in arrears with her rent to the previous owner, Leo Katzenberger, an amount of some 1,056 marks. In earlier days that wouldn't have been a problem. Back then, the apartment's rent wasn't as financially important for the businessman, and sooner or later a check always came from Father Scheffler. Now, however, Katzenberger needed every cent, and there was no check. Presumably Irene hadn't told her father about the outstanding rent because her finances were becoming embarrassing. She'd become a master photographer, was nearly twenty-nine, and had a fiancée who was living in her apartment — but she still couldn't pay the rent. Or was it that she just didn't want to?

Near the end of November 1938, when the shoe business was being liquidated, Katzenberger presented the photographer with a list of the outstanding rental payments, a record that still exists. The paper is indeed revealing, not only of Irene's financial circumstances but also of her morals concerning the obligation to pay. The rent amounted to 62.30 marks, but Irene frequently doled out the money in five-mark amounts over the entire month. When she was away from Nuremberg taking her journeyman's and master's examinations, from the fall of 1937 to early summer 1938, she paid nothing at all. There may have been a reason for her failure to pay: during the cram course with her sister in Guben and the master classes in Weimar that followed, she simply had no income.

By September 1938 one might have expected that her photography studio would bring in enough money so that she could at least make her five-mark contributions. And that was also about the time Hans Seiler moved into her apartment. He could have contributed to the rent. But Irene even stopped paying the small installments — she paid nothing at all in September, October, or November 1938. And she quite obviously remained unmoved when she received the list of her outstanding rental payments after the building changed hands.

It may be that Seiler was one of those profiteers who thought it no longer necessary to pay rent to a Jew. He might have convinced Irene not to bother about the bill. Perhaps, however, the photographer merely continued her usual slipshod ways because now she was so much in love that she didn't pay much attention to anything. But why then did she pay the new building owner, Müller, promptly starting in December 1938? No matter how one looks at it, there is good reason to believe that the political climate was having an effect on Irene Scheffler, because, in addition to everything else, the young photographer — who had never shown any interest in politics until then — took a significant step: She joined the Nazi Party, receiving membership number 5068732.

15

Hans Mäsel couldn't bear it any more. When the toolmaker sat in his small living room in the evening with his wife, talking over the day, a faint beam of light could often be seen coming from the front building. Sometimes the Mäsels heard laughter as well, and then there was that gurgling noise of running water. They were obviously having a high old time down there, the photographer and her fiancée. But during the day, Katzenberger was still stopping by — could things just go on like that?

Mäsel decided to speak to the photographer at the first opportunity, which presented itself on a summer day in 1939. Irene had driven to the country and brought back a basket of fruit for the Mäsels, something she occasionally did as a polite gesture toward her neighbors. When the machinist brought back the basket, he asked Irene if he might step in for a moment. "Then I told her that she shouldn't allow Herr Katzenberger in her apartment," was Mäsel's version of the conversation, claiming he'd warned her firmly to break off her relationship with the Jew once and for all, then told her, "There could really be a lot of trouble!"

Irene listened to Mäsel's warning, then shook her head energetically. No, she wasn't going to break off the relationship just like that — "The man has been very good to me."

That was certainly correct. In the spring of 1937, when Katzenberger pressured her to complete her training, Irene had been at a low point. She had allowed the business to slide and had few customers. Instead, she often sat over coffee with her girlfriends, smoking too much and chatting.

Back then she had willingly leaned on him for support. When he stopped by her studio for a moment, he always provided a welcome diversion. Irene actually seemed to be proud to have such a close relationship with the well-established businessman. She knew his wife in passing; they said hello whenever they met in the city, and once Irene had even paid a visit to the beautiful villa to deliver enlargements of photos from Israel. Irene called the businessman "LK," which meant that she belonged: in the Katzenbergers' shoe business and even within the family, the men were referred to by their initials, which may have been a fad among the brothers or perhaps an expression of their modernity. Irene did once confide to a motherly friend, however, that her relationship with the businessman "wasn't entirely innocent," that there was "something going on" between her and Katzenberger.

By the summer of 1939, things were somewhat different. Now Katzenberger, who had turned sixty-five, played the role of an old uncle. He was no longer the rich, busy shoe dealer who was driven all over the country in his big Chrysler. Irene was now more likely to see him looking a little lost as he walked through the neighborhood with his hat pulled down over his eyes. But if they met in the street or if Katzenberger visited her studio, he still gave her a pack of cigarettes or brought along a box of pralines — he still liked to play the gallant gentleman. Was she still pleased by that? When the businessman offered her shoes as the inventory was being liquidated, Irene took them, but secretly passed them on to someone else.

Irene's photography business had taken an unexpected turn for the better, thanks to her fiancée's help. Hansl, as she called him, had evidently not been successful as an automobile salesman, so for a while he switched to vacuum cleaners. But it was in the studio that his true talents were revealed. Irene thought he was "photographically very talented." And she had caused a stir at a recent exhibition; one of her photos showed the Führer at the Nuremberg Opera together with a local Nazi bigwig.

Thereafter, Irene's studio enjoyed increased popularity among party members. The Mayor Willy Liebel's wife even commissioned a portrait and invited the young photographer to her house. The finished pictures were then picked up, according to the recollections of a friend, by the mayor's adjutant. Irene wasn't afraid of mingling with the Nazi clique when there was something to be gained from it, which probably explains her party membership. And it may be that she enjoyed rubbing elbows with the best circles of Nuremberg Nazi society. Things were obviously on the upswing.

But Leo Katzenberger was now burdened by "many serious concerns," as he later explained to the court. The brothers had vacated the rear building of the Spittlertorgraben property and the storerooms with the freight elevator had been closed since the middle of 1939. Leo Katzenberger was now trying to find a place for his remaining Jewish employees. And some needy person was always asking the congregations for help; Katzenberger tried to be of assistance wherever he could.

At the same time, he hardly knew how he and his wife Claire were going to get by. Since the closure of the wholesale business and their stores, they no longer had a steady income and their assets were rapidly consumed by supplementary taxes, Göring's expiation payment, and by high rents and wages. There was certainly no way of getting cash; new currency regulations had gone into effect early in 1939. All bank accounts and safe deposits were blocked; Jewish account holders were permitted a monthly withdrawal of exactly 150 Reichsmarks for themselves and fifty Reichsmarks for their spouses. And now Leo Katzenberger was going to have to give up the gold pocket watch he always carried in his vest. That was a consequence of the February 21 decree that ordered Jews to bring their jewelry, candle holders, and table settings to the Nuremberg Pawn and Auction Center.

A beautiful old granary, located on Unschlittplatz in the middle of the old city, housed the Pawn and Loan Office of the Party Rally City. In the spring of 1939, sizable crowds could frequently be seen waiting at the entrance to the building. Jews with carryalls, suitcases, and pushcarts poured in, bringing things that were not merely of considerable material value, but were also the trappings of an upper-middle class lifestyle hated by the Nazis and often included valuable keepsakes that had been passed on for generations. Robbing people of their family silver or even valuable useful items, such as a pocket watch or cigarette case or cufflinks, was a particularly despicable Nazi touch.

Even Katzenberger had to resign himself to standing in line on March 27. When his turn came, the pawn clerks carefully recorded the gold and silver items he took from his bags: fish knives and forks for twelve people, two salt cellars with spoons, a silver toiletry set, two candlesticks, trays, a silver bowl and breadbasket, a diamond ring and a string of pearls, and finally Claire's gold wristwatch and Leo's beautiful pocket watch with chain. He turned in 103 items.

David Katzenberger stood in line with him. A widower, rather slender in comparison with his older brother, he made it a practice to dress elegantly. He ordered his custom-made shirts from Levinger, the well-known Nuremberg tailor. Now David, too, was forced to turn over his gold watch and chain with fob, his gold cufflinks, and his silver cigarette case, followed by silver place settings for twenty-two people, complete with soup spoons, fish knives, and dessert forks. Not to mention silver coins and a silver baby's rattle that a grandchild had left lying somewhere in his apartment. Then the meticulous clerks had him sign a receipt for the confiscated items.

Two weeks earlier, Max, the youngest brother, had turned over the first installment of table silver. On March 29 he returned and displayed various precious items in front of the clerks. There was a necklace with thirteen diamonds, bracelets, brooches, and a diamond earring, chains, rings, and a chatelaine with hanging purse. In addition, there were pounds of table settings, silver serving spoons, a gold money box, a silver umbrella handle, coins, salt cellars, and two silver cases in which Max kept his visiting cards. All in all, it came to some two hundred pieces. Max signed the usual declaration.

At the time, many people were still trying to sell their gold and silver valuables on the sly. Perhaps Leo and David kept some things from the pawn office for that reason. Max presumably wanted to scrape some money together for his daughter Hilde. The delicate, high-spirited girl had just turned sixteen and was traveling outside Germany. For some time, Max and his wife, "Little Claire," had been thinking about where their daughter could stay, because it had long been clear to the Katzenberger brothers that the younger people, at least, had to get out of Germany as quickly as possible.

There weren't many ways to escape the Nazi dictatorship. For years, the Gestapo and the Reich government had essentially forced Jews to emigrate, confiscating as much of their wealth as possible when they did; now the gates were closing. In desperation, Max first approached a banker's family in Manchester about adopting his daughter. But in the end he sent Hilde along with one of the last groups of the Alijah Youth, an aid society founded to help Jewish teenagers emigrate. The organization provided young people between the ages of fifteen and seventeen with ship's passage to Palestine, where they would find agricultural work. In the mid 1930s, chapters had been founded in many German cities. Prosperous Jewish citizens and noteworthies pledged a portion of their incomes to finance the society. Leo Katzenberger was a supporter of the Nuremberg-Fürth chapter.

Alijah Youth was quite controversial at first, since its sole offering was rural pioneer work in Palestine. But between 1934 and the beginning of the war, in 1939, the aid society rescued more than five thousand Jewish teenagers from Germany. The ship carrying Hilde Katzenberger to Palestine left Trieste on March 13. In her baggage her mother had hidden a gold wristwatch inherited from her grandmother. At the time it was necessary to declare all property to customs upon departure, and the Nuremberg authorities were considered especially tough. They demanded that the teenager fish the gold watch out of her paltry belongings. On March 17, Max took it to the pawn office, where it was weighed first, then valued and taken in like everything else. Two years later, on March 21, 1941, Max received 4 marks, 42 cents for the gold watch.

The employees at the pawn and loan office had a great deal of work. First, the jewelry was separated from the silver items. Elegant silver boxes, valuable bowls, and splendid candelabra — anything that wasn't obviously a work of art or a valuable antique, no matter how dearly their owners had loved them — ended up in the department for old, damaged, and used silver, destined to be melted down. The items were weighed and put in storage.

When it came to jewelry, the examiner picked up his loupe, looked for the engraved carat number, valued the piece as well as he could, and then conscientiously entered the value onto his list. The list for Max Katzenberger's consignment is still extant; it details many, but not all, of the pieces turned in. The diamond earring that Max took to the pawn office appears on the list as "one gram pendant/diamond, estimated value 300 Reichsmarks." Two brooches and one bracelet were classified together as "4g 8c" (four grams, eight carats) with an estimated value of 4.28 marks; two chains and a ring were appraised by the clerks at "21g 14c" and painstakingly entered on the list with their estimated value of 39.27 Reichsmarks. Of the eleven silver coins that one receipt indicates Max Katzenberger turned in, only ten are to be found on a later list; estimated value 3.87 Reichsmarks. There is no mention at all of the thirteen-diamond necklace in this list that otherwise gives the impression of being so precise. Whether it was separated out on the wish of some Nazi official or whether it disappeared into the pocket of some clerk is impossible to determine. It is part of that sunken treasure that presumably will never be found. What happened to the other meticulously registered pieces of jewelry belonging to Max Katzenberger remains a mystery as well. All in all, the jewelery was valued at the ridiculous sum of 399.42 Reichsmarks. As part of the Berlin Delivery, the Nuremberg office turned the items over to the Central Office of Municipal Pawnbrokers Institutions in the capital. There the trail disappears.

By the summer of 1939 the employees of the Nuremberg pawn house had collected so many valuables that the clerks were up to their necks in silver items; the storage area under the steep roof of the old warehouse was filled to the brim. The German Institute for the Disposal of Gold and Silver, abbreviated as Degussa, had the monopoly on silver melting in Germany. On August 23, 1939, a cry for help went from Nuremberg to Degussa: "My storage area is filled to capacity," wrote the head of the Nuremberg Pawnbrokers Office in his letter to Degussa, "and it would be a help if the silver could be taken for melting down as soon as possible," preferably before September 1, "since the streets are closed to vehicular traffic during the party rally." But Degussa never came, and the storage problem became even more pressing.

The Nuremberg office sent another urgent letter on September 2 — the war had just begun — pleading for Degussa "to initiate the transfer of the silver as soon as possible." Meanwhile, approximately six tons of candleholders, bowls, and cutlery had accumulated at the pawn office — in all, more than a truckload. The Degussa considered having the silver transferred by rail; obviously they were having difficulty getting a suitable vehicle for transporting it by road. On October 3, a furniture van towing a trailer appeared in front of the Nuremberg Pawnbrokers Office. The clerks were relieved.

It took hours to load the silver onto the truck parked there in the middle of the old city. It is hard to imagine that the scene failed to attract a crowd of onlookers. When everything had been packed, the truck drove to the Nuremberg coal depot, where the municipal truck scales were located. With just over six and a quarter tons of silver as well as a "considerable quantity of knives," the truck and its trailer drove off in the direction of Frankfurt. Several weeks later, the Degussa sent the pawn office a check in the amount of 130,653.95 Reichsmarks as payment for the silver. Through its own sale of confiscated items to local jewelers, the loan and pawn office took in another seventy-five thousand marks. The jewelers' interest in the items varied:

"Objects of lesser value are difficult to move," reported the clerks, "but diamonds and gold watches sell quite well."

Half of the money taken in up to that point, approximately one hundred thousand Reichsmarks, was to be turned over to the Reich's Ministry of Economics by the pawn office. Nuremberg was permitted to keep 10 percent; the remainder was to be paid out to the former Jewish owners. Most of the time, however, the Reich confiscated that money as well, since many of the Jews had already emigrated or had been deported by the time of payment, which in many cases had been delayed until 1942.

The order to turn in silver and jewelry was just one of many that had made life difficult since the beginning of 1939. Some restrictions sounded ridiculous, other decrees seemed insane, but there was method in the madness: step by step, with diabolic perfection, the Nazi dictators deprived the country's Jews of their freedom of movement and robbed their existence of happiness — the path to the "final solution" had already been taken. Soon, under threat of punishment, Jews had to be home by 8 o'clock in the evening; shortly thereafter they were no longer permitted to ride streetcars. Buying a newspaper was forbidden, as was going to a barber. Keeping a pet was forbidden. Telephones were disconnected. All useful, utilitarian objects, from binoculars to bicycles and sewing machines to typewriters, had to be turned in over the next few years. Soon after the war began, radios were confiscated and Jews were not permitted to listen to broadcasts in non-Jewish homes.

More and more families decided to emigrate, but the process became increasingly difficult. At the beginning of 1939, the Nuremberg congregations numbered about thirty-eight hundred, compared to the more than ten thousand members in 1930; at the onset of the war, there were only twenty-seven hundred. In the summer of 1939, Ludwig Rosenzweig, for years the Nuremberg congregations' chairman, was one of the emigrants. Like many other prominent German Jews, he took an opportunity to go to Switzerland. A year earlier, Leo Katzenberger supposedly had the opportunity to obtain a permit for Palestine. But "Uncle Leo turned it down," recalls Marga Weglein; instead, he suggested giving the visa "to someone younger." Until summer 1938, Leo's daughter Lilo reports, her father always argued that he was the oldest in the family and had to look after his sisters. That was why he was staying in Germany. "But there was no way he could look after anyone else," is Lilo's dry comment today. "He had to look after himself."

By 1939, Leo Katzenberger had clearly changed his views, as is evident in the letters he wrote to his children. Now the businessman would have given a great deal to get a visa for Palestine. Since his imprisonment as a result of the currency affair, even Leo Katzenberger wanted out of Germany. As early as November 1938, he begged his son-in-law in Jerusalem to "do anything to get us over there with you as quickly as possible." A little later he traveled to Berlin to plead his case at the Palestine Office. At first the chances didn't look too bad: Katzenberger knew Benno Cohn, one of the head men in the office, quite well. In addition, he looked up an old Nuremberger, Dr. Löwenthal, who was likewise active in the Zionist movement. In the meantime, Bernard Freimann had convinced Claire Katzenberger's brother, who lived in Palestine, to put up the one-thousand-pound security deposit. Leo had the tickets for the ship. "If all goes well," Freimann wrote to Germany on December 9, 1938, "the visa ought to be there in a few weeks."

But nothing went well. It appeared that the available visas were already used by others for travel to Palestine. "My connections are failing me," a disappointed Leo wrote to Jerusalem. It was "annoying that others, for whom one wishes all the best, are preferred." Katzenberger asked his relatives in Palestine not to give up: "One can't allow the officials to rest easy, because others aren't either." Their children were even to try "Alex in Brussels" — Leo and Claire didn't want to contact Dr. Jessel themselves. But there was no sign of gratitude on the part of Attorney Jessel — an attempt to emigrate with the help of a friend of Jessel's in Antwerp didn't work either.

Soon there was no one to talk to in Berlin; in the spring of 1939, Benno Cohn himself went to Palestine. "We've given up believing in miracles," Leo's wife Claire wrote to Jerusalem in resignation. At the same time, Leo was apparently making an attempt to emigrate to England. "It would be just too wonderful if the business in London went well," he remarked in February 1939. Even that was not possible, however, and so Leo and Claire Katzenberger settled back into their daily lives in Germany. First, they wrapped a package for their daughter Käthe. Six sheets and a pair of trousers for their youngest were to be included, but of course the items could only be sent after the foreign exchange office approved the export — things had gotten that complicated.

Leo Katzenberger now involved himself more than ever with the Nuremberg religious community, which had gotten into trouble immediately after Rosenzweig left. Up until that time, the large German congregations had formally retained their autonomy in spite of the repressions; since the summer of 1939, however, they were being pressured to join the newly founded Reichsvereinigung der Juden in Deutschland (Association of Jews in the German Reich), which had its seat in Berlin. All of the smaller congregations were being dissolved, and even the Nuremberg congregations feared for its independence. It was in these times that Leo Katzenberger was elected congregation chairman. He moved into the office on Lindenaststrasse, where the administration had been housed since the large synagogue on Hans Sachs Platz had been torn down.

Katzenberger worked from dawn till dusk, and the congregations even budgeted a small salary for him. Toward evening, he still liked to invite his card-playing cronies to his home, where, as they had at Café Gisela, the gentlemen played Tarock. Things were now somewhat cramped at the Katzenbergers', and in the fall it became rather chilly, because the heating system no longer functioned properly. But, for Katzenberger, playing cards was one of his last refuges. Without wasting words, the men slapped their cards on the table, then hurried home before dark. "We didn't talk about our situation," recalled Nuremberg metal wholesaler Hermann Fleischmann, "all that got mentioned was that things were terrible for us."

16

THE WAR HAD BEGUN! SUDDENLY CLIENTS WERE STREAMING into Irene's small studio — she'd never experienced such demand. The likenesses of young soldiers ordered to the front would soon be standing on dressers and chests in Nuremberg and stared at longingly. War brides had themselves photographed, and their pictures would march to the front in sweaty twill jackets. In strolled young couples who'd quickly sworn a lifetime bond, even if it might be put asunder by the first enemy gun encountered.

The rush had started a few weeks before the beginning of the war, when more and more young men were being called up for military maneuvers. Irene snapped away, her fiancée Hans helping. One day the two young people sat in front of the camera lens themselves, and Irene pressed the self-timer. It was July 29, 1939 — their wedding day. They were married quite simply at city hall: the salesman Hans Seiler, baptized Catholic and the photographer Irene Scheffler, Protestant. There was no celebration afterward; the only witnesses were the twin brother Josef Seiler and his wife, Vera, who had been married half a year previously. Sometime or other Leo Katzenberger looked in at the studio and added his congratulations and a bouquet.

A few days later, Hans Seiler reported for military maneuvers; after two weeks, however, he unexpectedly returned to Nuremberg. Overcome with happiness, Irene rushed out of the apartment to do a little shopping and bumped into Katzenberger on Dennerstrasse, right around the corner from Spittlertorgraben. The old cavalier had just bought flowers for his wife; despite the bad times, he wasn't inclined to give up the habit. When he heard how happy Irene was, he pressed some of the flowers on her, together with best regards for her husband. Even that bouquet was to find its way into the the investigation's records, third-hand of course. The milk lady from Dennerstrasse had observed the scene and passed it on to Mrs. Östreicher. She passed on the gossip to Betty Kleylein, who reported it to the police two years later: Katzenberger once "gave the photographer a bouquet, as a greeting to her husband, Seiler."

In the fall of 1939 several of the inhabitants on Spittlertorgraben and the surrounding area followed Katzenberger's every move with suspicion. Sometimes they saw the old gentleman, properly dressed in suit and hat as always, walking through the neighborhood. From her lookout post on the first floor, Betty Kleylein observed the businessman and Irene's husband "talking in front of the building, then shaking hands." Their neighbor Mäsel glanced "Katzenberger with the Seiler woman on Dennerstrasse." Paul Kleylein claimed to have seen the old man "repeatedly walking up and down Spittlertorgraben in the vicinity of the building around eight o'clock in the evening." What Katzenberger was doing there, Kleylein ventured to the police, was "waiting for the Seiler woman, without a doubt." There was a certain amount of malice in placing the time at "around eight o'clock," because back then everyone knew that Jews had to be at home by eight in the evening.

That Katzenberger was still walking through the neighborhood, which, after all, was in the vicinity of his own apartment, seemed to bother people like the Kleyleins. In imaginations poisoned by Nazi propaganda, some of them pictured a secret rendezvous with Irene if they only got a glimpse of him on the street. But there were all sorts of other reasons why Katzenberger was frequently seen around the Plärrer. For instance, he walked by the square if he was headed to upper Kanalstrasse, where Nuremberg's Jewish life was now concentrated. It was not only the meeting place for those members of Adas Israel left in the city; since the synagogues had been destroyed, religious services were held twice weekly in the former factory. The route to

the post office where Katzenberger sent his frequent letters to Palestine likewise led past the Plärrer.

However, Katzenberger also frequently visited his nephew Leo Weglein
and his wife, who were still living on Spittlertorgraben. The couple had been
waiting expectantly for some time for a visa for the United States. Soon after
the horrors of Kristallnacht, Leo and Else Weglein had gone to the American
consulate in Stuttgart with their son. There were already crowds of people
waiting in the large hall. The Wegleins took their place in line while people
in charge yelled out various orders. Suddenly someone in the hall started
screaming, "Get out of here, Jewish shits!" It was a drunken German, Walter
Weglein recalls, who was going to clean out the consulate. He was quickly
pushed out by the people in authority. The U.S. consulate was considered to
be the last hope for many Nuremberg Jews. Admittedly, things were not
always on the up-and-up there — some of the employees allowed themselves
to be paid for their favors. What counted first and foremost was getting the
best position possible on the unendingly long waiting list for visas. On a
printed form, a piece of paper no bigger than a cigarette pack, the U.S.
authorities noted down one's number on the list. That scrap of paper decided
life or death.

For four hours the Wegleins sat in the waiting room of the consulate, then
they were ushered into a small office where the woman clerk berated Leo
Weglein in a loud voice: Why he hadn't left long ago? Her voice only became
polite, according to his son Walter's recollection, "when my father pushed a
thick envelope across the counter."

The Wegleins returned to Nuremberg with the much sought-after piece
of paper. Now they were sitting on their packed bags — all they wanted to do
was to get away. Leo's younger brother Max tried to emigrate in the summer
of 1939. He wanted to go to Palestine, where his daughter had safely arrived,
but right then, after even Leo failed, getting another official entry permit
seemed hopeless. The English kept strict quotas on immigration. And at the
Palestine office in Berlin where the permits were issued, a non-Berliner
would have to have very good connections indeed.

There was another way — a dangerous one to be sure — to get to
Palestine: on the illegal refugee ships. Max and his wife, "Little Claire," were
uncertain about boarding one of them. Max was under the supervision of a
nurse because he had angina pectoris. How could he survive what was certain
to be a dramatic crossing? The refugee ship *Patria* had recently been sunk. In

a roundabout way, since the mails were watched, Max asked his nieces and nephews who were in Palestine, as well as his daughter Hilde, whether he should make the attempt. They advised against it "because of the great risk," as Hilde tells it. And so Max and Little Claire stayed in Nuremberg.

What dilemmas Leo and his brothers must have faced, vacillating between the love of their homeland and the vague feeling that life in Germany was gradually becoming life-threatening. The history books don't tell us much about the humiliation and fear of death that Jewish citizens in Nuremberg and elsewhere had to bear daily. Whether it was a walk around the block or shopping at the grocery store where Jews could only shop at certain times, nothing took place normally. Every path could lead to a trap; every errand could end up in a prison cell.

Cruel, absurd, and unforeseeable things happened. Fritz Söltner, eleven years old and in the Hitler Youth at the time — once entered a Nuremberg store where a Jewish customer was already standing in front of the counter. The man saw the boy with the Hitler Youth uniform, stepped aside, and motioned the saleslady to wait on the youngster first. But Söltner wasn't in a hurry and so the Jew was taken care of first. He hesitated a little, then got up his courage and asked for razor blades. Now that happened to be a commodity, relates Söltner, "that was subject to restrictions at the time and could not be given to Jews." The saleswoman looked questioningly at the Hitler Youth. Should she sell him the razor blades? The little guy was generous: "Ah, go ahead and give 'em to him," Fritz Söltner indicated to the woman behind the counter, who promptly handed over the pack of razor blades. The man quickly disappeared.

One had to be on guard, because there were informers everywhere. The Nazis had woven a tight net of "official" informants that extended even into people's living rooms. At the bottom of that hierarchy stood men like Heilmann. Even more important than the welfare contributions he collected as building warden was what he heard by chance in people's apartments. Heilmann's area comprised the row of buildings on Spittlertorgraben, where he regularly called on the inhabitants. He was visited in turn by a man from Blumenthalstrasse, who was the district warden in charge of the entire area around Rosenau Park. In addition to Heilmann, who was mainly involved with money, clothing, and other sorts of collections, there was a block leader, named Klein, who was more concerned with party matters, and he, too, called on Heilmann frequently. Marga Söltner recalls that Klein was unmarried and lived a few buildings away on Turmstrasse. Klein's superior was a district leader who functioned as a sort of political commissar for that part of the city. The block and district leaders reported to the city group leader. The larger cities had a local party chief who oversaw all. In Nuremberg, that post was occupied by City Councillor Georg Haberkern.

The network of block wardens and block leaders in Nuremberg was considered by the few remaining scouts from the Social Democrats reporting to foreign countries in 1936 "to have been set up in an exemplary fashion." "If you visit someone in Nuremberg who's been blacklisted, you're watched carefully from then on, and if they notice anything even halfway suspicious, you and your entire circle of friends and acquaintances are arrested and subjected to procedures designed to squeeze out confessions."

The police had eyes everywhere as well. They read all the mail to and from Jewish organizations, tapped the private phones of Jews, and took surveillance photographs when Leo Katzenberger and his fellow congregations members attended a meeting. In the Nuremberg police archives, various tattered and torn letters have been preserved, letters which were apparently intercepted and never reached the addressees. In addition there are a few police photos from the summer of 1936 that show several Jewish men entering Adas Israel's meeting rooms: slightly blurred, taken from a safe distance, the pictures reveal only older men in dark, double-breasted suits, with broad-brimmed hats and pince-nez; one of them looks like Katzenberger.

Professional informants under the control of the police or intelligence services are as much a part of totalitarian regimes as voting booths are of democracies. On the other hand, the level of voluntary informing is a revealing seismograph of a country's mood and the moral decline of its inhabitants. A pack of letters, some written in old-fashioned Sütterlin script, some typed on paper with official business letterheads, provides insight into that gloomy chapter of denunciation in Nazi Germany. They are letters written to *Der Stürmer*, found after the war in the bombed-out editorial offices of Streicher's newspaper and saved by Bernard Kolb and his son, Herbert. Today, many of those letters can be found in the Leo Baeck Institute in New York; others are preserved in the section of the Nuremberg municipal archives labeled "Stürmer."

The letters and cards collected were written over a period of several years and thus provide a cross-section of the era. But most date from the fall of 1939. In one, a *Stürmer* reader from Bingen-on-the-Rhine informs on a grocery store owner for a too-friendly attitude toward Jews. "At a time when we are fighting against our greatest enemy, World Jewry, and our husbands and sons are enduring exhaustion and privation on the battlefield and making the supreme sacrifice," complains the letter-writer, "the wife of the above-mentioned store owner goes so far as to serve Jews first, even providing them with margarine without ration coupons." Another letter talks about a hat shop on Frankfurt's Kaiserstrasse where, behind the scenes, the previous Jewish owner is still directing things — an untenable situation in the opinion of the writer, who demands that the party intervene. There is extensive correspondence about an Aryan lawyer in Hannover who dared to defend a Jew against a party member in a case involving rents. In September 1939, attentive *Stürmer* readers can look into the milk cans, so to speak, of a woman in charge of a dairy, who allegedly allowed a Jewish neighbor to enter her shop and provided her with milk and cheese.

In those letters, the names and addresses of the people being informed on were always provided. And that was not without consequences, because, for the most part, *Der Stürmer*'s editors passed the information on to the local party officers and to the police. They frequently inquired about what had happened as a result of that information. Malevolent neighbors could cause a good deal of trouble. In Nuremberg, and surely in other cities as well, the police had for some time been handing out a form labeled "Voluntary Testimony." It was hoped that through use of the form as many inhabitants as possible would help with investigations by describing their fellow citizens' activities. The form elicited a great deal of interest.

In the apartment building on Spittlertorgraben, life went on as before. After being fired by Katzenberger, Heilmann landed a new job as driver for a draftsman's supply store on Hefnerplatz. His daughter Marga, now twelve years old, was hurrying down the polished steps with her little sister, Betty. Marga often had to do the grocery shopping for her mother and went off with a big wash basket borrowed from the Kleyleins, accompanied by one of the Kleyleins' sons. In the afternoon, the girl still rang Irene's doorbell and took the dachshund Dommerl for a walk in Rosenau Park while the photographer frequently sat in the kitchen with her sister-in-law, blond Vera Seiler, smoking and drinking coffee. Sometimes the two young women, whose husbands had been called up by the Wehrmacht, strolled over to Café Gisela or tried on new hats somewhere. "We really had a thing about hats," Vera Seiler says.

Up to that point, the war had not yet influenced people's daily lives too much, but it was omnipresent nevertheless. Movie houses, theaters, and many

nightspots stayed open at first, even Müller's Musicals, the dance hall in
Rosenau Park that Irene had loved to visit, remained open for business. At the
same time, the entire city was shifting to a wartime footing. Large wooden
barricades were erected at several of the bigger churches to protect the valuable stonework from enemy attack. In previous years, the Nazi powers had
insisted on construction of air-raid shelters; now their locations were clearly
indicated in white lettering on building facades. Workers even painted the
big letters designating a shelter on the front of the apartment building as well
as thick white lines showing the way into the cellar. The air-raid shelter was
located beneath the Kleyleins' apartment but was not used at the time. On the
floors above, the tenants now hung blackish-brown paper pull-down shades
in the windows or put pieces of cardboard over the panes, because no light
from the building was to be visible outside. Even the street lights and shop
window displays had to be turned off at night; automobile headlights were
limited to just a small slit. As the blackout was decreed, the age of darkness
had begun in an external, clearly visible sense as well.

On an evening in the fall of 1939, "shortly after the Polish campaign," as
Paul Kleylein noted during his interrogation by the Gestapo, the orthopedic
appliance maker was coming home from his business, quite late as usual,
when he saw Katzenberger "leaving the apartment." Kleylein was just about
to enter the building but stepped away from the open door, stood off to one
side, and observed the scene. Irene appeared in the vestibule and looked in
both directions "to see if anyone was around." It was obvious to Kleylein that
she hadn't seen him. Then Katzenberger came out of the apartment and hurriedly left the building by the rear door that led to the courtyard. A moment
later, Kleylein claimed, he saw the old man walk through the courtyard
entrance, out onto the street, and quickly disappear.

"He's coming back again now that Seiler's away," he grumbled to his wife
that evening. And the resolute hausfrau, who didn't like Irene— she'd called
the photographer a "little tramp" — commented, "The coast is clear for
Katzenberger." It was perhaps on that evening that the Kleyleins finally
decided to involve block leader Klein. "The situation can't go on like this,"
Kleylein had often said to his wife. The relationship, he thought, was going
to end in some horrible tragedy — "Frau Seiler was a party member, Herr
Seiler was a soldier, Herr Katzenberger was a Jew." And Herr Kleylein and
his fellow tenants in the building on Spittlertorgraben? They were the fourth
and perhaps most important factor.

At the same time, neither Kleylein nor the other neighbors knew what was drawing the old gentleman and the young photographer together. There was no cause for the overheated imaginations of men like Mäsel or Heilmann to conclude that there was something untoward going on in the studio every time the rotund, ailing Katzenberger came to see Irene. Aside from the blurred kiss in the mirror that Mother Mäsel — who died in 1933 — claimed to have observed, no one had seen anything at all improper with his or her own eyes. By the fall of 1939 contact between Katzenberger and Irene had long since diminished. Katzenberger did indeed visit her apartment a few more times, but for the most part it was because he was helping the Seilers with their tax forms.

Nearly all of the tenants on Spittlertorgraben took part in the nasty chatter about the presumed love affair, but it was Kleylein who took the decisive step and raised the gossip to a new, more dangerous level by informing the party. In later years, he consistently denied having done anything at all against the young woman and the Jew. "I have a completely clear conscience," he said; and once when he felt that he was being forced into a corner during questioning, he protested, "I didn't do anything; that's the absolute truth." Kleylein, his wife Betty, and some of the other neighbors from the Spittlertorgraben apartment house afterward claimed not to have made certain statements taken down by the police in the 1940s, but their explanations in that regard got them tangled in so many contradictions that it is difficult to place much credence in their later remarks.

Presumably the old transcripts of the Gestapo interrogations, which Katzenberger's attorney, Richard Herz, made copies of at the time, come closer to the truth. The papers in the old folder are fragile, the pages tightly packed with small typescript. Stored for decades in an attic in Fürth, the copies were found in the 1950s among Herz's personal effects by Katzenberger's son-in-law Bernhard Freimann and taken to Israel. There they were preserved for many years, at times in a shoe box.

According to those transcripts, Kleylein consulted block leader Klein sometime in the late fall of 1939 and "told him about the relationship between Katzenberger and the Seiler woman." Klein immediately informed the next higher Nazi functionary and a "complaint was made to the proper local authority." Several weeks later — the year 1940 had already begun — Irene received a summons to appear before the party. She had moved into an apartment on Pfannenschmiedgasse at the end of 1939 but continued to operate her studio on Spittlertorgraben.

The distance to Nuremberg's party offices was short — the Nazi local authority, where Irene was to appear in March 1940, was in the building next to her new apartment. Georg Haberkern read the riot act to party member Seiler, wanting to know what she was thinking, consorting with a Jew. Irene replied that Katzenberger had merely come to her studio to collect the rent; otherwise there was nothing between them. Haberkern informed her that nevertheless, she "was not to meet him and not to speak with him hereafter." Irene promised the party functionary that she "would follow his directions." But she insisted on explaining that to the Jew personally, "in the presence of my husband."

A short while later, the Seilers invited Katzenberger to their apartment on Pfannenschmiedgasse. Hans Seiler explained to the old gentleman that they were no longer permitted to meet or visit each other. Later, Irene accompanied her paternal friend to the door one last time; as they parted, she gave him a kiss.

At the party office, Haberkern apparently believed that Katzenberger was only collecting the rent, and so he called in Betty Kleylein and told her about Irene's testimony. Kleylein was beside herself. Rent? There was no way that could be true — the stamp maker Müller had been the building's owner for a long time. There had to be another reason for Katzenberger's visits! The pugnacious hausfrau is said to have threatened to write to the Chancellery of the Reich about the affair.

But what Irene had said was true. On the few occasions that the old man had appeared at her apartment door in recent weeks, it was to ask her to pay the 1,056 Reichsmarks rent she still owed. Katzenberger now needed the money more urgently than ever.

17

SIRENS HOWLED. PEOPLE HURRIED TO THE NEAREST BASEMENT shelter from wherever they were on the streets: it was Nuremberg's first air-raid alarm. On August 16, 1940, the apartment building's inhabitants clambered down the steps to the basement. Only the Mäsels arrived later — they'd been at the theater. Irene was wearing a big swastika on her chest, Kleylein later claimed, the first indication he had that she was a Nazi party member. According to his testimony, she was an air-raid warden and gave brusque instructions to everyone — a version of events she later denied. It may be that Irene did boss the others around a bit. Perhaps, too, the fear brought on by the first air-raid alarm had everyone a little unhinged.

Suddenly the building's tenants jumped as a dull thud resounded throughout the dim, vaulted cellar. Something had fallen over, and Irene, who gave the impression of being fairly nervous, promptly snapped at one of her neighbors, telling him to stop behaving like a boob. With that, Östreicher exploded. "You Jew-lover, I'll teach you," screamed the salesman. Irene was shocked and said nothing; everyone else stayed quiet as a mouse. Finally someone had said openly what they all had been whispering for some time.

The incident in the air-raid shelter exploded like a land mine in the narrow-minded community. Irene was now branded as the "Jew's woman," as far as they were concerned. Irene didn't even seem to defend herself against it.

On the day after the incident, she met Katzenberger by chance in front of the Ludwigstor. Some of the Spittlertorgraben tenants watched as Irene gesticulated while she explained, obviously to them, the events in the air-raid shelter. Until then, she'd taken no notice of the neighbors' talk; she was actually under the impression that she'd been a good neighbor. Now it was suddenly clear to Irene "that the tenants were being nasty to me," as she said many years later, still in a naive child's language.

Irene was completely stunned. She informed her father, who immediately traveled to Nuremberg. The two of them went to a lawyer, but he advised them to "just leave things as they are," that things could be worse. So Irene acted as if nothing had happened. Such a failure to react, however, was immediately taken by the neighbors to be an acknowledgment of guilt. For instance, Kleylein noted that she "made no reply and didn't even take any action against Östreicher." And Östreicher's wife emphasized again and again that "no complaint was ever made" against her husband "because of the insult."

Irene was now regarded more or less officially as a *Judenschickse,* a Jew's floozy, and therefore on the blacklist. Accordingly, any association with her was almost as dangerous as associating with an actual Jew. Kleylein and his wife immediately came to that conclusion. Until then, the prosthesis maker, in spite of all the gossip that he and his wife indulged in behind Irene's back, enjoyed chatting with the pretty photographer when he met her in the stairwell. Now his behavior was definitely reserved. He didn't want to be accused of "having a close friendship with a Jew lover," because "for my business as a prosthesis maker being accused of having a friendly attitude toward Jews would have serious repercussions."

By that time, the community of tenants on Spittlertorgraben had turned into a community of informers. Fear and spitefulness subverted the building's inhabitants; public smear campaigns and crude demands for denunciation had had their effects. So no one was surprised when block leader Klein showed up at Spittlertorgraben shortly after the row in the shelter. Kleylein invited him into his apartment and told him about the incident, "but he already knew more than I did," was the prosthesis maker's comment later. The block leader rang other doorbells as well, inquiring about Irene and asking this and that. After Kleylein's tip in the fall of 1939, Klein had simply passed the information on to his immediate superior. Now, however, a real investigation was underway. Something was up, and everyone in the apartment house sensed it. Only Irene seemed to be unaware.

Perhaps she simply hadn't noticed what was going on around her because she had so much to do. Her photography business was better than ever, mainly as a result of the war. In the summer of 1940 the Nazis were attacking on one new front after another — they marched into Belgium, Holland, and France. The mood was still one of certain victory. When the warriors returned from a successful campaign, the attractive half-timbered houses in Nuremberg's old city were decorated with evergreen garlands and red swastika flags as in the days of the party rallies, while the victorious soldiers paraded through the marketplace and displayed captured enemy artillery pieces. The entrance to Irene's studio had turned into a revolving door of young men. "Every photographer does well during wartime," she stated later. "People sent pictures to the front and had reproductions made of pictures of those killed in battle."

Her photography business was going well for other reasons. For some time, Jewish citizens were obliged to carry special identification cards that they had to show under all sorts of circumstances — even to buy postage stamps. The person's photo was pasted on the left side of the so-called "Identification Card J." On the right was a copy of a fingerprint, and, underneath, vital statistics. The cards were required by a law passed in October 1938. Cards were made available in batches, a process that extended over a considerable period of time. The Jews needed new ID photos and it was clear that they wouldn't want to go to one of the city's well-known Nazi photographers.

Instead, many of them may have inquired at the Jewish congregations' office for the name of a photographer who was considered less friendly to the Nazis. In that regard, Leo Katzenberger, who had been working steadily in the office since August 1939, may have advised them, and Irene's studio may have benefited from tips passed through the Jewish community.

The Jewish customers usually entered the vestibule of the building on Spittlertorgraben fearfully and nearly standing at attention, as Ilse Gräntzel, one of Irene's employees, later recalled. In the studio, Irene tried to allay their fears and treated every arrival with great politeness. But when the Jewish clients had been processed there were new customers standing at the studio door — SS men who were stationed at the barracks nearby.

Katzenberger saw the photographer only rarely in those days. The old gentleman had a great deal of work to do for the Jewish community; he was considered one of the most respected representatives on the Council of Bavarian Congregations and frequently gave the farewell address when yet another congregational chairman left to go abroad. He himself had become resigned to staying. "I have my work," he wrote to Palestine in December 1940, "more of it every day, and that's good." Once that fall, when Irene's husband was on leave, Katzenberger met Irene on Dennerstrasse. Clad as always in a dark suit and vest despite his troubles, he refused to miss the opportunity to salute young love with a bouquet. And once again, malevolent eyes observed the scene. This time it was Gilger, the cigarette lady, who saw Katzenberger and quickly passed on her version of the meeting between the businessman and the photographer: the former had "walked up and down Dennerstrasse with the bouquet," and then Irene came along, took the flowers, and walked away quickly. The cigarette vendor, however, stood there and watched Katzenberger for a long time "because," as she later testified, "I knew about their relationship."

It is also possible that Katzenberger came to Irene's studio a few more times during those weeks. He, along with many other Jewish inhabitants of the city, had to make do with considerably fewer ration coupons than non-Jews. On their balcony on Praterstrasse the Katzenbergers planted tomatoes, chives, and parsley, and strawberries were ripening in their garden. But that alone was not enough to live on. So it may be that Irene showed her gratitude for Katzenberger's previous help by providing him with food. During the Gestapo interrogations, Irene always claimed that, at the time, she had simply met Katzenberger on the street by chance. However, she told a new friend after the war that the businessman had often visited her secretly; they sat in her little kitchen and then she gave him something to take along to eat, after which he disappeared through a rear exit. That story corresponds with Betty Kleylein's assertion that she'd seen Katzenberger in the building on Spittlertorgraben as late as the fall of 1940.

At that point, there were perhaps still places in Nuremberg where Jews and non-Jews could get together unobtrusively. Such meetings were impossible at the studio in the apartment house. The attentive neighbors, Hitler's willing accomplices, had their eyes on everything. But even the photographer's apartment on Pfannenschmiedgasse was not a place where Katzenberger could show up undetected, since it happened to be right next door to the local Nazi office. It was presumably a visit to that apartment that ultimately proved fatal.

In January or February 1941 Irene's father, Oskar Scheffler, spent some time in the city. The retired accountant was visiting his daughter, but he also wanted to see his old friend Katzenberger. And so he invited him to Irene's apartment. Presumably the two of them smoked cigars together as they did in the old days, Scheffler paid Irene's outstanding rent, and then the two former lodge brothers discussed the terrible turn of events. Toward evening Irene came home, followed by her soldier husband, who was stationed at a barracks in Nuremberg and permitted to spend the night with his wife. Irene greeted Katzenberger only cursorily, and the old businessman promptly said goodbye, since he wanted to be home before eight o'clock.

A short time later, on March 18, 1941, Katzenberger was arrested at his villa on Praterstrasse. The police photo, taken on March 19, 1941, shows him to be as elegant as ever. In black pin-stripe suit with vest and tie, his hat pulled down over his face a little, he is looking at the camera with a serious expression. It is the last surviving picture of him. Not long after the incident in the air-raid shelter, a "confidential report" reached the police. Who made it is still a matter of speculation. Bernard Kolb reported later that Leo had been "under surveillance for months," until finally a witness came forth who "had seen Katzenberger leaving the apartment of a German married couple."

Kolb's statement makes sense. According to it, the police had been unable to make any progress following the anonymous tip in the fall of 1940, because Irene and Katzenberger had broken off contact for some time. Since Irene had been instructed by the party in March 1940 to avoid all contact, the businessman had no longer visited her; at the most, he merely went to her studio a few times. But even those visits tapered off, so the investigators were unable to catch him *in flagranti,* although perhaps he had been shadowed since the incident in the air-raid shelter. When the old gentleman showed up on Pfannenschmiedgasse months later at Father Scheffler's invitation, the trap was sprung.

The first person from the apartment house to be interrogated after Katzenberger's arrest was Margarete Östreicher. She had always taken part in the gossip about Katzenberger and Irene, but showed unexpected strength of character. She claimed to know nothing specific about the relationship and referred her questioners to the Kleyleins. Later, Frau Östreicher was said to have made a few remarks about the presumed intimacies between the Jew and the young woman. Betty Kleylein, it seems, heard that her neighbor had suddenly "kept her trap shut," so the pugnacious housewife marched off to the police station on her own accord to discredit her. She claimed that the Östreicher woman had kept quiet about what she knew because she'd bought a suite of furniture from Katzenberger after Kristallnacht.

Sergeant Hans Zeuschel was assigned to investigate. A member of the vice squad since 1936, he was an inconspicuous fellow — Irene couldn't even remember him later — but he would never forget the photographer. "By my standards, Frau Seiler was a very beautiful woman," was the way he described the suspect thirty years later. The first thing he did in the spring of 1941 was to call all the tenants in for interrogation. Heilmann and Mäsel both brought up the ancient story of the shoe boxes that Irene carried across the courtyard now and again, back in the days when the shoe business still existed. They claimed practically in one voice that it was certainly just "camouflage" for some sort of sexual dalliance.

In addition, Mäsel claimed to have "constantly seen Katzenberger going into the Seiler woman's apartment." How he came to that observation he didn't say; from his lookout in the carriage house he couldn't have seen anything of the sort since, for years, Irene had always pulled the curtains when she had visitors. Heilmann came out with his favorite tale: Irene had received money from Katzenberger, something she could "easily work off" with the Jewish businessman. In addition, he claimed that after a prearranged signal the two of them used to go off together, presumably to go shopping. When Irene came home later, she'd "often have a package under her arm." With a solemn tone of conviction, Heilmann then declared to the investigators that he was "certain that there was a sexual relationship between the two of them."

The cigarette vendor, Frau Gilger, likewise proved cooperative, revealing that the Seiler woman had "lived beyond her means" and was constantly in debt.

Only the flower lady from Dennerstrasse, Rosa Haselbacher, remained silent. If she had wanted to, she could have told just as much as the tobacconist from the Plärrer. After all, the flower-lover Katzenberger had made purchases as frequently from her as from the cigarette lady; he was always taking a colorful bouquet home with him. Sometimes he'd even bought flowers for the photographer; presumably no one knew that better than the flower lady. Yet Rosa Haselbacher had never had anything to do with the nasty rumors about the old merchant. When Sergeant Zeuschel interrogated her, she simply declared that she was "unable to provide any details."

Paul Kleylein and his wife, Betty, on the other hand, provided extensive testimony. The housewife told about an alleged "secret telephone" in Irene's studio. And she could not be budged from her statement that she'd seen the businessman with Irene as late as January 1941. Anyone who claimed otherwise "was telling a lie," she said in a shrill voice. But then she had to meekly confess that she'd made a mistake: "It wasn't at the beginning of 1941, but in the fall of 1940 when I saw Katzenberger going to visit the Seiler woman."

Paul Kleylein gave even more detailed testimony. Whatever he'd heard from one of the tenants was passed on with a precise indication of the source: from Heilmann he knew that Katzenberger had bought a car for Irene; the tobacconist reported that the businessman always took cigarettes along for her; Katzenberger had indeed given the photographer money in his office, and details could be provided by "a worker who's an invalid." Irene lived beyond her means; she "spent a lot of money on clothing and hats." The prosthesis maker claimed to know that himself and went on: "She even hit me up for money." Once Kleylein claimed to have seen Katzenberger coming directly out of the Seiler woman's apartment: "He was taken aback and got out of there in a hurry."

A few minutes after his interrogation that morning, Kleylein himself was in for an extremely unpleasant surprise. It was nearly eight in the morning. Kleylein was just walking out of the imposing portal of police headquarters when he saw Irene walking along Ludwigstrasse on her way to work. He would have liked to quickly sneak back into the foyer, but it was too late — Irene had obviously seen him. She was not being interrogated at that point, but she knew of Katzenberger's arrest, of course. Standing there in front of the entrance to police headquarters, Kleylein felt like a thief caught in the act, he later admitted. "Lord Almighty," it dawned on him, " the woman's certainly going to think I informed on her."

A few days later, Irene was ordered to appear at the ornate, ostentatious building that housed police headquarters. At first she didn't want to say anything at all — there was nothing between her and Katzenberger. But Sergeant Zeuschel, thirty-two years old, knew his business. "It's always that way. No one ever walks in and starts to tell everything right off the bat."First, he took down Irene's personal information, then asked her about her photo shop and the rent she owed Katzenberger. Then the officer asked about her visits to the shoe firm's office, then inquired in passing about the shoes she'd been given, and suddenly the young woman cracked. The businessman "became intimate now and then," admitted Irene. "Katzenberger kissed me on the mouth, and I responded."

Carefully, Zeuschel now asked more detailed questions. And Irene, naively unaware of how charged the situation was, willingly told all that had happened over the course of the last ten years. Sometimes she'd sat on the old man's lap and "he patted my upper thighs through my clothing." Once Katzenberger had even "put his head against my breast," but, of course, the merchant was appreciably shorter than she was, Irene explained good naturedly, so it was natural that his head would be at the same level as her breast during such a friendly sit on his lap. Zeuschel wanted to know if her touched her breasts. No, replied Irene, then thought it over. "Well, but he did caress my bosom," was her statement.

Sergeant Zeuschel was beginning to enjoy the conversation, and so he went through the entire litany of possible sexual advances. Hadn't the businessman gotten "under your skirt," or "even reached for your genitals"? Hadn't he "exposed himself" and demanded that she "take hold of his sex organ"? The questions couldn't have been more direct, but Irene answered them conscientiously. No, "such improprieties" had not occurred; she had "not indulged in any sexual congress" with Katzenberger and "had not undertaken any abnormal acts with him."

The sergeant even wanted to know if the businessman had "gotten excited," and what she could say about his potency. But by now the possible consequences of her admissions were probably dawning on her, and she tried frantically to backpedal. The caresses described had been completely harmless, in truth, and were "not the result of any erotic feelings," stated the photographer. She considered Katzenberger merely her "old uncle," or even her "Nuremberg Daddy."

Hans Zeuschel, visibly impressed by Irene's charm, could not believe that this "pretty, tall, and slender woman" had been the object of purely paternal caresses. Instead, she gave the impression that she was "not disinclined to flirt and enjoy intimacies with men." And so he became convinced, as he explained later, "that any man who gets a woman like that on his lap is not likely to stop with kissing, but is at least going to try to get somewhere beyond her thighs."

18

IN THE NUREMBERG PRISON, LEO KATZENBERGER was listed as "personal file No. 428981." Sergeant Zeuschel summoned him to police headquarters for questioning. The door to the interrogation room opened; a short man with a goatee was ushered in, and Zeuschel studied the man for a moment. According to his file, Leo Israel Katzenberger was sixty-seven years old, but the officer thought he looked "considerably younger." Zeuschel imagined that the stocky gentleman would certainly stand a good chance with women. "Judging by his appearance," the policeman's assessment was that one could still "credit him with sexual activity." To someone from the vice squad, therefore, it was out of the question that the intimacies admitted by the photographer were "free from sexual implications."

At the interrogation Katzenberger at first claimed, as Zeuschel recollected later, that he had not exchanged intimacies with Irene. But the officer was ready for that. He read the photographer's testimony, and then Katzenberger basically admitted that there had been intimacies. But he too sought to have the relationship understood as purely paternal. At the same time, the Jew emphasized that he had "not caressed the young woman's thigh" and had "not kissed her in her apartment." Zeuschel drew up a brief report. Katzenberger's basic confession sufficed — the photographer had already provided all the details.

As Katzenberger was being taken back to his cell after the interrogation, he probably sensed for the first time the extent of the trouble that was brewing. Irene had related a number of things that could do terrible damage, and he was not sure whether the interrogating officer had understood or believed his testimony. Katzenberger resolved to write a letter to the state's attorney, stating unambiguously that "sexual things" had "really not played a role" in his relationship with Irene.

On the outside, meanwhile, David Katzenberger had been looking for a lawyer, which was not easy because of the more than eighty Jewish lawyers that had practiced in Nuremberg there were now just a handful. And since the fall of 1938, they were only allowed to call themselves "consultants," meaning that they were restricted to "providing legal advice and representation for Jews." In addition, the affair at hand was most delicate: David and Max had certainly warned Leo earlier not to flirt so openly with the photographer. But an attorney was found to take over the case: Dr. Richard Herz, whom Leo Katzenberger presumably knew from the Adas Israel. On April 4, 1941, Herz submitted his credentials in the case of "Leo Israel Katzenberger," and shortly afterward visited the businessman in jail for the first time. Katzenberger was not in good health. He had tried several times to get visiting privileges for his wife, but his application was always rejected. "My nerves and heart are going on strike," he wrote to his lawyer on May 12.

At first it seemed as if Leo Katzenberger had some good luck in the midst of all the bad: Investigating Judge Hans Groben, thirty-four years old, gave an affable impression and obviously did not consider the facts presented so damning. Groben worked out with Herz that, for the moment, there was no point to pleaing for a suspended sentence, because the investigation had to be concluded first. Then he would give Herz "the nod," and the affair could perhaps be concluded quickly. Meanwhile, Katzenberger's former chauffeur, Fabro, drove to the jail daily, bringing the old gentleman a tin canister with kosher food. For his trouble, the prison warders called him a "Jew's lackey," recalls his wife.

In June 1941, Attorney Herz applied for "permission for regular visitation" for Claire Katzenberger. There were important questions Claire needed to discuss with her husband. She had begun making renewed attempts to arrange for emigration for herself and Leo. Presumably Claire had gone to the

American Consulate in Stuttgart and had stood in line to get one of the much-sought-after slips of paper with the waiting-list number. She was not trying for just a U.S. visa — it could be for Cuba, Ecuador, or any other country on the face of the earth. The main point was to get out of Germany. In those weeks in mid-1941, Claire and others in the Katzenberger family still cherished the hope that they could get Leo out of jail and then out of the country as quickly as possible. "Leo healthy, hope for favorable settlement," wrote Claire Katzenberger in a terse Red Cross letter to Palestine in July 1941.

The basis for their hope may have been provided by a parallel case, the tattered records of which are in the archives pertaining to the Fürth congregations. A Jewish merchant from Fürth had been sentenced to eight months' imprisonment in the spring of 1938 on a morals charge: the man had allegedly touched the breast of a female coworker. During his imprisonment, his relatives arranged for his emigration. All of the requirements for an America visa, such as guarantees by friends or relatives in the United States, had been provided, but the waiting-list number from the consulate at Stuttgart, 7961, made the man's case look hopeless. A member of the Nuremberg Aid Society, a Jewish organization whose central office was in Berlin, approached the authorities.

The Aid Society representatives wanted to obtain a temporary travel permit for the merchant so that he could go abroad to wait while the formalities for his U.S. visa were being taken care of. The police were open to that suggestion and, after being released, the man traveled to Berlin under discrete police surveillance. His passport was issued a short time later. The police showed themselves similarly helpful in the case of a second citizen from Fürth who had been sent to Buchenwald in the fall of 1938. When presented with his ticket for ship's passage, they indicated that the man had good prospects for receiving a passport and certified that he had a clean police record. Unfortunately, the records do not make it clear whether or not the two men were actually able to emigrate. The cases do fit, however, with the policy of Nuremberg Police Chief Benno Martin, who had the reputation of supporting the wishes of Jews to emigrate.

An ambitious Nazi, Martin had maintained contacts with several representatives of the Jewish community in Nuremberg and had become stronger politically. Step-by-step, the police chief had worked to reduce the power of Gauleiter Streicher, whose corrupt, unpredictable, and arbitrary regime Martin found offensive. In the spring of 1939, the Göring Commission, whose activities Martin strongly supported, went after Streicher. By fall 1939, Hitler banned Streicher, his old comrade-at-arms, from making public speeches. When he failed to obey and instead embarked on a speaking tour throughout Franconia, the Führer began disciplinary proceedings against him. The party's committee declared the Franconia Gauleiter "unfit for a leadership role." Thenceforth, Streicher was banished to his estate at Pleikershof. Benno Martin won.

When Katzenberger was arrested in the spring of 1941, his wife and brothers presumably hoped for help from Martin. They had always thought of Leo's relationship to the chief of police "as a sort of insurance," Lilo later recalled. Thus it seemed logical to arrange for a visa. How they were going to get Leo out of jail remained to be seen. Nevertheless, the businessman had gotten out of the currency imbroglio barely three years earlier and the present affair was not considered hopeless, even by Groben, the investigating judge.

The complicated procedure that was necessary to obtain the hoped-for U.S. visa was something Claire Katzenberger learned from Leo Weglein and his wife. The first thing the Americans required from every applicant was a packet of paperwork: birth certificate, marriage license (both in duplicate), a valid passport, a police certification of a clean record, four loose passport pictures, a ten-dollar visa fee, and, in addition, the "affidavit of support," a guarantee on the part of friends or relatives living in America that their yearly incomes would suffice to support the immigrant if need be. Finally, the ship's passage had to be prepaid — assuming, of course, that one could find space on a ship.

Since the beginning of the war, a berth on a ship was harder and harder to come by as one harbor after another was closed to German refugees. The Aid Society was now arranging the greatest number of passages, but there was a problem: the farther one lived from Berlin, the less likely the prospects of getting a ticket. Nuremberg was fairly far away from Berlin. Not even 10 percent of the applicants from Nuremberg, according to Bernhard Kolb, "got their passages directly through the Aid Society — all the rest had to get theirs through middlemen in ways that were not quite aboveboard."

With the outbreak of war, a desperate competition began for the few berths still available. Several Jewish organizations that tried to help people emigrate, such as the Hebrew Immigrant Aid Society (HIAS) in New York, which ran a European office in Paris under the initials HICEM, saw confusion approaching. "The more difficult the situation becomes, the more precisely the general rules of our common endeavor must be observed if we wish to avoid disorder, not to mention chaos," warned the Paris office in a circular letter of December 29, 1939. HICEM workers were afraid that "panic would overwhelm our unfortunate, cruelly persecuted fellow believers," and that it was therefore "all the more necessary to keep a cool head."

Like a gigantic, slowly closing trap, nearly all of the exit points from Europe were sealed. The German harbors had been closed to emigrants since the war's outbreak; the path through Holland or Belgium was blocked when those countries were attacked in the spring of 1940. After the Nazis marched into France, the HICEM office moved to Lisbon, the last open harbor, in July 1940. Refugees from all over Europe tried to fight their way through to Portugal; for many it was a horrible odyssey, because almost every country required a different transit visa. And yet some ten thousand people were said to have succeeded.

Since 1940, Bernhard Kolb had been trying to get his two children, Herbert and Erna, out of Germany. The Kolbs made it over the usual hurdles: travel to Stuttgart, a place on the waiting list, then the affidavits, records, and on and on. Things didn't look so bad, because a relative of the Kolbs' lived in America and was quite well-off. He put up the financial guarantees for Herbert, by now eighteen, and Erna, sixteen.

The affidavits arrived and the waiting list numbers were about to be issued. The Kolbs traveled expectantly to Stuttgart. "But things somehow got snarled," recalls Herbert Kolb. "They said they hadn't gotten our papers." Someone else must have bribed his or her way onto the waiting list instead. The Kolb family had another uncle in Uruguay who'd left Germany in 1933. The Uruguay Consulate was in Hamburg. Kolb twice made the trip north and paid money to a consular officer; the uncle in Uruguay put up considerable sums in South America. But nothing happened. Some corrupt consular clerk presumably made off with the money.

Not much was able to get Bernard Kolb down, but now he felt limp, defeated. In his role as congregations secretary, how many people had he helped to get away? But now he couldn't get his own children out. He had a premonition of the horrors that faced them. Thanks to some edict or other, he had to constantly report to the Gestapo, so he in turn was well informed. In the spring of 1940 the news made the rounds that the entire Jewish population of the harbor city Stettin had been shipped off to Litzmannstadt (Lodz) and Pieski, in Poland. Faced with inquiries from the Jewish congregations, the Reich Security Office in Berlin explained that Stettin was a special case; but the shrewd, experienced Kolb remained skeptical.

In Germany and the occupied countries, a feeling of panic began to spread, one confirmed by officials at the Joint Distribution Committee, an international Jewish aid organization, in the fall of 1941. The committee had received reports concerning the first deportations. They also noted a brisk upswing in business dealing with Cuban entry visas, one of the emigrants' last hopes. Black marketeers demanded a good deal of money for tourist visas to Cuba, but "anyone in a position to come up with these astonishingly high sums is scrambling to get one." According to the committee's report, "numerous agencies have sprung up overnight" to sell visas — "some are trustworthy, others not."

Claire Katzenberger was hoping for such a visa in the fall of 1941. Soon after a visit to her husband in prison, an active correspondence developed between the Nuremberg Aid Society, its central office in Berlin, and the HIAS office in New York. Airmail letters, cable messages, and telegrams were sent back and forth; clearly, everyone seemed to think they could get Katzenberger out of prison if he just had a visa. Relatives in America could help obtain documents and tickets for the ship. Sally Weglein was now living in New York; his brother Leo Weglein had ended up in Youngstown, Ohio.

However, they were both earning rather meager salaries. Sally was driving all over the country as a shoe salesman, and Leo had gone to work in a shoe factory and was earning just $30 a week. Nevertheless, the Nuremberg Katzenbergers still nourished the hope that the Wegleins could help. In a cable dated August 13, 1941, the people in Berlin urged their opposite numbers in New York to "get the Katzenberger relatives to help with their emigration to Cuba." Presumably the primary concern was to cover the travel expenses, which generally had to be paid abroad, because German money had become virtually worthless. In mid-September 1941, a terse, three-line letter from the Nuremberg Aid Society that reached Katzenberger's attorney, Richard Herz, stated "Herr Weglein is not in a position to raise the necessary funds." One month later, on October 14, 1941, the Berlin Aid Society sought to get through to New York again — the situation had become extremely pressing, and yet the HIAS office had only mentioned dealings with a single relative. Hence the question from Berlin: "Have you heard anything in the meantime of the other relatives who should be contacted?"

No answer has been preserved. But Marga Weglein, Sally's widow, recalls that her husband was once called to the New York office of the HIAS at 425 Lafayette Street. "I went, because my husband wasn't home," relates the old woman, "but I told them it was hopeless; we couldn't raise the money."

19

THE INVESTIGATING JUDGE, HANS GROBEN, did not feel entirely happy about the proceedings against Leo Katzenberger. Groben later asserted, "it went counter to my feelings for justice." And so the judge felt positively relieved when the public prosecutor's office issued orders to reinterrogate the witness Irene Seiler under oath. On July 9, 1941, Groben had the photographer shown into his interrogation chamber; he instructed the witness that this time she really had to tell the truth. Irene began her statement.

She alleged that she'd sat on the businessman's lap as well as kissed him on the mouth, and that at times Katzenberger involuntarily put his head against her bosom, "because he's shorter than I am." For the same reason, he'd occasionally touched her thigh and "stroked it once." It had nothing to do with "intimacies like with lovers," but affection "of the kind a child would show toward her father." Irene acknowledged that "Katzenberger had taken my father's place in my life."

The photographer had made these statements already, but without the salacious questions of the vice-squad officer it all sounded basically innocent. As far as Groben was concerned, there "was no longer any pressing suspicion," and he made a notation that he was considering canceling the arrest warrant and sent the files back to the prosecutor's office. He then told Counselor Herz that this was the proper time to file for a dismissal and went off on vacation.

Herz was an extremely proper man. Rather corpulent, his remaining hair closely cropped, he was prone to withdraw into himself — he was only forty-seven, and yet his life seemed to have run its course. The attorney formulated a punctilious and dispassionate motion for release: Katzenberger had been detained for five months by then, and revelations had been developed to the point that there "was no longer any danger of obfuscation." Beyond that, the accused "was suffering from heart troubles, according to his own statements," and Herz petitioned that the accused be "released on bail." How bail money was to be raised can only be a matter of speculation — according to official account balances, Katzenberger no longer had any significant financial assets.

A piece of scrap paper on which Herz scribbled all sorts of notes during a visit to Katzenberger in jail gives at least a hint. On that piece of paper, an old envelope, Herz wrote down a short wish list of daily necessities that he was to bring to Katzenberger on his next visit. The old gentleman had asked for toothpaste, coffee, various books, and a package of corn plasters. On the very top of the scrap of paper is the note "Adas 10000." It is possible that the ortho-dox religious organization, which had lost its independence by then, still had sufficient assets to put up bail. Or it may be that Katzenberger, who, like all Jews, was limited to bank withdrawals of two hundred marks since the decree of January 1939, had earlier deposited a large amount of money in the organization's account.

The answer to Counselor Herz's motion to dismiss charges came promptly, almost by return mail. On September 5, 1941, he received a letter from the court that stated "by judicial decision" he had been "rejected as the accused's defense attorney" and that therefore his motion for release was "without basis." With its dry legal language, the letter had an unpleasant sound; but it had to do with a purely formal rejection, not a decision in the case. What was worrisome, however, was that the sender was not the forth-right Judge Groben. The postmark indicated that the rejection had come from the feared Special Court of the Superior District Courts of Nuremberg.

Jurisdiction over the proceedings had been assumed by the District Court Director Oswald Rothaug — the very man who was called the "executioner" at the Blaue Traube. Several weeks previously, without anyone's knowledge, he had taken the reins in the Katzenberger criminal case and was already engaged in spinning a complex net of judicial intrigue which would soon put Irene in the dock as well. Whenever Rothaug got his hands on a case, Nuremberg Public Prosecutor Hermann Markl stated later, he "acted like a dog working a bone."

The sentencing guidelines at the Special Court were considerably more severe than in other courts; therefore it had to be taken as a bad sign when Rothaug contrived, in the summer of 1941, to have the files "reassigned in the register." Henceforth, Katzenberger's case was known as Criminal Case 1b / Sg / 1074 / 41.

Rothaug presided primarily over offenses that came under the Volksschädlingsverordnung (Law Concerning Acts Detrimental to the People), a sort of martial law that severely punished even minor crimes if they were carried out through the exploitation of wartime conditions. For instance, a thief who stole a chicken at night could be condemned to death, because he exploited the blackout orders for his purposes. From his reading of several interrogations conducted during the investigation of the Leo Katzenberger case, Rothaug concluded that the "offense against racial purity" most certainly had occurred at night, in other words, during darkness. Rothaug considered Katzenberger, therefore, as potentially guilty of a "detrimental act against the people."

The judge sought out cases such as this one — he had a fine nose for whatever might benefit Nazi propaganda purposes. A Jew and an Aryan, an old man and a young woman. The Jew was not just any Jew, but the chairman of the Nuremberg congregations. It had the makings of an excellent case. He would invite his friends from the Blaue Traube to show them what a capable judge he was. Rothaug wanted to further his career, and the regulars from the pub in the shadow of the St. Lorenz Church played a decisive role in those plans. The District Inspector Haberkern's inn was frequented by all the important people: Deputy Gauleiter Karl Holz, Police Chief Martin, SS Security Services member Fritz Elkar, and, before he'd been banished to his farm, there was even a good chance of catching sight of Julius Streicher. Rothaug had known the Gauleiter for a long time — in 1938 Streicher had pressed hard for the judge's promotion. At the time, Rothaug, who'd only been in charge of the Special Court for a year, wanted very much to be vice president of the Nuremberg District Courts. Streicher wrote to the justice minister that Rothaug was "not only politically completely trustworthy," but "from the standpoint of ability, one of the most competent judges in my entire district." But the president of the Nuremberg District Courts, Friedrich Döbig, did not care for Rothaug and presumably discretely prevented the ambitious Nazi from becoming his deputy. On December 13, 1938, the Justice Ministry in Berlin answered Streicher: Rothaug, at just forty-one years of age, was a bit young for the vice presidency. From then on, Rothaug, consumed by ambition, hated President Judge Döbig, whom he considered responsible for his rejection, and plotted against him whenever an opportunity presented itself.

Soon Rothaug was regularly writing bulletins for the SD, the Security Service of the SS, and functioning as a sort of unofficial collaborator for that Nazi counterintelligence service. He spent an hour almost every Sunday in his office talking informally with SD man Elkar. The code name for the informant Rothaug was Tante (Auntie).

Rothaug was not a National Socialist from the beginning. Originally he supported the arch-reactionary German national movement led by General Erich Ludendorff, who had helped involve Germany in World War I. It was not until 1937 that Rothaug joined the Nazi Party. However, he was surely a "National Socialist of the purest water even before that," his one-time colleague Dr. Martin Dorfmüller stated. Rothaug had once taken the jurist to task when they were on a court-related train trip because he was reading a biography of Goethe. "It's unbelievable that you're reading that," scolded Rothaug, "because Goethe was a potential emigrant."

What linked Rothaug to Streicher was his outspoken hatred of Jews. He maintained his contact with the Gauleiter even after the latter had been forced to the sidelines. To his colleagues, Rothaug occasionally boasted that he'd been invited to the Pleikershof estate once again. It's possible that the two of them discussed the Katzenberger case. It may well be that Streicher remembered the painful slander suit that Katzenberger brought against him in 1933. In addition, Streicher doubtless had an ear for cases involving "racial purity." In *Der Stürmer*, he made sure that such things stood out boldly.

The ambitious Rothaug had every reason to assume that he would attract a great deal of attention from the Nuremberg Nazi hierarchy with a trial against Katzenberger. In a fashion worthy of an army general, the judge now plotted his moves: first, he delegated prosecutor Markl to conduct follow-up investigations to be sure that Katzenberger had indeed paid a nighttime visit to the presumed object of his affections; with that information the trap of the Detrimental Acts Law would snap shut on the businessman. Markl had the

Kleyleins visit police headquarters again and the investigators promptly got the answers they'd hoped for.

Paul Kleylein reported that it "was already very dark," when he saw Katzenberger coming out of the apartment on one occasion — he was, of course, able to recognize the man despite the darkness. Another time, Kleylein claimed to have seen Katzenberger "going to Irene's apartment toward eight o'clock at night." "In my estimation," intoned Kleylein, Katzenberger had "used the blackout to more easily carry out his visits to the Seiler woman." And Irene herself had confirmed in the repeat interrogation that the businessman had often come around five in the afternoon, "when it was already dark since it was winter." Of course, she added, the only reason he'd come so late was that he wanted to meet her husband —who came home from the army barracks at around that time — because the Seilers had asked him to help them with their tax return. The only thing disturbing Rothaug now was Irene Seiler's testimony, in which the photographer spoke of a purely paternal relationship. If the young woman was going to insist upon the innocence of her romance with the Jew, he had to get her out of the way as a witness. He came up with a legalistic trick: he accused the photographer of perjury, whereby she herself became a defendant and could no longer be called as a witness for the defense.

On December 3, 1941, Irene was arrested. Markl hastily composed a new version of the indictment. The three-page, closely written document is bursting with unproven accusations, ones that would have been news even to the Spittlertorgraben tenants. It claimed that "sexual intimacies of all types" had occurred between Irene and Katzenberger, "including sexual intercourse." The accused, according to Markl, "exchanged kisses frequently in the Seiler woman's apartment and in the Katzenberger's business offices." In addition, Irene had "very often" sat on the businessman's lap, and he had fondled her thighs "with the intent of obtaining sexual satisfaction," while at the same time, according to the state's attorney, "they were holding each other very closely."

"In view of those evil deeds," concluded Markl, "the people's healthy sensibilities demand, in view of this particularly reprehensible crime, that the regular limits of punishment be exceeded." With that, the first indication that the state intended to seek the death penalty was provided.

Markl's indictment did not merely reflect his bending to political pressures; it also reflected his own impression of Irene, gained during one of the interrogations: "Herr Katzenberger, as a man, would have had to be very strong indeed to actually restrain himself with such a pretty woman." Markl was of the opinion "that an actual love relationship" had formed between the old man and the young woman, a liaison "with a sexual basis" — especially in view of the fact that the state's attorney had obtained from Dr. Armin Baur, the court's medical expert, a report that Katzenberger was "still able to indulge in sexual intercourse."

Slowly the trial date edged closer. On the session calendar of the justice department, the proceedings were set for February 21, 1942. Rothaug marked an exclamation point on the date with a red pencil, a signal within the legal system that the death penalty was anticipated. His friends from the Blaue Traube were informed, and the judge even sent them reserved seat numbers. Rothaug was already smugly anticipating his "close-up performance," as he called it, when he suddenly recalled the one condition that received great emphasis in those days: before a defendant could be condemned to death, investigations had to prove that he was mentally competent. Order reigned in the National Socialist State.

There was insufficient time for such an investigation before the trial date and so Rothaug had to delay the proceedings three weeks and had an announcement printed in the party's *Franconian Daily News,* so that the Nazi leadership would be informed. Soon the telephone lines between party head-quarters and the courthouse were heating up — several of the top people from the Gauleiter's office were upset. Dr. Baur was escorted to the business-man's cell once again at the behest of the judge. Baur did the usual tests on the accused and pronounced him mentally competent.

"Katzenberger was, in fact, neither mentally ill nor feeble-minded," Baur related, "quite the contrary — he knew exactly what he could expect from Rothaug."

20

ON FRIDAY MARCH 13, 1942, IRENE LOOKED anxiously around the gigantic room. The walls were paneled in dark wood. Above the high entry portal, framed in dark green marble, hung showy, dark, bronze reliefs portraying original sin and the expulsion from paradise. The photographer saw several black-robed men sitting on a high, paneled platform. Behind a balustrade of turned wooden spindles sat Leo Katzenberger, flawlessly dressed as always, in a black pin-striped suit with vest. But his shoulders were a bit slouched and his head drooped slightly; the year of imprisonment had already visibly affected the old man. Irene felt small and shabby in Courtroom 600.

When she looked in the direction of the spectators' benches, her view was totally blocked by uniforms, each with a big swastika on the glowing red armband. The photographer immediately recognized District Inspector Haberkern in his brown jacket. Karl Holz was in his dress uniform. Streicher's deputy for many years, he was now considered the strong man in Nuremberg; before the end of March, Holz would be named Gauleiter. There was also another man in civilian clothes whose face Irene did not recognize at all. It was Reich Inspector Öchsle from the Munich Central Party Office.

Rothaug had reserved the first three rows of spectators' benches for prominent members of the party. There were three men from the Sicherheitsdienst
(the SS's security service), several department chiefs from the Nuremberg
court system, and a few Wehrmacht officers. Almost all the Blaue Traube
regulars had shown up. Only Police Chief Benno Martin was missing.

Every one of the Spittlertorgraben tenants had come to Nuremberg's
Palace of Justice as well.

At the entrance to the spectators' area, which was separated from the party
grandees by a barrier, the police checked every visitor. Among the people
holding out their identification cards was a young Wehrmacht officer in civilian clothes, Gerhard Hopf. Hopf, age twenty-five, happened to be on leave
from the front. A friend had dragged him to the trial because it was something he "just had to see." By the noon recess the soldier had left the courtroom, revolted. "I still get sick," says the old gentleman today, "if I even think
about those awful hours."

Hopf is apparently the only living witness to Katzenberger's trial who can
still recall some details. Documents have survived, however, that permit one
to reconstruct the proceedings. There are brief notes that Katzenberger's
attorney scribbled during the sessions in writing so small that they are nearly
illegible. Associate Judge Ferber made a few notations on a piece of paper. An
old transcript of the verdict, properly notarized, survived, together with
interrogation records.

In a loud, rasping voice, Judge Rothaug opened the proceedings. Rothaug
was a rather short, stocky man with closely cropped hair; a broad pug nose
dominated his face; a cynical smile often played around the corners of his
mouth. He was capable of furious outbursts but was almost completely hidden
behind the judges' bench. The first thing he did was to misspeak the name of
the accused, reeling off a list of Jewish first names. When Defense Attorney
Herz politely objected that one or another name was incorrect, Rothaug
screamed down from his desk, "It doesn't matter what the man's name is."
Then he turned to Katzenberger, who was sitting quietly in the dock, and bellowed, "Are you the Jew Katzenberger or not?" Katzenberger merely nodded.

The judge then inundated Irene with a flood of poisonous words; her public interrogation had begun. How could she have forgotten herself to the
point that she entered into a relationship with that "little, syphilitic Jew," while
her husband was at the front defending the Fatherland? Later, when Irene
pointed out that her husband was not at the front at the time under discussion,

but at the barracks a few hundred meters away from their apartment, the judge changed directions, thundering, "That's just fine. Your husband is hanging around at home while our best are dying at the front!" He persistently belabored Irene, saying that if she made a clean confession she could be sure of leniency. The judge was obviously still disturbed by Irene's persistent refusal to confess to having had a sexual relationship, even if he had long since neutralized her testimony by accusing her of perjury. It may be that there was still a hint of judicial ethic motivating Rothaug's demands for a confession. If Irene had admitted to a real love affair, the situation would have been unambiguous.

Actually, Irene was not at all the heroic type; not one to hurl herself against tyrants. She was quite happy to swim in the current of the times. But Irene did not envy or mistrust others. Perhaps because of her childhood, which former neighbors describe as exceptionally loving and happy, she had gotten the dash of humanity that allowed her to stand firm against every challenge in spite of her fear. "I can't admit to something that didn't happen," she informed the courtroom defiantly.

With that, the little man up on the rostrum exploded with rage: "Indeed, but you could be lying!" Then Rothaug delivered a long speech criticizing Irene's lack of party discipline. Apparently party friends had told him that the photographer had never attended meetings or the Evening Conversations in her neighborhood and that she did not regularly pay her membership dues. The young woman, Rothaug asserted, was completely under the Jew's influence. He had taken advantage of Irene's youth to make her compliant. If she'd read *Der Stürmer*, Rothaug went on, she would have known that "shaming her race is worse than murder." Anyone so little interested in "the life of the nation" needed to be punished for her actions. "If you have nerve enough to set yourself apart from the society of our people by the life you lead, I have nerve enough to make an example of you for doing so."

The photographer stood motionless. She related later that she was deeply shaken "that a man who was supposed to be a judge could behave that way toward a woman." But of course the good-natured, good-spirited person had no idea how she would be described by the men behind the judges' bench. During the interrogation, Rothaug asked about her love life in general: whether she had lived with a man before she was married and whether she had "cultivated friendships with men earlier." Irene affirmed both questions without realizing how it would sound. The associate judges to the right and left of Rothaug, however, were listening closely. Associate Heinz Hoffmann, a thoroughly modest man of thirty-five with a wife and two children, studied the accused — her unruly, dark curls, the way she unconcernedly revealed what in his view was a rather risqué lifestyle — and presumed she was "a somewhat loose woman."

His colleague Karl Ferber, age forty, who functioned as the court recorder during the proceedings, had paged through the files before the beginning of the trial and gathered from the neighbors' insinuations that men had frequently visited the photographer. Irene's answers to Rothaug's questions supported his judgment that Irene appeared "not at all adverse to relations with men." The jurist investigated the family trees of couples who wanted to get married as a sideline job for the National Socialist Office of Racial Affairs and thought he was a good judge of people. The flighty, high-strung person in front of the judges' bench seemed to embody "the characteristics of a barmaid."

After Irene's testimony, it was Katzenberger's turn. Rothaug now turned the trial into a degrading spectacle, ordering Katzenberger to turn toward the onlookers and show himself full face and in profile while the judge delivered a short lecture on racial politics. "Now you can see what a Jew looks like." Rothaug tore everything Katzenberger tried to say during his interrogation to pieces. "Katzenberger hardly got to say a word," recalls Hopf. "The presiding judge kept cutting him off."

When Katzenberger related that he'd met Irene in her parents' house, the judge mocked it as "real Jewish cunning." When Katzenberger testified that Irene's father had asked him to look after the young photographer, the man behind the bench made a sarcastic aside: "That's like hiring the fox to look after the henhouse"; the spectators responded with loud laughter. Many of them, observed Irene, were now thoroughly enjoying the sight of a Jew being beaten down. Very few of the spectators felt, as Hopf did, that sitting in that courtroom became more and more unpleasant.

But Katzenberger fought in his own way. He calmly explained that he was not guilty of anything. And he had certainly not met the photographer behind her husband's back. On the contrary — more often than not, her spouse was present, and Katzenberger had even given him financial advice. Judge Rothaug, however, took that statement as an opportunity to indulge in a tirade against Hans Seiler. Anyone who put up with such things wasn't a real man, in Rothaug's opinion, and he went on to inform his listeners that that sort of incomprehensible tolerance could only have one explanation: the man was "in complete sexual bondage" to Irene.

Judge Rothaug was enjoying himself, to the point where he could hardly stop his lectures even when the witnesses' interrogation was underway. Babette Gilger, the cigarette vendor, took the stand. She disclosed the brand and the number of cigarettes Irene smoked each day. With a sidelong glance at Katzenberger, she revealed that "the Jew" had always purchased Irene's brand. It was welcome evidence for Rothaug, who castigated Irene for her cigarette consumption — after all, German women do not smoke.

Mäsel told about the shoe boxes that Irene always had under her arm when she walked across the courtyard, boxes that were presumably just camouflage for the love affair. He told about how he had observed Irene's visits to the firm's offices from his kitchen window. When questioned, he added that Katzenberger frequently had been red in the face and looked embarrassed when he emerged from the office in the rear building after a rendezvous with Irene. Mäsel presumed that the blush "came from excitement."

Hopf recalls how Heilmann approached the witness stand: "He was wearing a brown uniform, clacked his heels together, and gave the Nazi salute with his right arm."

What Heilmann had to say was less noteworthy. The one-time stockroom clerk seemed to have forgotten almost everything in his excitement. He knew about the signals in the courtyard and that Irene and Katzenberger had greeted each other on the street. He claimed that from his post in the stairwell he'd seen Irene kissing the businessman in front of her apartment door as he was leaving.

After Heilmann's testimony, a female spectator addressed the judges. In a shrill voice, the woman related how Irene bought a dress back in 1933 that was eventually repossessed by a Jewish lawyer, since she couldn't pay for it. One could see, the self-appointed witness went on, how dependent Irene was on Jews even back then.

Next, Betty Kleylein took the witness stand. The housewife claimed to have often seen Katzenberger sneaking out of Irene's apartment. Furthermore, during those visits she could hear water running in the bathroom, which she considered proof of intimacies. Once the old gentleman had not left Irene's until late at night.

When Katzenberger heard that, he jumped up and yelled that there was absolutely no truth to her statement. Rothaug overruled his objections as "real Jewish insolence." But Katzenberger had struck at the crucial point of the indictment — the charge that he had violated the Detrimental Acts Law. Until

Katzenberger's trial, not a single violator of the Racial Purity Laws had been condemned to death in Germany, even though *Der Stürmer* had frequently demanded it. The Racial Purity Laws mandated prison terms of up to just fifteen years. However, if it could be proved that Katzenberger had used the nightly blackout to carry out his detrimental acts, he was as good as dead.

In his boundless ambition the judge had set out to sentence a "racial defiler" to death, in keeping with *Der Stürmer's* demands. He was especially persistent about the details of evening meetings and visits under cover of darkness, and even called for a recess so he and the associate judges could go over a map drawn by the investigating officers. On it, every street lamp on the route between the Praterstrasse villa and the apartment building was indicated. "All in all, six lighting installations," Ferber recalled precisely.

At that point, Irene did not understand why Rothaug always wanted to know the exact times of the various encounters. "It never crossed my mind," said the photographer later, "that darkness could mean death." Katzenberger, on the other hand, knew from the very beginning where the greatest danger lay. With every conceivable argument he resisted having a visit under cover of darkness pinned on him. Several of the witnesses seemed to be telling such wild stories, the old gentleman stated, that he felt as if he were "a character in a trashy romance novel."

Katzenberger still believed in some remnant of the rule of law. And he wanted to survive. His attorney, however, had already ceded the outcome. Herz obviously considered it pointless to challenge the witnesses by demanding supporting evidence. During a lull in the proceedings, Werner Endress, Irene's attorney, considered calling her husband as a witness; Endress remembers his Jewish colleague just gave him a tired wave. "It doesn't really matter whether Katzenberger is sentenced to death now," whispered Herz to Endress, "or whether he dies in a concentration camp in a few months like the rest of us."

In the meantime, Paul Kleylein was on the witness stand. The prosthesis maker first rambled on about Irene's immoral behavior, which had thoroughly offended him and his wife — after all, Irene was married to a soldier. And Katzenberger's activities in the building were, he indignantly stated, "just not to be tolerated any longer." When asked for the pertinent details, Kleylein rattled off everything he'd heard at one time or another. Mention was made of the insulting remark in the air-raid shelter to which Irene hadn't objected, "out of shame and guilt," Kleylein assumed. He quoted Heilmann's statement about "paying it off easily," which the former store-

THE MAIDEN AND THE JEW

room clerk had forgotten to mention in his excitement. And he claimed that Irene had been financially dependent on Katzenberger, citing as evidence that Irene once owed his wife five marks, which she'd paid back only after a visit from Katzenberger.

Kleylein conducted himself just as Rothaug had hoped. The judge sang a seemingly endless hymn of praise for the orthopedic technician, saying he had expressed himself in a way that should stand as an example for his fellow German citizens. After all, remarked Rothaug, Kleylein had lodged the complaint about Katzenberger's "scandalous activities." That sentence caught Irene's attention. In her mind's eye she remembered seeing him emerge from police headquarters several months previous. Back then, the man had seemed so embarrassed that she immediately became suspicious. Now she knew for certain that Kleylein was the informer.

Irene turned away from the man on the witness stand with a feeling of revulsion. She wondered what his motive could have been but came to no conclusion. Irene was torn out of her thoughts by a loud voice that constantly cracked — the public prosecutor had begun his summation. He poured insults over the two accused, treating everyone to a few sayings from *Der Stürmer*. According to her subsequent recollections, he mentioned, "The Jews are our misfortune," and managed to get "The Jews are guilty of this war" into his address as well. With sharp words he castigated Irene for her recalcitrance and the lack of insight that led her to take Katzenberger's side. "But," concluded Markl, "whoever gets involved with the Jews will perish with them."

It was not just careerism and political blindness that led the state's attorney to be so vehement in his arguments against the accused. The men who functioned as investigators and judges into the inquiry of the relationship between Irene Seiler and Leo Katzenberger were without exception men. Irene's appearance and bearing apparently reinforced their prejudices. And thus it was not merely Nazi justice that the two faced; there was also a large element of masculine bigotry. That element would persist well beyond the end of the Nazi era.

Markl was questioned about the case in the 1960s. Even in retrospect he could not imagine that there had been nothing between Katzenberger and Irene. If it had not "come to sexual relations," then the merchant had to have been "a hero of a man," Markl pronounced, for not trying to "get someone that good looking into bed."

The two associate judges shared his view. Hadn't the Jew been in Irene's apartment "for thirty to forty minutes" each time? What could they have possibly been doing, if not sharing intimacies? Rothaug never entered into such complicated speculations. In the trial's early stages, during a pause in the proceedings, he had said to his colleagues, "For me, it's enough that this Jewish pig admits to having had a German girl on his lap." In his view, that alone justified the death penalty.

And so the verdict had long been clear by the time the defense began its plea. Herz was quite brief and limited himself to claiming that the application of the Detrimental Acts Law was questionable in this instance, and therefore recommended that the judges not pass the death sentence. Irene's attorney emphasized that she had consistently told the truth and likewise made a plea for more lenient sentencing. Only Katzenberger fought for complete acquittal. He had prepared a speech while in prison. The handwritten text, seven pages long, was later copied in Herz's office. That single-spaced, typed paper — which survives to this day — lay before him on the table. He stood up and began a somewhat lengthy monologue. Rothaug interrupted him constantly, so much of what Katzenberger's said was drowned out. But the old gentleman calmly started over, picking apart the alleged observations by the neighbors on Spittlertorgraben and clarifying his relationship with Irene. It was indeed correct that he considered her a close friend, as he did the whole Scheffler family — "We all used the informal word for *you*." The generous help, solidarity, and love that Father Scheffler lavished on his children had impressed Katzenberger, "because they were feelings that I myself strongly cherished."

Katzenberger had indeed given Irene small amounts of money. "Once, when I was struck by how poorly she looked," he said, "she admitted that she didn't have any money and hadn't eaten in two days." Whereupon, he continued, he gave her ten marks and told her she had to let him know if she ran that short again, "because I couldn't stand the thought of her going hungry." But the sums that he gave her were so small "that they never were a burden." And besides, he hadn't helped just Irene but other people in difficulty as well, "whether Christian or Jewish." Both Heilmann and Mäsel could testify to that, stated the businessman, as he looked around the courtroom.

Mäsel was then called up to give a statement. He coolly denied Katzenberger's claim. "That has nothing to do with this," he said. Then, turning toward Katzenberger, continued, "You never did anything good for me."

Of course it had come to kissing in his relationship with Irene, continued the defendant. "Exchanging a kiss when we arrived or left," he explained, was the completely normal "result of our friendly relations." However, in reference to all the statements and questions as to "whether I touched her breasts," or had touched her somewhere with his hand in any immoral way, he wanted to make himself clear: "Nothing of the sort ever occurred for the purposes of gaining sexual satisfaction." If Irene had sat on his lap at his office, "it was something that she did with her father, too."

The fond relationship with Irene had developed as a result of his close acquaintance with the Schefflers, "but it was and remained just a friendship," Katzenberger emphasized. He then asked, "How could it have been anything else? I was an old man of sixty to sixty-eight years of age, with heart problems, and she a desirable young woman, twenty-two to thirty years old." No one could seriously claim that one could win that young, attractive woman with cigarettes and an occasional gift of pralines. "I am innocent, and I ask to be acquitted."

Katzenberger turned directly toward Judge Rothaug. "You have branded me a Jew this entire time," he now said in a somewhat softer tone. "I would like to point out that I am also a human being." Katzenberger then wanted to quote a sentence by Frederick the Great, but Rothaug interrupted him brusquely, saying he was not going to allow the name of the Prussian king to be "dirtied by a Jew." The sentence that Katzenberger wanted to quote is: "Only justice ennobles a nation."

The recess that followed was extremely brief. "There was nothing in the case that required deliberation," thought Ferber. He shared Rothaug's view that only the death penalty was applicable. And he felt somewhat as if he were being benevolent, as he pointed out later, because the deportation of Jews had already begun in the fall of 1941, and so the death penalty was "the only thing that the rule of law could offer to oppose the arbitrariness of the SS." Similarly absurd was Hoffmann's thought process. He later confessed to being relieved, because "Katzenberger, as a Jew, was already a dead man." Rothaug, on the other hand, viewed this, to certain extent, to be a competition with the SS. His objective, Ferber later revealed, was to send condemned Jews to the gallows himself rather than let them be murdered by the Gestapo or the SS.

Back in the courtroom Rothaug, in a thunderously loud voice, passed down his judgment. He first mentioned the amount of time that had passed since the two had met and claimed that Irene never minded "sexual advances" from her friends. The presumption that an erotic relationship between Irene and Katzenberger never developed was in his view "opposed by every experience of ordinary life." In view of the "limitless number of opportunities for seduction," there could be no doubt whatsoever. The court was convinced, he continued, that Katzenberger had "regularly had intercourse with the Seiler woman," because "everyday experience makes it impossible to think otherwise." Therefore, the deed "could only be atoned for by the physical destruction of the perpetrator." There could be no leniency for Irene, who had "tried to protect the cornered criminal." The sentence read "two years imprisonment."

Katzenberger sat in his chair, struck senseless. Motionless, he watched as the courtroom slowly emptied and one witness after the other left; the red-haired Babette Kleylein walking beside her strong-looking husband, the frail Heilmann marching in his uniform toward the exit in a zigzag course, the toolmaker Mäsel striding out in his deliberate way. Irene, likewise, had remained seated and spoke briefly with her sister's boyfriend, the only representative of her family in the courtroom during the proceedings. Father Scheffler never recovered from the shock of events and had died, grief-stricken, in January 1942. Two bailiffs appeared and led Leo and Irene from the room at approximately 2:30 P.M. on March 14, 1942. It was the last time they saw each other.

2 I

ADOLF HITLER WAS SITTING IN MASURIA, far from Nuremberg, in the Wolf's Lair, a complex of bunkers built in the summer of 1941, the beginning of the Russian campaign. The isolated, carefully guarded settlement consisted of seven buildings that had trees growing from their roofs. Surrounded by swamps, the complex lay in the midst of the forest belonging to the little town of Rastenburg, today called Ketrzyn, in eastern Poland. Sealed off from the rest of the world by concrete walls five meters thick, Hitler directed most of his attention toward reports from the front, which hinted that things were not going well in snow-covered Russia.

The news from Nuremberg, however, did pique his interest. Under the headline "Racial Offender Condemned to Death," the March 18, 1942, edition of *Berliner Illustrierte* (Berlin Illustrated) detailed the trial of Leo Katzenberger and Irene Seiler. Hitler presumably received the newspaper excerpt a week after sentencing, on Monday March 23rd; it had been handed to him by his adjutant, Julius Schaub, whom Hitler had known from the days of the Munich Putsch.

There was a brisk traffic in telephone calls and teletype messages between the bunkers in Masuria and the seat of government in Berlin. In addition, couriers were constantly shuttling back and forth, carrying orders, reports, and documents. In one of those ways, presumably, the news from Nuremberg arrived at the Führer's headquarters, "FHQu" in official shorthand. As Hitler studied the report, he was less disturbed by the Katzenberger's death sentence than he was by the fact that a Jew and an Aryan had been found guilty in the same trial — this displeased the Führer mightily.

In Hitler's view, Jews and Aryans should never be seen together on the defendants' bench. And what had happened in Nuremberg, moreover, seemed to run counter to an earlier edict, one in which the chancellor placed considerable importance. Hitler had insisted from the very beginning that women should not receive sentences when "racial offenders" were tried. In keeping with that, when the Racial Purity Laws went into effect in mid-September 1935, the section relevant to the severity of punishment mentioned only men, not women. The decision had a certain amount to do with Hitler's warped sexual views — he considered the man active and responsible; the woman was merely the innocent object of masculine desire.

At the same time, however, there was an entirely practical side: women who did not fear punishment were more likely to tell. By the very nature of things, it was hard to prove what had gone on during a discrete love affair, and thus judges were often dependent on the testimony of the woman who had been "racially harmed."

As time went by, however, several courts began to sentence women during racial purity trials if, for instance, the woman was found guilty of obstruction of justice by giving false information. Such women were not charged with racial offense but rather with being an accessory to the fact. That did not please Hitler, who intervened as early as 1939. Chancellery Secretary Lammers made it clear in a letter to the Minister of Justice, Franz Gürtner, that the Führer's decision was that women should go unpunished in cases involving a breach of the Racial Purity Laws. In February 1940, the Ministry of Justice issued a revision of those laws with the formulation that Hitler wished. Accordingly, women guilty of incitement, complicity, and accessory to the fact received no punishment. In the category of "separate offenses," however, only false testimony not given under oath was excluded from punishment — perjury under oath was not mentioned, and thus not excluded from sentencing.

The report of the Berlin paper's evening edition conveyed the outcome of the Nuremberg trial correctly: Irene Seiler had been sentenced for perjury, not a racial offense. That the woman had even stood before the court together with the "racial offender" was, however, extremely unusual. At the time, Hitler was generally uncomfortable with the court decisions. He had intervened at the Ministry of Justice a short while earlier over a case where a man fatally mistreated a woman; in Hitler's view, the five-year prison term was too lenient. In the case of Irene Seiler, on the other hand, the Führer obviously had some feeling that the two-year prison sentence passed against the photographer was unjustifiably high. He ordered Schaub to get hold of the verdict as quickly as possible.

Schaub picked up the telephone and soon things went into high gear. Lammers, the chancellery secretary, was notified, as was the Ministry of Justice in Berlin. The correspondence between the various authorities has survived, and several of those involved provided extensive commentaries later, which are to be found in the court records. On Monday, March 23 at around 10 A.M., Secretary Roland Freisler of the Reich's Ministry of Justice phoned the Nuremberg courthouse. He demanded to speak with the chief state prosecutor, but he was not present; Senior Public Prosecutor Georg Engert accepted the call as his deputy. Freisler's instructions were brief and to the point: by nine the next morning, Engert was to be in Berlin with a written transcript of the judges' deliberations.

An official from the prosecutor's office hurried across the broad colonnade of the Nuremberg Hall of Justice to the District Court. But on that Monday morning, there was still no transcript. Associate Judge Ferber had taken his time getting to it; now he had to transcribe the deliberations within a few hours. Around five that evening Engert had the transcript. Engert later indicated he was not entirely in agreement with the basis for the judgment; the application of the Detrimental Acts Law seemed particularly questionable. Accordingly, he drew up a criticism on behalf of the State Attorney's office. That evening at nine, Engert boarded the express to Berlin. The cars were so packed "that I hardly had room to turn around," he reported. The next morning, he shaved in the station's men's room and headed directly to the Ministry of Justice.

Freisler appeared preoccupied and could only spare ten minutes for the jurist who had traveled so far. Engert explained his doubts regarding the Detrimental Acts Law and even Freisler expressed concern as to whether the verdict was entirely proper. Obviously he did not find the judicial grounds convincing, but he made no mention of the fact that Hitler wanted to see the deliberations. Engert caught the next train back to Franconia. Freisler ordered the transcripts of the deliberations, opinions, and sentencing to be taken to Chancellery Secretary Lammers.

On Thursday, March 26, Lammers read to Hitler the judgment's essentials; the bureaucrat realized to his relief that the Führer's anger was the result of his assumption that Irene Seiler had also been found guilty of racial offense. That was easily clarified. Lammers explained that she had been found guilty of perjury. "That sufficed for the Führer," Lammers noted afterward.

The storm clouds had blown away and now it was Lammers' turn to get upset with Schaub, the adjutant, who had stirred up all the excitement. "The Führer had clearly been falsely informed," Lammers noted in an April 1 letter to the SS officer.

The functionaries had smoothed everything over quite nicely. However, the judgment was highly controversial, even in Nazi circles. State Secretary for the Ministry of Justice, Roland Freisler, who later became the feared "hanging judge" of the Volksgerichtshof, the Peoples' Court, mentioned the Nuremberg verdict shortly afterward at a meeting with presiding judges and other high-level justice officials.

Freisler pointed out that he considered the evidence raised against Katzenberger "somewhat forced." A few weeks later, ministry officials in Berlin had an opportunity to express their doubts again: they had to render a decision on Katzenberger's plea for clemency. The plea had been promptly drafted by Richard Herz, but first of all — and this was one of those greater or lesser bits of chicanery that Jews had to endure at the time — it had to be certified as admissible by the Association of Jews in the German Reich. The association had been created in 1939 as the overall administrator for Jewish affairs and was the successor to the older Reich Council of Jews, which had its offices in Berlin and which represented all of the congregations.

The certification came by telegram on March 27, 1942. Immediately afterward, Herz presented his plea for clemency to the District Court at Nuremberg. Ever since the trial, even the reserved Herz seemed completely convinced of Katzenberger's innocence; in any event, he formulated his plea much more energetically and with far less restraint than he had the motion for release. Herz emphasized that "no direct proof that Katzenberger was guilty of the crime had been presented" and that both of the accused had "protested their innocence throughout the entire trial." Hence one was forced to consider the possibility that "the current case did indeed represent an exception to the experience of everyday life" — meaning that nothing at all erotic had occurred. Katzenberger was, "considering his entire personality, not unworthy of clemency," since he had stepped in to help the poor and the sick, contributed considerable amounts to charity, and was "energetically involved with social projects." For all those reasons, Herz "respectfully requested that the plea for clemency be honored."

Meanwhile, Leo Katzenberger was sitting in prison in a suburb of Munich, having been transferred there on March 20, 1942, a few days after sentencing. He had been given a room on the prison's first floor with a window facing the courtyard — cell number 12. From his prison file, it can be seen that he suffered greatly, tormented not just by psychological distress and fear for his life, but by entirely banal things as well, including pain in his feet. The prison administration had not returned his oxfords, which had inserts for his flat feet, nor his handkerchiefs with the embroidered initials LK. As he pointed out in a petition to the prison supervisors, he needed the latter to use as bandages for his corns, which were causing a good deal of pain.

The handkerchiefs and shoe inserts were turned over to Katzenberger after a week. On the other hand, the request to have his Bible returned was denied without explanation. The diet was marginal — "one kilogram of bread and one kilogram of fruit every fourteen days" — which led Katzenberger to request his attorney arrange for more food, "doubtless permissible and even desirable." After the businessman was executed, the finance authorities withdrew 105 Reichsmarks from his Nuremberg account to cover his board.

Stationery was available only by request. Katzenberger wrote several letters to his wife, with whom he obviously shared the greatest rapport. Whether a single one of those letters ever reached her, however, is uncertain. Some days after the verdict, on March 24, 1942, Claire was deported to Izbica, a town in Poland near Lublin, along with Max Katzenberger and Little Claire. "No news of my dear wife and the others?" Leo Katzenberger asked Herz in a letter dated April 14.

The plea for clemency was discussed at the highest levels in Berlin. Albert Hupperschwiller, a former ministry official and, at the time, the Ministry of Justice's expert on the "death sentence in non-political offenses," recalled later that the Katzenberger case had been the subject of an in-house discussion during which several of the ministers expressed reservations about the unusual coupling of the Racial Purity and Detrimental Acts Laws. An offense against the blackout regulations seemed to the officials present to be far-fetched. The State Secretary and Interim Justice Minister Schlegelberger likewise thought the punishment too severe and recommended clemency.

Other officials disagreed. Nuremberg's Nazis tried to influence Berlin. The current Gauleiter, Streicher's long-time deputy Karl Holz, maintained a cordial relationship with Judge Rothaug. It can be assumed that Holz frequently discussed things with Streicher, who was still living on his Pleikershof estate. It is completely possible that Streicher lobbied against the clemency request indirectly, through Gauleiter Holz. Overcoming initial reservations, State Secretary Freisler came down on the side of the hardliners, and asked that the death sentence against Katzenberger be carried out.

The deliberations dragged on for several months. The case was eventually presented to Hitler, together with Schlegelberger's recommendation for clemency, but the Führer, who had initially been upset by Irene Seiler's perjury conviction, was no longer interested; he was indifferent to the fate of the Jew Katzenberger. On May 23, 1942, the Ministry of Justice issued its official rejection of the clemency plea. Its instructions were that "Justice should be allowed to take its course."

On Tuesday, June 2, 1942, around six in the evening, a warden opened the heavy iron door to cell number 8, into which Leo Katzenberger had been moved. A member of the prison administration informed the old man that the death sentence would be carried out on the following morning, whereupon Katzenberger asked for a little paper. That evening he wrote three letters: one went to an old business friend in Munich, the second to his brother David in Nuremberg. The third letter was a Red Cross telegram, used to send wartime messages abroad. It went to Palestine, where it was preserved for more than half a century. "I kiss you warmly," the old man wrote to his daughter and other relatives, mentioning each of them by name, "God bless you and keep you, with love, Father."

The next morning, before six, they took Leo Katzenberger from his cell; shortly afterward, he was decapitated by guillotine. In the Mortality Register of the Ministry of Justice, Nazi bureaucrats painstakingly listed every death sentence that was carried out. Katzenberger's execution is filed under the designation "initial K, no. 1367." There is no grave. His body was turned over to Munich University's anatomy department, a fact Marga Weglein learned from Bavarian justice officials after persistent questioning many years later. "Well, at any rate it's better," remarks the old woman dryly, "than if they'd thrown him to the dogs."

2 2

LEO KATZENBERGER, CONSCIENTIOUS MAN THAT HE WAS, left behind in his cell a tiny, handwritten note indicating in a few, bare letters, that the "Katzenberger effects" were to be sent to David Israel Katzenberger, Praterstrasse 23, Nuremberg. A few days after the businessman's execution, a prison clerk sent the note through proper channels to the Nuremberg's Probate Court, with a request for "further instructions regarding the personal effects deposited here."

The clerk had appended an exact list of the few belongings that Leo Katzenberger had brought with him to prison: his gold wedding ring, the oxfords with inserts, a black suit with vest, a tie, a neckerchief, five handkerchiefs with the embroidered monogram LK, eyeglasses, a mechanical pencil, a packet of old letters, a lighter, and "one book," — presumably that very Bible that was never returned to him.

Scarcely a year later, the prison communicated with Nuremberg's Probate Court again, "repeating the request for further instructions concerning the effects of Leo Katzenberger deposited here," and pointing out that thus far, no answer had been received. The person in charge of personal effects in

Munich asked whether there were any reservations about shipping the things to Katzenberger's wife, Claire. One word is typed beneath the letter: "Yes." Someone still objected to sending the businessman's modest effects to his family.

But at that point, late May 1943, there no longer was a Katzenberger family in Nuremberg. All of Leo Katzenberger's relatives were dead or had been deported, and most of the other Jews in Nuremberg, originally more than ten thousand souls, had disappeared. By the spring of 1941, when Leo Katzenberger had been arrested, the congregations' membership had been reduced to barely two thousand; many had emigrated or died in the previous years, or had been picked up by the SS or Gestapo and taken to concentration camps. During Katzenberger's imprisonment, the Nazi authorities were making their final preparations for the ultimate destruction of Jews.

Bernhard Kolb was now beginning the most difficult phase of his life. At the beginning of September 1941, the Gestapo gave him the task of handing out the yellow Star of David badge to all members of the congregations, with instructions to sew it onto their jackets in a visible place. The insignias arrived in Nuremberg as thick, yellow rolls of fabric on which palm-sized stars had been stamped, along with the word "Jude" in black letters imitating Hebrew script. Geitel and Company, a Berlin flag maker, had printed around a million of those stars on long rolls of fabric for some thirty thousand Reichsmarks.

For three cents a piece — "at cost," as the Gestapo officials pointed out — the Nuremberg congregations had to take delivery of the stars, then sell them to individual members for ten cents "to cover the expenses of distribution." After September 19, 1941, Jews throughout the entire Reich had to wear the yellow patch on the left breast of their coats. Many non-Jews in Nuremberg seem to have been pleased by the cruel touch: a government memo written in February 1942 states that the introduction of the Jewish star in the Franconian city "has had a generally favorable reaction from the populace," reflecting a "long cherished wish throughout broader circles of the population."

While distributing the yellow stars — "four per person" according to Gestapo instructions — Kolb and his colleagues also handed out mimeographed sheets with tips on behavior. "Show yourself in public as little as possible," says one. "If at all possible, walk alone on the street, or at most, in twos," and "Do not stop in front of store windows." Even in their apartments, Jewish citizens were urged to "maintain the utmost calm in all situations." Loud conversations on the stairs or in hallways, as well as at open windows, were "absolutely to be avoided," as was "looking out of front windows for long periods of time."

Those matter-of-fact sounding recommendations reveal how lonely and miserable life must have been for Nuremberg's last Jewish residents and, at the same time, how risky. "Keep in mind that every aspect of your conduct is now being scrutinized," concluded the memorandum, "even when you believe yourself to be unobserved." By that time, party members were to report any Jew not wearing a yellow star. According to Kolb's recollections, "a high-grade competition" broke out among informants — "the police received tips almost daily." But the police were obviously more indulgent than the ordinary citizens. "Fortunately," reported Kolb, "the Gestapo paid no attention to the denunciations in most cases."

For some time, rumors had been circulating in Nuremberg and elsewhere about impending mass deportations of Jewish citizens. There had been considerable unrest the previous year, after word had gotten around that the Jewish inhabitants of Stettin had been deported. In fall of 1940, two Jewish women from Nuremberg who had wanted to visit Mannheim accidentally boarded a deportation train going to France. No one in Nuremberg knew anything for certain until October 18, 1941, when the Gestapo summoned Secretary Kolb for one of the increasingly unpleasant discussions at police headquarters. "In the near future," the officials revealed at that meeting, "we foresee that one thousand people will be sent away from Nuremberg," but the deportations would be limited "to people under the age of sixty-five, that is, those capable of working." Kolb was instructed by the Gestapo to select Jews who fit that description and to maintain strict silence concerning the plan.

Bernhard Kolb was a man who could bear a great deal. "A brave man," according to his son Herbert, "who always kept his presence of mind, right up till the last moment." The horrible task of picking out his fellow believers for deportation must have caused him tremendous emotional distress. And it may have been on that evening that Kolb walked into the room where his two children, Herbert and Erna, were and made them swear the secret oath that Herbert would remember his entire life. "We had to swear to him," states the old man, "that we would kill as many Germans as possible."

The Nuremberg Gestapo prepared with the thoroughness of a military operation. In ten pages of procedural guidelines the police central command spelled out the details of the impending deportation, placing emphasis on "procedures relating to the property law" as well as necessary preparations for impounding Jewish dwellings and possessions. The director of operations specifically directed the authorities in Nuremberg, Würzburg, and other towns to prepare "seals, candles, and No Trespassing signs," as well as "clamps for applying lead seals to locked dwellings." The overall implementation of the deportation rested with none other than Police Chief Martin, who until then had always managed to keep himself in the background during actions against Jews.

Some of the orders issued under Martin's authority were found after the war at the Gestapo headquarters in Würzburg, which belonged to Nuremberg's administrative district. Those documents reveal the painstaking industry with which not just the Gestapo but an entire army of civil servants in regional government offices, mayors' offices, finance and registration offices, as well as in the railroad all participated in the greatest homicide and robbery in history. From old files and bank account records concerning the Katzenberger family, one can get some idea of the degree to which bank employees had been drawn into secret complicity. Even private individuals — business people, innkeepers, shipping and hauling contractors, and local artisans — worked as helpers during the Holocaust.

First, the authorities drew up lists of inhabitants and indexed their dwellings. In local finance offices, clerks made preparations to process as swiftly as possible the massive shifts of private capital to a state account. Meanwhile, Gestapo officials discussed train schedules with representatives of the Reichsbahn, the state railway. The coordination of individual "loading schedules" seems to have given the greatest difficulty to death's logistical planners. There is, for instance, a drawn-out teletype dialogue in which Dr. Theodor Grafenburger, the Nuremberg Gestapo's director of operations, and his colleague in Würzburg discuss the difficulties in coordinating the "transfer of Jews from Würzburg to Nuremberg, up to one thousand units," with convoys coming from other localities. During their exchanges, the bureaucrats shunted various empty passenger and freight trains back and forth in their minds until they finally worked out a solution. The dialogue ended with: "Slick as a whistle! Heil Hitler!"

The Nuremberg municipal authorities combined the first deportations with the eviction of Jewish inhabitants from certain districts of the city; presumably there had long been applications for the apartments about to be vacated. Kolb was now obliged to draw up the lists of people to be deported in conformity with such plans.

The remainder of the operation would take place with Germanic precision: first, every person affected had to "conscientiously prepare a listing of property," and enter it onto a special form, to which were to be appended all documents relevant to the property, such as "sales contracts, promissory notes, mortgage agreements, and insurance policies." Eventually, even such things as bicycles, binoculars, and cameras — if anyone still had them — were to be turned in immediately. People had to move all the furniture in their apartments into one room that would be sealed by the police; the other rooms were to be cleaned. Gas, light, and water had to be turned off and all outstanding municipal utility bills paid.

Outside the city, meanwhile, five barracks were set up on the very tract of land where, in years past, the party rallies had been held with such ostentatious pageantry. There the Jews were to spend several nights while awaiting their final departure. Kolb had to arrange for a field kitchen in the camp and in addition had to collect fifty Reichsmarks per person for the transportation costs plus another ten marks each, on account, for expenses. The money allegedly would be paid out again in local currency at their destination. Then there was a long list of things that people were supposed to take with them on that strange trip: window glass in prescribed sizes, iron stoves, cooking pots, and barbed wire for fencing, together with mattresses and sewing machines. The Gestapo used moving vans to pick up such unwieldy objects at Jewish homes; but many things, according to eyewitnesses, disappeared right on the spot.

On November 25 and 26, 1941, 512 people were picked up and taken to the assembly point in the Langwasser section of Nuremberg. As the Jews were saying goodbye to their homes, "people on the street indulged in insults and vile remarks," Kolb reported. At the camp, the Jews passed through various rooms in which they had to submit to different searches, all with a single purpose — to take the last few personal possessions from them before their planned murder.

In the first room, all suitcases were opened and searched for jewelry, currency, or other "disallowed objects." The guards confiscated pocket- and wristwatches, rings, chains, and cuff links. According to the lists later found in Würzburg the Gestapo even took mechanical pencils, a notebook with postage stamps, and 31 six-cent postcards. In the second room, the guards collected all identification papers; in the third, the deportees had to undress completely and be examined to be sure they had not concealed anything. That third room is probably where gold teeth were extracted. An SS man held the person while another Jew was forced to grab his fellow-believer's tooth.

From that point, people were permitted to carry a Jewish identification card only, a "utility watch," and a wedding ring. Finally, in the fourth room, a bailiff handed out receipts indicating that their total assets had been confiscated and then stamped EVACUATED on the identification cards. The legal justification for this robbery was provided by an ordinance in force throughout the Reich, passed on November 25, 1941, and based on the Citizenship Law devised at that night-time session of parliament during the 1935 Reich Party Rally. According to it, Jews "taking up residence abroad" immediately relinquished their total assets to the Reich.

Of the 512 Nuremberg Jews in that first convoy, only sixteen survived the journey. In a forest near Riga, Latvia, people were shot in groups, Arnd Müller writes in his comprehensive work, *History of the Jews in Nuremberg 1146–1945.* Two large pits had been excavated ahead of time with dynamite. According to an eyewitness quoted by Müller, small bridges were laid over these pits. The naked prisoners were forced to walk across them, and they were "shot by SS men so that they fell into the pits."

In the second convoy, readied in March 1942, everyone perished. That time, the journey was to Izbica, a small Polish town near Lublin. Bernhard Kolb now had to put his own relatives on the list — including his brother Hugo. All tolled, 426 people traveled to their deaths on that train, among them Claire Katzenberger, her brother-in-law Max, and his wife, Little Claire.

Bank employees in Nuremberg had a great deal to do every day. Huge transfers of money were all going in the same direction — to the Reich's coffers in Berlin. From Max Katzenberger's account with the Bavarian Mortgage and Exchange Bank, for example, the Reichsjudenvereinigung, the Reich Association of Jews, in Berlin withdrew 539.40 Reichsmarks. But the money was only passed through; the Nazis had long since degraded the association to a financial processing station. Little Claire's account yielded 418 marks to the main Finance Office in Berlin. In November 1942, when Max and Claire were presumably dead, the Berlin Finance Office withdrew the remaining twenty-one marks from Max's account.

Ten days after the death sentence was pronounced against Leo Katzenberger, Max and the two Claires left for Izbica on the deportation train. At the bureau of vital statistics, municipal employees made the following notation under Claire's name: "Emigrated 24/3/42, destination unknown."

Izbica presumably served as a transfer station for Belzec, the nearby death camp, where the first three gas chambers had been constructed at the end of February 1942. People were herded from the train directly into the chambers, which the guards then filled with carbon monoxide. It was an assembly line: as Jewish slave laborers were removing the corpses through a rear door and a special group of workers called "the dentists" were pulling any remaining gold teeth from their dead fellow-believers, the next trains were rolling up with their cargo of candidates for death. Approximately six hundred thousand people are presumed to have died at Belzec, all within a very short time indeed, because by December 1942 the Nazis closed the camp. Before the end of the war it was leveled, and the site made to appear as if there had been nothing there. Just when Max and the two Claires were murdered has never been discovered. An inquiry at the municipal bureau of vital statistics in Nuremberg during the 1950s merely received a shrug of the shoulders and the answer, "Nothing known here about deportations."

In the previous convoys from Nuremberg, only people under sixty-five who were capable of working were deported. David Katzenberger, now sixty-seven, remained behind. He now lived entirely alone on the top floor of the beautiful villa on Praterstrasse. The residents of Leo's former apartment were the building's new owners, business people named Kuhn. Approximately 570 Jews were still living in the city when the Reich Association of Jews in Berlin appointed Bernhard Kolb chairman of the Nuremberg Jewish community. By that time, the Association of Jews of the German Reich was used by the Gestapo, for all practical purposes, to carry out its orders. The umbrella organization had become "a well-organized mad-house," as a clerk later recalled. Kolb attempted to maintain some remnants of the Nuremberg congregations life, arranging, for example, that religious services be held twice weekly at the Jewish School on upper Kanalstrasse. At the same time, he was always hurrying off to Gestapo headquarters to prepare new deportation lists. In Nuremberg, as in many other cities, the Nazis increasingly forced Jewish community leaders to become collaborators.

So far, the SS and Gestapo had deported nearly one thousand Nuremberg Jews to the east. At the end of August 1942, the third, final, and largest deportation was imminent. This time, 533 older people were to be evacuated to Theresienstadt. Once again, the Gestapo's organizers used every available trick to get the deportees' money. Theresienstadt was reputed to be an old people's home and sanitarium, and it was necessary to sign an entry contract agreeing to a yearly fee of eighteen hundred Reichsmarks. David Katzenberger, who was to be deported, transferred 523 marks to Seiler and Company, a Munich banking institution, on September 9, 1942. The purpose listed was "Entry fee for home." The Association of Jews withdrew an additional 500-plus Reichsmarks. Judging by what was packed into his suitcase the businessman, who always had an eye for elegance, obviously had no idea that he was traveling into the unknown. He included two brand-new suits, three new pairs of shoes, a "nearly new raincoat," as he stated later, and fifteen new, custom-made shirts from Levinger, the well-known Nuremberg tailor. He never unpacked a shred of it. David Katzenberger was deported on September 10, 1942, along with the 532 other Nurembergers. Only twenty-seven people returned from that journey; David was one of them.

The Jewish departure could not have been unknown to citizens of Nuremberg and other cities, if for no other reason than because so many agencies and institutions were involved. What, for instance, could bank clerks have thought when they suddenly had to process so many transfers of funds, all going to the same recipient? How did workers at the housing office explain the large numbers of apartments that suddenly became vacant? Where did the people participating in public auctions of household items think all those things came from?

In the Main-Franconian district of Bad Neustadt, which belonged to the Nuremberg Gestapo district, such auctions are recorded in several towns after the mid-1942 departure of the Izbica convoy. Furniture, silver, and even linens came up for bid. "The local inhabitants," reported an area councilman, "went crazy and bid prices that were out of proportion to the actual value of the objects, which were mostly old Jewish junk." In the marketplace of the small town of Bad Neustadt, the local newspaper displayed photos shot during the Jewish deportation. The city of Nuremberg preserved a memo from the Chief Public Prosecutor to the Minister of Justice of the Reich: the populace "seemed to be in agreement" with the first deportations.

Meanwhile, Grafenberger, the Nuremberg director of operations, remembered the "strenuous but satisfying days" of the Izbica convoy, as if he'd been involved in organizing a factory picnic. "Such a common task," he wrote to colleagues in Würzburg, with whom he'd organized the Jews' journey to death, "really does bring people closer together and furthers cooperation between comrades carrying out their duties."

23

BUSINESS WAS GOOD AT THE BLAUE TRAUBE. Otto Thierack, Justice Minister of the Reich since the fall of 1942, was sitting in a cozy circle of local judicial and Nazi officials; Judge Rothaug was at his side, and Gauleiter Karl Holz was present as well. Nobody was holding back. Plates of bratwurst were carried through the dining room and the beer flowed in torrents. According to eyewitness reports, as the evening wore on many of the assembled gentlemen could be found lying under the tables, drunk.

But the drinking companions had sorted out some important personal details that evening in January 1943. Rothaug was to be promoted to public prosecutor at the People's Court in Berlin; official notification of his appointment was to arrive on March 8. The position was not in keeping with Rothaug's wishes — he would have much preferred to be named a judge at the People's Court, in order to let an even larger public see him "close-up." An in-house notation made by Minister Thierack and later found in Rothaug's personnel file reveals that he became prosecutor "because he appears completely unsuitable for the post of judge."

Leo Katzenberger's legally sanctioned murder raised a huge furor in

Franconian Nazi circles and noticeably strengthened Rothaug's standing with leading party members. *Der Stürmer* carried the case on its front page and its display cases featured two photographs of Leo in the courtroom. One showed the old gentleman standing in the dock, looking quite cowed by Rothaug; the second, retouched around the mouth, eyebrows, and ears and distorted to a caricature, was supposed to reveal his typically Jewish features. "This is the racial offender Katzenberger," read the caption, "the Shoe-Jew and Chairman of the Israelite Congregation in Nuremberg." The scandal sheet seized upon the show trial of the "last Jew in Nuremberg," as Katzenberger was called in SS circles, as a welcome propaganda event that provided their comrades with additional ammunition in their campaign to exterminate the Jews.

Even among the citizens of Nuremberg, Rothaug the Executioner enjoyed considerable sympathy. The judge's boisterous courtroom monologues, called "phonograph records" because they kept repeating the same Nazi slogans, obviously appealed to people. Whenever the judge passed a milder sentence at the end of proceedings, Groben related that "the public grumbled." But Rothaug rarely disappointed. After he presided over his last session at the Palace of Justice on Fürtherstrasse in March 1943, spectators put a bouquet of flowers on the judges' bench.

Less favorably impressed by Rothaug was Hans Seiler, Irene's once dashing husband. The soldier had appeared before Rothaug in the summer of 1942 to plead for clemency for Irene. Seiler emphasized that he would never divorce her because he knew she'd done nothing wrong. Rothaug presumably smiled in his cynical way and curtly dismissed the young soldier. Seiler visited Irene once more; he'd found out that she was being held in a prison camp at Griebo, near Coswig on the Elbe River. It was the last time they saw each other. On October 31, 1944, Hans Seiler died, as his death notice states, "in a desperate forest battle" near the French town of St. Die, in the Vosges.

After sentencing in March 1942, Irene remained in the Nuremberg jail for a time. On June 15 at nine o'clock in the evening she was taken to the women's prison in Aichach. At that time prisoners were not simply locked away behind bars — the Nazis needed anyone who could work. And so, a week later, Irene was in a sizable prison convoy with other female convicts headed for Griebo. Convicts at the penitentiary in Coswig worked for different armament companies. Irene was assigned to Reinsdorf Explosive Works. Working under the worst conditions, she and some fifty other prisoners produced gunpowder for Hitler's final victory.

In Nuremberg, Herbert Kolb, Bernhard Kolb's son, contributed compulsory labor as well. Since May 1939 the Nazi leaders had been ordering more and more of the Jewish inhabitants to work, most in armament-related industries. In June 1943 the Kolbs received orders to join their own convoy. They left the city with several other Jews who had previously been resettled in Fürth. The train was headed to Theresienstadt. On the same day, sixteen more people were deported from Fürth, among them Katzenberger's defense attorney, Richard Herz. The destination was Auschwitz.

The journey to Theresienstadt, paradoxic as it sounds, at first seemed to Bernard Kolb like a vacation. After the terrible stress that he had recently suffered, the bookkeeper, now sixty years old, could finally relax. "It was as if he were relieved," remembers Herbert. "Suddenly he had nothing more to do with the Gestapo's constant terror." Compared with that perpetual psychic tension, hunger, poor hygiene, and confinement in Theresienstadt seemed almost bearable to Father Kolb.

In the camp, the Kolbs met up with David Katzenberger. The camp administration had given him a job in the "shoe store," the building whose show window was decorated like a retail store, but, of course, there were only used shoes on display. As the director of the Used Shoe Retail Department, David was in charge of twenty-five workers, most of whom worked as cobblers. "There was a lot of work, but it did me good," Katzenberger told his relatives after the war, and related that he'd had customers "from Germany, Holland, Denmark, Poland, Vienna, and so on" who were clearly selling confiscated shoes for the Nazis — among them there were "some pleasant people and some others."

Leo Katzenberger's sisters Meta Schwarzenberger and Clothilde Weglein died in Theresienstadt. There is no record of Rosa Ledermann or Recha Rosenthal, two Katzenberger sisters who had also been in deportation trains headed east. David eventually volunteered to join a convoy that was said not to be going to Auschwitz. Not a safe thing to do, but he was lucky. On February 5, 1945, he traveled to Switzerland with other prisoners who were the beneficiaries of a ransom effort arranged by Count Bernadotte, president of the International Red Cross. Shortly before war's end, David was sitting in a sports hotel in the Swiss Alps with others who'd been freed and sounded like he was in quite good spirits again: "We're surrounded by beautiful, 3,100- to 3,200-meter-high mountains, and can see down into the Rhone Valley," he wrote to relatives in America. "It's a splendid view."

Meanwhile the Nuremberg Nazis were in the midst of their last battle. From behind the barricades at police headquarters, Gauleiter Holz issued orders that the city be defended "to the last man." On the night of April 19, 1945, Holz sent one last radio message to Berlin. "My Führer!" he began, "Nuremberg surrounded on all sides." Then, boasting till the very end: "Twenty-four tanks destroyed so far, eighteen of them with our handheld rockets." By then the Americans had fought their way to the ring of streets surrounding the inner city. "Day-long artillery and mortar bombardment of the burning city," the report went on in the Gauleiter's telegraph staccato. "Our losses heavy as well . . . running out of ammunition!" Praising the "splendid cooperation" from the battle-group leaders, he maintained enthusiastically. "Comrades in the streets are greeting us with Heil Hitler!" That same night, in the Palmenhof Bunker not far from police headquarters, Nuremberg's mayor, Willy Liebel, shot himself in the head with his gold pistol.

The following day — Hitler's birthday — the indefatigable Holz appropriated that very pistol and marched off to his final encounter. A short while later, he died in a hallway at police headquarters after an exchange of gunfire; whether he was killed in battle or took his own life remains unclear. The Americans had Chaplain Max Pfuhlmann of the nearby church of St. Elisabeth remove the bodies from the police building and bury them. Pfuhlmann later stated in a letter that he had graves dug for the dead veteran Nazis "in the only spot where the ground was soft enough" — what turned out to be a children's playground. The Nuremberg Nazi heroes ended up being interred beneath a kindergarten play area.

In the spring of 1945, the old town on the Pegnitz River lay in ruins — even the building on Spittlertorgraben had burned. Sixty-two members of the Kolb family had been murdered in the death camps. No one has yet established how many Katzenbergers perished. David was the only one of his generation to survive. Of the Nuremberg Jews, 1,626 died in the Holocaust.

2 4

THE VILLA, IN ONE OF NUREMBERG'S PRESTIGIOUS neighborhoods, seemed like a dream to Irene. Stockings torn, completely exhausted, she had endured a bumpy Jeep ride through the demolished countryside from Guben to Nuremberg, past burned-out cities and blown-up bridges. When she finally reached Nuremberg early in March 1947, she saw nothing of the old city but heaps of stones, charred beams, and ruins. Now she stood in front of a magnificent dwelling that seemed to have been completely spared.

Fir trees framed the facade, which still displayed blotches of the dark brown paint used as camouflage against air attacks. Inside, things looked comfortable. She saw a long dining-room table, an imposing sideboard, and a big Telefunken radio in the drawing room. A friendly woman led her across the creaky parquet floor and up to one of the bedrooms with windows that looked out onto a large garden filled with chirping birds. Irene closed the door and took a deep breath. She was in the house reserved for witnesses at the Nuremberg war crimes trial.

At supper, Irene met the other guests at the suburban villa. Gathered there were people whose names Irene was already familiar with. There were old

Nazis, sympathizers, opponents of the regime, and concentration camp survivors. That they were all sitting so peacefully side by side at the supper table seemed uncanny. A rather dignified woman by the name of Anna Maria von Kleist, whom people addressed as "Baroness," was in charge. After dinner, the Baroness played bridge with several guests; over in a corner a circle of men discussed the political events of the day with muted voices; and off to the side a woman sat quietly in an armchair, reading a book.

Irene did not feel at home with the group that had assembled at number 24 Novalisstrasse. At first, when an emissary of the American military located her at her home in Guben, she didn't even want to come. He informed her that Judge Oswald Rothaug was being tried by the American Military Court at Nuremberg because of the brutal way he had conducted courtroom proceedings during the Nazi era. The trial was to take place in the Nuremberg Palace of Justice, which had survived the hail of bombs with only slight damage. Irene was an important witness, she learned, and her testimony was required. But Irene had been trying to put those terrible events out of her mind.

Her prison term in the munitions factory on the Elbe had been horrible. The yellowish powder that had to be poured into the shell casings ate into one's skin and hair, and the workers lived in constant fear that at sometime or other the whole place would blow sky-high. Only after her mother's third application for clemency was Irene Seiler set free — on June 19, 1943. When she was released, at around nine in the morning, the warders, according to her release form, handed her "bread for one day" as sustenance for her journey. She went to Guben, where she later fell ill with typhoid fever, which was soon followed by frequent gallbladder attacks. Her high spirits had evaporated. But she was still tall and attractive, capable of making a good impression; for her age, however, her face was deeply lined. Irene often seemed gloomy; an old medical file indicates that she was suffering from depression.

She was now working in a photo shop. Her sister Hertha directed the technical aspects; the business manager was Irene's brother-in-law, Paul Ladiges. When the Russians came to Guben, the Schefflers had to vacate their beautiful brick villa on the eastern shore of the Oder River, which would soon belong to Poland. But they were able to move into a pretty, art nouveau villa on the west side of the river. There Hertha opened a new photography business. Everything ran smoothly; soon the firm had a near-monopoly on new passport photos, which everyone needed, since the Oder was now the country's border. It was exactly what Irene had experienced in Nuremberg — she

once again confirmed that "the photography business is good in wartime" —
and directly afterward, too.

Robert Kempner, one of the chief prosecutors at Nuremberg, later stated
that cases were still being sought for the judges' trial. The American investigators had managed to find the Reich's Ministry of Justice records in the
Russian zone. If the accusations were to stand up, however, court-worthy documentation was needed. One day, Kempner was strolling across the courtyard
of the Palace of Justice with Camille Sachs, a respected Nuremberg discrict
attorney who had returned from exile. When Kempner told him about the
planned Judges Trial, Sachs pointed to the roof and said, "Up there are all the
transcripts." In the attic, U.S. prosecutors did in fact find fairly complete
records of the barbarous verdicts handed down by the Nazis' Special Court.
The verdict against Katzenberger was not among them — to this day the
court files with the registration number 1b/Sg/1074/41 have not been found.

One of the main prosecution witnesses against Rothaug was his sometime-
colleague Karl Ferber. Because he behaved so servilely toward the presiding
judge at the time, his colleagues belittled him, calling him "Rothaug's office
manager." When Rothaug was later transferred to the People's Court, Ferber
succeeded him as presiding judge of the Nuremberg Special Court.

Like so many other jurists who wanted to continue their careers during
the Nazi era, Ferber had joined the National Socialist Party in May 1937. He
also functioned as block helper from time to time, taking up collections for
the National Socialist Welfare Society. Beyond that, he had been a "sustain-
ing member" of the SS since 1934 and worked for the Nazis' Office of Racial
Policy. "I was taken in by the spirit of the times," he explained after the war.
Then, at the behest of the Communist Party, Ferber spent four days clearing
debris, contributing his salary to help care for former concentration camp
inmates. To him, that should have been sufficient atonement, and he could
now be back on top during the new era. The only awkward thing was that
Associate Judge Ferber had composed and signed the written verdict against
Katzenberger — that very bundle of papers that had disappeared without a
trace from the attic file repository in the spring of 1947.

Judge Ferber soon had his own desk again at the Nuremberg Palace of
Justice. When Irene Seiler ended up in Nuremberg, the jurist immediately
took her under his wing. Five years previously, as a Nazi judge, he'd considered the pretty photographer a barfly for whom anything would go as far as
sex was concerned. Now he hastened to explain to her that the judgment back
then had been "far-fetched."

Irene also came across the last of the three judges who condemned Katzenberger to death and her to two years' imprisonment — completely at liberty. Judge Heinz Hugo Hoffmann, a narrow-shouldered man with glasses and neatly parted hair, forty years old and rather unremarkable in appearance, was having supper at the witness house. Irene hadn't even noticed him; someone else called him to her attention. When asked, Hoffmann immediately brought up the judges' 1942 verdict, which had been "disturbing and depressing . . . the verdict was untenable, unjust, and inhuman."

During those days at the witness house, the erstwhile Nazi judge's knees were shaking with fear, he later admitted. "My back was against the wall." Originally, by his own estimation, he'd been "moderate, liberal, and nationalist . . . an outspoken opponent of all radicalism." Hoffmann had studied in Munich and Geneva, won a scholarship to England, and had written his doctoral dissertation on English administrative law. All in all, he was a splendidly educated jurist. But when the Nazis came to power, Hoffmann saw his chances for a career disappearing. "I thought to myself, 'Well, you'll have to ante up, too — go along with it.'" In 1937 Hoffmann joined the party; in 1938 he became a district court judge in Nuremberg. "When the war broke out, my attitude changed," Hoffmann stated, "then you had to keep a stiff upper lip — Germany was in danger." And so he never protested when Rothaug wanted to pass yet another death sentence. Together the two judges had sentenced at least twelve people to death. "It was all Rothaug's fault; we were lowly associates who couldn't risk doing the wrong thing," Hoffmann later explained. "It was impossible to resist his incredible drive."

On the sideboard in the witness house the Baroness had placed a little book bound in brown artificial leather — her guestbook. On one of the gilt-edged pages Hoffmann penned a bit of fustian that revealed a little of his discomfort: "Dark days, wild days, a dancing witches' whirl, / but look, an island here offers kindly respite from the swirl."

The witness house on the edge of the woods had its own, very discrete style. The lodging house was organized in the fall of 1945, shortly before the legal proceedings brought by the Allies against Nazi war criminals started. An annex was maintained in the neighboring building. Prosecutor Kempner recalled in his memoirs that it had been "a work of art in and of itself" to house such disparate witnesses "with empathy." The first to be trusted with the sensitive task of hostess was a Hungarian, the thirty-six-year-old Countess Ingeborg Kalnoky, whom the Americans happened upon in a Nuremberg hospital where she'd just become a mother for the fourth time. A noblewoman, politi-

THE MAIDEN AND THE JEW

cally untainted, and fluent in several languages, she was just right for the position. The countess was hired while still convalescing from delivery. Kalnoky
ran the house for a year; it was then taken over by Baroness von Kleist.

Room and board were provided to the witnesses free of charge, and the
meals were ample. Food was brought in three times a day by an American
jeep, and included things unknown to the Germans at the time: corn flakes,
grapefruit juice, peanut butter. And while the inhabitants of Nuremberg's
inner city had to find shelter in drafty ruins, the guests at the cozy inn on the
edge of the woods slept between fresh American linens. It was "quite wonderfully feudal," recalls Otto Kranzbühler, Karl Dönitz's defense attorney.
Kranzbühler always wore his snappy navy uniform to dinner and regarded
his time at the guesthouse as "an amusing entryway into the new era." For
many an antifascist, however, it was very uncomfortable. "The food stuck in
your throat," a guest from Munich stated afterward.

There were many noteworthy guests at the witness house, but for Irene, it
was an odd scenario. Almost every day she went to the Palace of Justice to swear
affidavits with her interrogator, Henry Einstein. First, Einstein asked whether
she might "have a guilty conscience." Irene was taken aback: How did he come
up with that? Then Einstein told her about Hoffman's testimony. At the witness house, Hoffmann was said to have displayed great cordiality toward Irene.
In court, however, Hoffmann asserted that the young woman would probably
have pangs of conscience because she'd implicated the Jew. Such a bold rever-
sal of the relationship of guilt and innocence — yet it was coin of the realm in
those days when they were all just trying to save their own skins.

Karl Ferber had two faces as well. Years later, whenever the jurist was
backed into a corner, he always told an anecdote that was intended to compromise Irene: When they met back in 1947, he asked why she had never
entered a plea for clemency. "I got off easy, considering what happened," she
allegedly said, which in his mind amounted to a confession of guilt. In truth,
Irene's mother made several pleas for clemency. Furthermore, Irene had not
meant her statement to be construed in that way. What she meant was that
she had suffered relatively little, compared to the frightful sentence
Katzenberger received.

The Americans shielded Ferber, their key witness, from all complicity, and
their strategy paid off. Ferber testified that Rothaug had instituted a virtual
"derby" for the quickest death sentencing. In addition, Rothaug made it clear
by the way he conducted the proceedings that he "was the executor of the
party bosses' destructive urges." Rothaug sat with fourteen other judges on

the defendants' bench at Nuremberg. Among the accused was former State
Secretary for Justice Franz Schlegelberger, accused of collaborating in the
design of the criminal anti-Jewish laws. Otto Thierack committed suicide
shortly before the trial began; Roland Freisler was killed in an air raid on
Berlin in February 1945.

Soon Ferber and Rothaug were involved in a mudslinging contest, in
which the two judges hurled insults and attempted to implicate one another.
From prison, Rothaug threatened his one-time associate, saying "I'll pursue
you for the rest of your life." Ferber struck back by bringing up Rothaug's
"despicable behavior," castigating his "fanatic anti-Semitism" and attributing
to him the "morals of a predator." "A slimy character, that Ferber," fumed
Rothaug, even in his latter days. "It'd be hard to find anything worse than
that lying, slinking dog."

The Nuremberg judges were not the only ones competing to save their own
skins. Some of the former tenants of the Spittlertorgraben apartment house
were afraid of unpleasant questions as well. Johann Heilmann was listed as a
Nazi sympathizer because of his activities as a house warden. He carefully followed the newspaper reports about the judges' trial. When he met Mäsel, his
old neighbor from the carriage house, the two discussed the courtroom devel-
opments with a certain amount of apprehension. Heilmann expressed his
worry that "they'll give us no rest with the Katzenberger business."

Heilmann and Mäsel never had to appear before the Americans, but their
former neighbor Kleylein was sought out by the U.S. military authorities.
The prosthetics maker was interrogated by Henry Einstein, who wanted to
know if he had been the one who denounced Irene Seiler. Kleylein denied
that vigorously, afraid that he already had one foot in prison, since Irene was
present during his interrogation. But he was in for a surprise. As he later
recalled, "Irene didn't disagree with a single word." One year later, Kleylein
and his wife were completely cleared. The certificate stated: "After a thor-
ough investigation, the origin of the denunciation in the Katzenberger-Seiler
case could not be determined." The couple had it in writing — they were not
informers. However, the officials hadn't seen the files from the original
investigation, which were missing at that time.

Irene Seiler had other worries. On March 26, 1947, knees trembling, she
stood in Courtroom 600, where she had been sentenced five years before. This
time she was appearing as a witness for the prosecution, but Rothaug's
brusque defense attorney, Josef Koessl, was so hard on Irene during his cross-
examination that it looked as if she were the accused. The transcripts of his

endless questioning, which resulted in yards of documents, is a record par excellence of an attempt to wear down a person with the sheer weight of words. Using brutal intimidation, suggestion, and prejudgment, Koessl attempted to discredit the witness — she was to appear a simpleton who had been seduced by a Jewish businessman.

The attorney questioned her as if the Third Reich had never ended: didn't she know that "it wasn't just sexual relations with Jews that got people into trouble in Nuremberg, but any relationship?" Irene responded calmly that that hadn't occurred to her, and if it had, it wouldn't have made any difference. "To toss out a friendship from one day to the next just because of laws like that," the photographer declared firmly, "never entered my mind. I would have thought it inhuman, and wouldn't have done it." Then Koessl asked in a sharp tone what sort of dealings she "had admitted" to the judge in the 1942 trial. Irene answered calmly that "Herr Katzenberger was good to me, paid his respects by way of a few flowers, a little chocolate, and cigarettes." Koessl: "Didn't you admit something else at one point?" Irene said she didn't understand: "What was I said to have admitted?" Koessl replied in a cutting voice that he "just wanted to know what else you admitted to." Irene continued to respond calmly, saying that "Herr Katzenberger had gotten a kiss from me."

Koessl kept at it. Hadn't Irene admitted to having kissed Katzenberger "quite frequently?" "From 1932 to 1941 is a long time," she retorted, close to tears, and "that's still quite a way from proving that the two of us committed any racial offense." Irene was now nearly done in, but Koessl bored on. Hadn't she "admitted that she'd taken him on her lap?" Irene said no, but that she'd "sometimes sat on his lap," just like she did at home with her father, "because I looked upon Herr Katzenberger as a fatherly friend."

Attorney Koessl had further questions: "Can you recall Herr Katzenberger admitting that, despite his age, he was still able to have sexual intercourse?" Irene, exhausted by now, answered evasively that Katzenberger had been asked that question by the court "and he answered it." The attorney then wanted to know how he answered it. "With 'yes' as far as I can recall," replied Irene. Then she dissolved completely. In the affidavit taken by Henry Einstein she had said, "He was my best friend, like a father to me, and his horrible fate has depressed me my entire life." But "natural feelings like that," as she called them, didn't interest Koessl in the least.

Tired and worn out, Irene went back to the witness house, packed her bag, and left. She wrote a simple proverb in the guestbook: "Sunshine follows rain."

25

"IT WAS THE FAULT OF THOSE DAMNED ESKIMOS!" complained prosecuting attorney Ted Lawson to Judge Haywood over drinks at a dance hall. They seemed to have been the ones who brought Hitler to power, murdered the Jews, and cooked up the world war. The American was tired of hearing the citizens of Nuremberg claim they "didn't know a thing about it." In Courtroom 600 of the Palace of Justice on Fürtherstrasse, Irene Seiler was being badgered on the witness stand by an attorney for the defense. One of the accused, Judge Janning, stands up and shouts, "Stop it! If there is ever to be any salvation for Germany, we who know our guilt must admit it, whatever the pain and humiliation."

In reality, those scenes never took place; it occurs in *Judgment at Nuremberg,* a Hollywood drama of the 1947 judges' trial filmed in 1961, starring Marlene Dietrich as a German general's widow and Spencer Tracy as the American judge. Burt Lancaster played a Nazi judge, a combination of Oswald Rothaug and Franz Schlegelberger; Judy Garland was Irene Seiler. Rothaug-Schlegelberger's evil defense attorney, who reduces Garland to tears, is played by a German, Maximilian Schell. Hollywood celebrated the opus of guilt and atonement: Oscars were awarded to Schell and to Abby Mann, who wrote the screenplay.

The movie was not so well received by German audiences. "The response was rather cold," reported Abby Mann after the 1961 premiere in Berlin, which he was visiting along with Spencer Tracy, Judy Garland, and Richard Widmark, who played Lawson, the American prosecutor. Willy Brandt, mayor of Berlin at the time, invited the stars to dine with him. "But he didn't know what to say about the film," reported Mann; the Social Democrat merely mumbled that he'd have to "study the background facts first."

The reporters at the subsequent press conference likewise failed to understand the monumental film. The cold war was on and Berlin was the front-line city in the East–West conflict; the boundary ran right through the middle of the city, and it would soon be strengthened by thick walls and barbed wire. In East Berlin, Russian tanks were rolling down Stalinallee; on the west side, politicians ostentatiously rang the Freedom Bell. They were rallying their citizens for the ideological battle against the Red enemy in the East — Germany was the last bastion against communism. And Hollywood wanted to judge former Nazi war crimes in a film?

The movie was destined to be a flop in Germany, and yet its political analysis was astute and intelligent. At the end of the film the trial is over, the defendants have been sentenced to prison for life, and the German defense attorney is saying goodbye to the oldish American judge who surprised everyone by passing draconian sentences. The attorney offers the judge a wager: "In five years the men you sentenced to life imprisonment will be free." Tracy doesn't take the bet: "It is logical in view of the times in which we live," says the old judge thoughtfully, "but to be logical is not to be right."

In fact, reality had already overtaken cinema. By the time the movie made it to the theaters, Rothaug was sitting comfortably in his living room, having long since been released from the prison for war criminals at Landsberg. The Nuremberg court had found him guilty early in December 1947, asserting that Rothaug had "turned the court into an instrument of terror" in a series of legal cases. In the Katzenberger case, the alleged "racial offense" had never been proved; the American judges found that Katzenberger "was brought to trial and executed because he was a Jew." Rothaug and three other defendants in the judges' trial were given life sentences. In 1954, Rothaug's penalty was commuted to twenty years. Two years later, on Christmas Eve 1956, the judge was freed on probation after serving nine years. On June 13, 1958, he was formally pardoned. He settled in Cologne, where he promptly applied for a state pension.

Karl Ferber and Heinz Hoffmann, the two associate judges in the Katzenberger trial, as well as prosecutor Hermann Markl, appear to have moved on fairly quickly: Ferber was working in industry as a legal advisor, Hoffmann was running a flourishing legal practice in Darmstadt, and Markl had managed a government career — he had become an official of the State Superior Court in Munich. Obviously, there weren't any investigators interested in these three men. The prosecution of Nazi perpetrators, carried on with considerable commitment in the years right after the war's end, generally slackened after the mid-fifties. In any event, there is no particular inclination within the legal profession to put fellow members in the dock — one crow isn't likely to pick another's eye out. Nevertheless, on April 19, 1960, a directive, stamped PRIORITY, from the Bavarian Ministry of Justice arrived at the Palace of Justice in Nuremberg. In it, the Minister of Justice, Dr. Albrecht Haas, instructed the Nuremberg Public Prosecutor's Office to immediately open investigations against Ferber, Hoffmann, and Markl "concerning manslaughter and accessory thereto, respectively." The haste was necessary because on May 8, 1960, exactly fifteen years after the Third Reich's collapse, the statute of limitations would expire. According to records, investigations against Ferber, Hoffmann, and Rothaug were initiated on April 26, on charges of "perversion of justice, willful manslaughter, and being accessory to the fact." Their colleague, Markl, was overlooked initially.

The case against Rothaug was dismissed, since the Nazi judge had already been convicted by the U.S. military tribunal. But the public prosecutors soon wanted to abandon their investigations into the other jurists as well: in mid-July 1961 they submitted a "Proposal to Cancel Proceedings" to the Ministry of Justice. The nearly one-hundred-page document read like a rehash of the old verdict, espousing the view that during the 1942 trial, "factors had come to light that forced one to assume a sexual relationship between Katzenberger and Seiler." And what was formerly said to be "people's normal sensibilities" was now called the "experience of ordinary life." The Nuremberg prosecutors found it "scarcely believable that an adult, a thirty-year-old woman, sat repeatedly on the lap of a man, exchanged kisses with him, put his head against her bosom, and let her thigh be touched, without sexual motivation playing a role." Indeed, the assumption was "that, judging by ordinary life experiences, such intimate association over the years is bound to lead to sexual intercourse in most cases."

In addition, in 1961 the prosecuting attorneys could not see how the Nazi judges who had condemned Katzenberger could have incurred guilt, since the verdict, though "horrible and depressing," was in accordance with the law at the time. "It is my intent to suspend proceedings," the Nuremberg senior prosecutor wrote to the Bavarian Ministry of Justice in a letter dated July 18, 1961. The authorities there, however, demanded that investigations continue, which set off a long, drawn-out exchange between bureaucrats in Munich and in Nuremberg. If the ministry instructed the Nuremberg prosecutors to proceed with the Katzenberger case, the prosecutors always complied while simultaneously looking for the first opportunity to suspend their investigations. This back-and-forth went on for five years, during which time the Nuremberg prosecutors applied for suspension on four occasions, always presenting lengthy justifications that all came down to one essential point: "life experience" led the investigators to surmise that there must have been a sexual relationship between the businessman and the photographer.

Suppression, postponement, refusal — civil servants throughout Germany acted in accordance with those precepts when reappraising the Nazi era. In Bavaria alone there were several offices for processing victim's claims for restitution.

Today the files from those agencies are stored in various depots. When a worn cardboard folder is opened, bugs crawl out from between the dusty pages. The battered documents reveal the soul of the German civil servant, which remains for the most part unmoved by individual tragedies. Rigorously they insisted on proof that the Gestapo had long since destroyed. With exaggerated correctness they demanded statements from witnesses when there were none who survived. But however assiduously they may have demanded proof, in many instances the servants themselves were slipshod with the victims' vital statistics — names were misrepresented and dates of death transposed, information sloppily evaluated or overlooked and false deportation dates reported. And when it had to do with the state's purse strings, the first thing the officials did, out of principle, was to voice their objections. Thus the proceedings dragged on for years. Frequently those concerned were dead by the time a decision was reached.

In March 1950, David Katzenberger, by then seventy-five, had come to Germany to apply for compensation on behalf of himself and his brothers' and sisters' heirs. He presented a packet of notarized declarations given under oath in which he detailed the loss of various possessions, including the

destruction of apartments and stores during Kristallnacht, the forced liquidation of the shoe business, the compulsory share paid to the state at the sale of
their homes, and the deportation luggage with the custom-made shirts.

All in all, David, then living without means in Israel, valued Katzenberger
losses at just about a million Reichsmarks. And that amount reflected only
what could be reimbursed by the state under the Federal Republic of
Germany's Compensation Laws. Items pocketed by individuals during the
forced Aryanization of buildings and shoe stores was not taken into consideration. Those losses, comprising at least another half million Reichsmarks,
had to be made good in time-consuming negotiations between the Jewish
merchant's family and private individuals.

For the first two years, David Katzenberger heard nothing substantive
about his application. Then he was granted a lump-sum compensation of
4,650 deutschmarks, paid in two installments during the summer of 1952.
With that, the officials considered the claim satisfied. In 1954, Katzenberger
hired an attorney. The authorities had demanded new documentation and
raised doubts as to whether the Gestapo had confiscated valuable furnishings
at the time of his deportation. They didn't even believe the extent of the devastation in the Katzenberger stores after Kristallnacht.

A year-long contest began, during which the businessman had to fight for
every penny. Meanwhile, he had no idea what he was supposed to live on.
When he went to Israel in 1945, he was too old to start over, and he didn't
know enough Hebrew to compete in business anyway. His relatives gave him
emergency help. In 1954, he contracted typhus. Desperate for funds, he submitted his physician's bill of nearly 1,200 marks to the German authorities,
requesting that they grant him an advance on his claims, "since otherwise I
will find myself in great distress."

Six years after he applied for compensation the German authorities finally
granted a small pension of 429 marks per month, an amount equivalent to that
received by someone at the lowest level of German public service. Instead of
using his previous income as the basis for determination, the compensation
clerks had gone strictly by his level of schooling. Katzenberger had never grad-
uated from high school, and that his jobs had paid incomparably more than the
wages of a worker in public service played no role in their decision. One year
later, the pension distribution was revised to 600 marks. Katzenberger didn't
see much of it; he died in early 1960. Max and Leo's survivors received nothing.
Rationale? "Both had died before the compensation laws went into effect."

By law, the descendants of Nazi victims were to be paid a state compensation for "restriction of liberty" if their parents had been forced to wear the yellow star; the payment agreed upon was 150 marks for each month. From September 19, 1941, the "Jewish star" was considered compulsory, and so Claire Katzenberger's heirs claimed compensation payment from then until May 8, 1945, the day of liberation from the Hitler regime. At first, authorities in the Federal Republic of Germany investigated thoroughly to determine whether this countrywide obligation actually pertained to Claire. Eventually the Munich compensation office recognized that she had indeed worn the star.

In order to keep the payments to the descendants to a minimum, the civil servants now churned through books about the Holocaust. "The female victim," they subsequently confirmed, had been deported to the Izbica camp "at age fifty-seven." From the *Literature of the Persecuted* and the resolutions of the Wannsee Conference, it was known that the Nazis had considered "women over forty-five incapable of working." Accordingly, the Munich bureaucrats decided Claire had died immediately upon arrival at Izbica.

To the admirable servants of the state, therefore, it appeared probable, "without the need for further investigation," that Claire Katzenberger died five months after her deportation, on August 30, 1942, at the latest. They therefore wanted to pay only for the time from September 19, 1941 until the presumed date of her death. "Given the situation," went the absolutely unbelievable rationale, "it could be considered as proven" that Claire Katzenberger "had only suffered compromise of freedom or withdrawal of freedom, respectively, from 9/19/41 to 8/30/42." After the date of her death, there was no further "restriction of liberty" for Claire Katzenberger to complain about.

The response, despite its cynical sound, was meant seriously. The descendants received compensation for "twelve full months," a total of eighteen hundred deutschmarks. The office wanted to pay even less, because at first a death date of June 3, 1942, drifted in and out of Claire's files, as well as those of her brother-in-law Max and his wife. A clerk had confused the presumed dates of their deaths with the date of Leo Katzenberger's execution. When legal action was threatened, the authorities implicitly acknowledged the shaky basis for their decision by immediately offering a compromise: they came up with another fifteen hundred marks and paid for a total of twenty-two months.

Whether damages stemming from Kristallnacht, the theft of table silver, the refund of special taxes, or the loss of insurance policies or bank accounts, it still took several legal proceedings until the files were finally closed on the Katzenberger compensation case. Concomitantly, claims for restitution were most vigorously resisted by the individual profiteers who had acquired shoe stores, real estate, and inventories from the Katzenbergers for very little money during the Nazi years. It was asserted that the sales had taken place "completely voluntarily," and that the Katzenbergers had even made a favorable deal — their wares were basically junk and the buildings high-quality ruins.

The Kuhns had purchased the beautiful villa on Praterstrasse for the low price of fifty-three thousand Reichsmarks, only thirteen thousand of which had to be paid; the mortgage made up the difference. In 1949 they claimed that the building had been "badly in need of repairs" when they bought it in the fall of 1940 and that they'd only lived in it for four years, because it was destroyed during an air raid in January 1945. "We've never profited from the house," lamented the Kuhns, then made an offer: "If Herr Katzenberger's heirs refund us the sum of fifty-three thousand marks, we'd be happy to place the property at their disposal."

The Kuhns wanted their money back and said so without any trace of shame. It was not their fault that in the interim Germany had initiated a world war and that millions of Jews had been murdered. They felt themselves totally blameless. Nevertheless, the married couple must have had some Nazi party connections, otherwise they would never have gotten the villa. And the building can't have been in such incredibly bad condition; faced with legal action, the Kuhns quickly agreed to a compromise payment of ten thousand marks.

Nor did any of the former neighbors on Spittlertorgraben feel any sense of guilt. Paul Kleylein was working away on his back braces, artificial legs, and knee supports, and he and his family would eventually open a second store. When public prosecutors interrogated Kleylein at the beginning of the 1960s, he represented himself as a threatened opponent of the Nazi regime. Back then, according to him, the Nazis had accused him of "trying to protect Katzenberger," because his "testimony exonerated Katzenberger."

In the spring of 1968, legal proceedings were actually opened against Judges Ferber and Hoffmann. Prosecutor Markl merely had to appear as a witness; the justification for his not being tried was that he had only "acted on orders from the court," though the fact that he'd previously hired a defense attorney who happened to also be a member of parliament obviously had its effect. For nearly a month, the trial proceeded in Courtroom 600, a chamber that had been presided over by Rothaug and later by the Allies. Paul Kleylein and Johann Mäsel took the stand, as well as Wilhelm Fabro and the now rather elderly Margarete Hölzel, who'd entered those columns of numbers so accurately in Katzenberger's office. Johann Heilmann had died in the interim. Irene Seiler, who was now living in East Germany, was unable to attend the proceedings because of illness. On April 5, 1968, the court handed down its verdict: guilty of manslaughter. Ferber received a three-year prison sentence, Hoffmann two years. However, no arrest warrants followed.

The verdict was halfhearted. On the one hand, the court reprimanded the two Nazi judges, because following Irene's marriage there was no proof of a sexual relationship between the photographer and the businessman. On the other hand, for the period before that, in the opinion of the 1968 judges, there were "several important indicators of repeated sexual intercourse between Frau Seiler and Herr Katzenberger." And once again, ordinary life experience, once called "the people's normal sensibilities" provided the final remnant of proof: "the presumption of a sexually charged relationship" between the two was " a conclusion based on life experience" the verdict continued, because "excited sexual passions demand satisfaction in the natural form of sexual intercourse." Irene had indeed admitted that "before her marriage she had several boyfriends with whom she'd had sexual relations," and therefore it could be attributed that "she would not be disinclined to have sexual intercourse with Katzenberger as well."

26

LUDWIG PRANDL WAS A MAN OF FIRM PRINCIPLES. He hated injustice and shirkers and valued personal reliability and individual responsibility. Prandl was somewhat stocky, and behind his glasses a wreath of white hair wound around his broad, bullish head; when he appeared professionally, he always wore a white collar and bow tie. The lawyer had intended to spend his retirement writing a book about the history of the papacy — in Latin. Whenever he dedicated himself to something, he did it wholeheartedly. "What's important in life is to be serious about your calling," he used to tell his colleagues.

Inclined to be politically conservative, Prandl had found his calling early — as a public prosecutor. But it was only in his later years that he was confronted by the Katzenberger case, which he considered the most important case of his life. After the 1968 verdict, Prandl lodged an appeal with the federal Supreme Court. In his opinion, the accused had been guilty of "murder in judicial guise" in 1942, not the lesser charge of manslaughter. The defense attorneys appealed as well, and so the Supreme Court vacated the verdict in August 1970.

The high court found inadequate clarification of the degree to which the

Nazi judges' decision had been determined by "professional ambition and compliance toward an influential — especially in personal affairs — superior" instead of, as the jurists had claimed, by fear for their safety and their lives. Beyond that, the censure went on, the verdict contained highly contradictory answers to the question of whether there had been a sexual relationship between Katzenberger and Irene. If "a conscientious and experienced judge might have considered that the witnesses had been led" to testify that sexual intercourse had taken place in the time before Irene's marriage, the Supreme Court asked why that objection would not be equally valid for the time after her marriage.

The case had to be unearthed again, that was clear. Prandl prepared the new indictment with extreme care. Right at the outset, the defendant Ferber, then sixty-nine years old, was found incompetent to stand trial, medically certified as suffering from cerebral arteriosclerosis and severe arthritis of the spine. Shortly thereafter, an investigating judge suspended the proceedings. Just thirty years after the original trial, efforts toward atonement seemed to have run aground. Prandl was horrified. But then something unusual happened: on the very day proceedings were suspended, two elderly women from Israel lodged a complaint — Leo Katzenberger's daughters had come forward.

Robert Kempner, the former Deputy Chief Prosecutor at the Nuremberg war crimes trials, had become an attorney in Frankfurt, but always kept one eye on the progress of the trials against Nazis in the Federal Republic. He searched out the two women, and they were prepared to appear as accessory plaintiffs in the case. For Lilo and Käthe, it must have been like awakening from prolonged anesthesia. The two women were now over sixty; no one had asked to hear from them during the decades-long investigation into their father's murder. "I assume that you wondered why we had never put in an appearance," Käthe Freimann wrote to Kempner in January 1971.

Back when Leo Katzenberger was sitting in prison, communication with relatives in Germany had become extraordinarily difficult. Up to the point when the Americans entered the fighting, Käthe and Lilo had been able to find ways to communicate with Nuremberg, but afterward there were just the three-line Red Cross telegrams.

In one such telegram, dated February 1942, Leo Katzenberger's daughters asked how he was; it was returned in August with the news, "Sorry to inform you Grandfather Leo died June 3." Just about the same time, the last telegram from Leo Katzenberger arrived, the one sent from prison on June 3, 1942, the day of his execution. In early July, the emigrant newspaper *Aufbau* ran a small notice: "In Nuremberg the 68-year-old congregations official Dr. Katzenberger was condemned to death for 'racial offenses' at the instigation of Julius Streicher." The paper soon carried eulogies by Nuremberg emigrants, in which Katzenberger's social activities were effusively praised: "His heart never failed us" and "To all of us he was a warm friend and trusted advisor, an example of Jewish kindness and humanity, full of boundless willingness to help."

Katzenberger's daughter Lilo, thirty-one at the time, went into shock. Some years later at the Holocaust memorial in Yad Vashem, Käthe was horrified when she saw an issue of *Der Stürmer* with her father's photograph; only then did she learn all the details of the terrible trial. For years, the two sisters were unable to get over the execution of their father. All of the older generation, with the exception of their Uncle David, had been murdered in the Holocaust. The two women were still suffering the effects of the shocking revelations when Kempner contacted them in Israel.

Their action against the suspension of proceedings against Judge Hoffmann garnered results; the trial was continued. Scarcely had it become known in Germany that the Katzenberger daughters had entered the case when a curious letter from Otto Scriba, a priest in Darmstadt, reached them in August 1971. The pastor represented himself as a "friend of Jews" who "himself had lost friends in Auschwitz." He wrote that Hoffmann's life "has been burdened by guilt that no court can lift from his conscience." The man knew, he went on, "that he stands guilty before God and you" and that "Herr Hoffmann has not only realized the errors of his youth, but has consciously departed from them." Hoffmann had, claimed the cleric, "done thousandfold penance and atonement for the grief he has caused you." Then he came to what was really on his mind: the sisters should withdraw their case because "Dr. Hoffmann's inner peace has been disturbed" for years. "Show him the greatness of spirit of your religion," implored Scriba, "give him your forgiveness for the 'sins of thy youth' (Psalm 25:7)."

The women in Israel did not respond to the letter.

The penitent sinner Hoffman next tried to use illness to get out of the situation and was examined in January 1972 by the Darmstadt court physician. His diagnosis: Hoffmann was "fit to stand trial." When Kempner asked Hoffmann at the beginning of the trial if he did not at least feel some sense of guilt, the defendant looked straight ahead with an agonized expression. "I regret," he said, as if the question had been directed to someone else, "that one got involved in those things."

On January 16, 1973, Hoffmann's new trial began; it was the last time legal proceedings would be carried out in the Federal Republic of Germany against a Nazi judge. Once more, the event took place in Courtroom 600. Hoffmann had managed to have himself declared "of limited ability to stand trial" because of a slipped disc. He appeared in dark glasses and sat listlessly in the dock, slumped forward. Irene Seiler came from East Germany. Once a striking young woman to whom judges had attributed all sorts of love affairs, the sixty-two-year-old entered the room wearing grandmotherly lace-up shoes and a woolen coat with matching cap and set her unwieldy handbag down next to the witness's bench. Her heart pounded wildly as she again stood in the room where such unhappiness had entered her life.

In response to the judges' questioning, she began to tell the whole story yet again: her father's friendship with Katzenberger, the money problems with her photography studio, her love of riding in automobiles, the scene in the air-raid shelter, the Party warning, and, finally, the frightful trial in that very courtroom. Judge Rothaug's shrieking resounded in her ears again, along with his demeaning treatment of Katzenberger and his hateful question to her: "How could anyone kiss that Jew mouth?" It had been the most horrible experience of her life — "that trial was worse than the experience of being a refuge at the end of the war."

When asked by how many weeks her prison term had been shortened after her conviction, the old woman suddenly broke into tears. Her words, "twenty-five weeks," were lost in a fit of sobbing. The court ordered a recess and Seiler pulled herself together, standing in the broad vestibule of the Palace of Justice, surrounded by well-wishers saying she would make it through the trial. "I owe Katzenberger that much." Back in the courtroom, Irene once again broke into tears. It seemed to her, she stated, that someone was going to stand up any moment and announce that she was the accused.

The court reassured her that she was now living in a state governed by law. But when the defense began to question her, it was nevertheless as it had been earlier. Irene had already spent hours testifying about the kisses with Katzenberger and the business on his lap. She explained that it had been just like it was with her father, to whom she sometimes said, "Come father, be nice to me, I want to be your little girl again." She stated, "But I didn't do anything with him."

The defense attorney pushed on: Why had she sat on Katzenberger's lap? "Where did he caress you?" the judge now wanted to know. And one defense attorney asked, "Where did you kiss each other — just on the cheeks?" When Irene, now quite flabbergasted, said "I don't know anymore," the lawyer said in an easily heard aside that he had indications that there had been "kisses on the mouth."

The neighbors from Spittlertorgraben, now well along in years and gray-haired, also appeared during the course of the trial. Once again they were as innocent as little lambs. Seventy-two-year-old Paul Kleylein repeated, in his broad Franconian accent, the thirty-year-old statement "The sparrows were shouting from the rooftops" that there was something going on between Seiler and Katzenberger. He, of course, hadn't been involved in that kind of talk. Johann Mäsel, now seventy-one, suddenly told a completely new story: he'd once seen Irene and a friend going over to Katzenberger's shoe storeroom wearing bathrobes. Once again the same old testimony was repeated: the running water in Irene's apartment, the frequent visits from men, the flowers on her windowsill. Mixed in with the former neighbors' statements about her alleged love affair were nasty remarks about her lifestyle and protestations that they themselves really hadn't talked about those things, which were public knowledge, anyway. "We took the blame," complained Betty Kleylein, but somebody else did the informing. It had been Heilmann and Frau Östreicher, but "that Heilmann was the worst one." Heilmann and Frau Östreicher couldn't defend themselves; both were dead. But of course everybody knew about it, hissed Betty Kleylein, "somebody was always saying 'Katzenberger's been over at Irene's again today.'" Paul Kleylein suddenly interjected that he'd had a long talk with block leader Klein after the business in the air-raid shelter, but with an entirely different purpose than what the court supposed. "I was trying to protect Katzenberger." When he was asked to repeat the statement under oath, one of the defense attorneys caught him surreptitiously crossing the index and middle fingers of his lowered left hand as he said "So help me God," a trick used to "lead off" a false oath and make it nonbinding.

The duplicity enraged Prosecutor Prandl. The Kleylein couple, he thought, were "despicable beyond belief." Although he wanted to clear things up, Prandl was overcome by serious doubts that this "phalanx of tenants who could only express envy and dislike toward Irene had anything at all worthwhile to contribute to the matter." What they offered instead was "household gossip, assumptions, but no proof."

Month after month the proceedings dragged on and more and more wit-nesses were interviewed. In the summer of 1973, Irene appeared again. Now she had to testify about the bathrobe scene recalled by Mäsel and — of course — be questioned over again about kisses and other intimacies. And again there was the forty-year-old story about how Mother Mäsel saw Katzenberger and Irene kissing. In all seriousness the court concerned itself with that third-hand report of a kiss allegedly seen in a mirror, even though the kiss would not even have been against the law, since the Racial Purity Laws were passed two years later, in 1935.

The summations were drawing closer and the accused looked more and more frail. Emaciated and slouched forward, Hoffmann sat at the defendant's bench until one day he simply disappeared behind the gates of a sanitarium for neuropsychiatric disorders at Hofheim, in the Taunus Mountains. A short time later, Hoffmann was declared unfit to stand trial due to severe depres-sion with "psychomotor incapacity"; he had managed a last-minute escape from impending justice. Prandl never got over the blow. He had worked out his summation in great detail, all 134 pages lay ready on the desk. It would have taken many hours to express all aspects of the carefully weighed argu-ments. The prosecutor wanted to give proper consideration to everything that spoke for or against Heinz Hugo Hoffmann, because Prandl had made it his goal that "He should receive a more just verdict than he ever passed himself."

Prandl had tried to think his way back into the past, and indeed, did so more thoroughly than Hoffmann's defenders, who merely conjured the spirit of long-gone times to exonerate their client. In his prepared summation, Prandl had sketched out a fictitious verdict that he was convinced could have been handed down in the Katzenberger case, even in times of Nazi justice: "Innocent by virtue of insufficient proof." The witnesses' testimony, Prandl argued in his fictitious role as a Nazi judge, had not been "conclusive beyond doubt." Even "life experience" could not serve in lieu of proof, because it might lead one person to think one way, another a different way. "The only thing definitely established was a friendly relationship between the two peo-ple that lasted from 1932 until 1940." And the "numerous opportunities" that the accused had had during that time to indulge in sexual relations actually spoke against "there having been anything between them." If there had been, said the prosecutor, concluding his presentation as a Nazi judge, far better proof should have been forthcoming, since the two people were under con-stant surveillance.

According to everything he had learned about legal practices under the Nazis, Prandl was firmly convinced that even under their laws, a more lenient verdict would have been possible. He also felt that the motivation for Hoffmann's action had less to do with fear than with "opportunism, sycophancy, and compliance toward an influential superior." Prandl intended to plead for a sentence of life in prison for murder, carried out by perversion of the law.

Instead, the proceedings against Hoffmann were irrevocably suspended on August 20, 1976, based on extensive expert psychological opinion certifying Hoffmann's absolute inability to stand trial. Included was the statement that Hoffman was "an introverted person, nearly disabled by shyness . . . who prefers to adapt and compromise rather than swim against the current."

Later, Hoffmann resumed his Darmstadt law practice for several more years.

27

HER LITTLE HOUSE WAS CONCEALED behind two large oak trees. From the street, all that could be seen was a meadow with blue hepatica. Farther back, a broad, weathered stone staircase led uphill to the end of the promenade — a small house with Swiss-style woodwork. Inside was a tiny living room with creaky wooden floors, cozily furnished in the old-fashioned style with a Biedermeier sofa, a cherry secretary, and a Flemish chandelier.

In the secretary the old woman kept a folder with articles from *Der Stürmer* concerning the "racial offenders' trial," a few letters, and her prison release certificate. Irene's story to her friends in the little East German town of Apolda, where she spent the rest of her life, was that she'd "hidden a Jew" during the Nazi era. "Katzenberger came to my studio at night, through the back door," she went on, "and I gave him something to eat and made him some coffee." She never mentioned a love affair.

In 1946 she applied for recognition as a Opfer des Faschismus (Victim of Fascism, abbreviated as OdF). Anyone officially confirmed as an OdF had a privileged position in the Workers' and Farmers' State. At first the comrades rejected Irene's request, but after she returned from the U.S. tribunal at

Nuremberg in 1947, she was recognized as an OdF. Her red identity card dates from July 27, 1947. At that point, Irene was still working in the large photography studio that her sister Hertha ran in Guben. One year later, however, she went to Weimar, where she opened her own small studio on Prellerstrasse. Her sister, meanwhile, resettled in Hamburg.

The comrades on the Committee for the Victims of Fascism in Weimar checked their more carefully scrutinized applicants for proper evidence of resistance against the Nazi terror than did their counterparts in the state of Brandenburg, where Guben is located. A conscientious activist named Kiliani went over Irene's records in April 1950 and noted: "The relationship with the 68-year-old Katzenberger has to be termed unusual to say the least — she herself was 31 [during the trial] — received various amounts of money from him, etc." The affair, concluded Kiliani, "appears to have been a completely personal one, without political motivation, judging from the documents." Even the fact that her prison sentence had been shortened by half a year following the third plea for clemency appeared suspicious: "If she had conducted herself as an antifascist in prison, that probably would not have been approved." Two years later, Irene's OdF status was revoked.

Irene had apparently gone to Weimar because she still had contacts there from the master class that she took in the spring of 1938. She continued to live there until 1960; aside from the early days in Nuremberg they were presumably her happiest years. Later, she often spoke warmly of her many friends and of the artistic aura that surrounded her in the one-time domicile of Goethe, Herder, and Liszt. All that Apolda offered, on the other hand, were knitting machines and Philistines. In 1960, Irene moved to the small textile center between Weimar and Jena because of a man. Her marriage to photographer colleague Justus Helmerichs must have been a catastrophe; she was divorced just six months later.

Now Irene was sitting in boring Apolda, her studio in Weimar long since rented to someone else. She supported herself with part-time work, but her thoughts and energies were directed toward being recognized as having been persecuted by the Nazi regime. She filled out applications over and over again, but they were always rejected. The comrades on the committee at Apolda wrote that "the cause of the conviction in 1942," in light of their examinations, was "of a private, not political, nature." Irene became embittered.

"At that point she was said to be in a state of confusion," reported Stasi observers sometime around 1967. A few months later, Prandl directed his first request to East Germany's Attorney General, asking that Irene be permitted to testify at the trial of Hoffmann and Ferber, scheduled for the spring of 1968. Irene gave illness as a reason for being unable to go to the West; in reality, as revealed by files kept by the Stasi, her appearance at Nuremberg was never approved because there was some fear the photographer might defect.

Irene presumably had no intention of doing that — since 1961 she had been in charge of the small, state-run photography shop and laboratory on Pushkin Square in the center of Apolda, next to the People's Beauty Parlor. The photographer had four employees and received a monthly salary of 431 marks. "She gave absolutely no impression," said her colleague Christa Schindler, "that she was on the lookout for a man or interested in any sort of affair." Photographs from the time show slanted eyebrows, a careworn face, and the usual East German permanent. Irene smoked like a chimney and was always worried about heart problems. "She suffered from loneliness," said Schindler, "but when she did come into contact with other people, she wanted to monopolize the show, run things."

In 1972 the photographer received a letter from Prandl: a second request to be questioned as a witness. This time the East German authorities considered the photographer "politically reliable." After the Katzenberger case had been reviewed a second time in the West and even garnered considerable publicity, it appeared politically opportune to various East German officials to classify fellow citizen Seiler as an antifascist. This would not only help her, it would, calculated the political functionaries in East Berlin, have a beneficial effect on the international standing of the German Democratic Republic.

On January 29, 1973, shortly after Irene's appearance before the Nuremberg court, the Berlin office of the Committee for Nazi Persecution Victims recommended that their colleagues in the Erfurt district "forthwith announce the recognition of Irene Seiler," because she represented "a special case." While she had not carried out any "illegal antifascist activities," the motive behind her imprisonment had not really been of "such a private nature," since it had been "an exclusively political trial."

Then the letter came to the heart of the matter: "From considerations that reach beyond the borders of our republic," the commission considered Irene Seiler's recognition "as mandatory," since she had "also made a positive impression before the court in the Federal Republic." Press reports following her testimony, which included criticism of West German dealings with the Nazi past, had helped to bring about the desired recognition.

Irene was delighted. Instead of her ridiculous pension of four hundred marks, she now received a Pension of Honor amounting to eleven hundred marks, a considerable income in 1970s East Germany. The old woman bought a refrigerator with her first payment.

A second trip to the Hoffmann trial, where she was to state her views on the original interrogation records, was authorized in the summer of 1973 — only after, of course, the East German bosses had been reassured by Irene that nothing could go wrong. She was carefully questioned by the Stasi as to whether the new evidence might, in the end, implicate her as a "racial offender."

When she returned from Nuremberg, Irene was a changed woman. She stormed into a neighborhood friend's apartment, pulled a pack of West German newspapers out of her bag, and remarked happily, "Look here! They admired me!" Then, with great satisfaction, she read the headlines: Eine tapfere Frau (A Brave Woman).

But Nuremberg, the trial, and the publicity — all of that was over. At times, Irene could be seen pulling a child's wagon filled with groceries along the promenade in the narrow valley where her little house stood. Somewhat bent over, she would pick her way along the brook; then her silhouette would disappear behind the trees. Often she sat on a bench outside the door of her house, at her feet the two dogs, a collie and a Pomeranian, who had become her faithful companions. Or she worked in the tiny attic space that she'd turned into a darkroom.

There was no mention of friendships with men in Apolda. After her failed marriage in 1961, she seems never again to have taken up a serious relationship with a man. The few people with whom she maintained contact were mostly environmentalists or animal lovers. If friends came to her chalet for coffee, Irene sometimes used a few silver spoons taken from the china closet. They had finely worked handles that resembled snakes' heads. A Jewish businessman from Nuremberg had given them to her, she said. "They're all I have to remember Katzenberger by."

Irene Seiler died of stomach cancer in 1984, at the age of seventy-four. Her two dogs were put to sleep shortly afterward, as their mistress had directed in her will. Her furniture and valuable items, such as the chandelier, Chinese porcelain, and the silver spoons, were promptly carried out of the house by movers. Whatever remained was tossed out in front — kitchen utensils, personal items, newspaper articles, old photographic files, and a few rolls of film.

The last physical reminders of her life stirred in the wind. Gusts blew the rolls of film away one by one. After a few days, the garbage truck came and took what was left.

The judgment passed against Leo Katzenberger by the Nuremberg Special Court on March 14, 1942 was vacated in 1983 thanks to the efforts of Robert Kempner and Ludwig Prandl.

After this book was published in Germany in 1997, the city of Nuremberg named a street after Leo Katzenberger; it starts at Hans Sachs Platz, site of the synagogue destroyed by the Nazis in 1938. A stone commemorating the synagogue bears the following inscription:

UND WENN MAN SAGT, SIEH', WIR WUSSTEN NICHTS DAVON! GLAUBST DU DICH, DASS, ER, DER DAS HERZ DER MENSCHEN KENNT, IHN DURCHSCHAUT? ER VERGILT DEM MENSCHEN NACH SEINEN TATEN.

SPRÜCHE 24/12

If you say, "Behold, we did not know this," does not he who weighs the heart perceive it? Does not he who keeps watch over your soul know it, and will he not requite man according to his work?

PROVERBS 24:12

AFTERWORD

A NUMBER OF COINCIDENCES LED ME to write this book. More than fifteen years ago, a small, brown, gilt-edged book came into my hands — the guest registry from the Nuremberg villa where witnesses for both prosecution and defense were housed during the war crimes trials. Along with many prominent contemporaries, collaborators, and members of the anti-Nazi resistance were the names of Irene Scheffler Seiler and her one-time judge, Heinz Hugo Hoffman; both stayed at the house during the Judges Trial, conducted by the Americans from February until October of 1947. These entries attracted my attention more than any of the others. How extraordinarily unpleasant it must have been for Irene to sit at the supper table with the man who had sentenced her to prison and ordered her friend's execution.

Several years later, I sought out Robert Kempner, one of the chief prosecutors at the Nuremberg trials. He and his assistant, Jane Lester, received me at Haus Sonnenhof, a wonderfully situated pension with a view over the rooftops of Königstein in the Taunus highlands. That conversation, which took place in 1987, awakened my interest in the Katzenberger case. Kempner, who had represented the co-plaintiffs, still recalled quite well the 1973 proceedings against Hoffmann. He told about the revolting court sessions in the town hall at Hofheim in the Taunus, describing the malevolent impression made by the witnesses who had brought up the business of the running water as evidence of sexual goings-on. My discussion with Kempner and Jane Lester was wide-ranging and detailed, and I recorded it word for word; however, I was unable to investigate the Katzenberger case at that time.

Years later I was drawn to look more closely into the fates of Leo Katzenberger and Irene Seiler. In the spring of 1996, I had written an article in Der Spiegel about the history of the Witness House at Nuremberg, briefly mentioning their story. Shortly thereafter, I received a telephone call: the voice said, "I knew Irene Seiler, I lived right across from her photography studio." It was Ulrich Koch from Berlin. His boyhood years were spent in Apolda, the last place where Irene Seiler lived. Koch strongly urged me to explore her story. I began to investigate the "judicial murder" of Leo Katzenberger. I went to Apolda and Nuremberg and traveled to the United States and to Israel. The Internet was helpful as well.

It was my goal to reconstruct the situation in which Leo Katzenberger and Irene Scheffler Seiler found themselves, as well as the exact circumstances of their denunciation and the judicial persecution. I would like to thank all of the members of the Katzenberger family, who have actively helped me; I especially thank Lilo and Hilde Katzenberger and Marga and Walter Weglein, whose precise memories directed me to important details. I thank David Seldner and Joach Freimann from the younger generation of the family for their interesting comments and their critical examination of the manuscript.

Even though many of the later witness statements from the Spittler-torgraben tenants were self-serving, primarily glossing over details and proclaiming the innocence of their own actions, the testimony nevertheless offered a wealth of details and provided insight to the ideas and motivations of those involved. There is much information stored by the city of Nuremberg, particularly archives of old office files and material from the examining board that Göhring appointed in February 1939 to investigate the Nuremberg real estate deals. In this respect it was a stroke of luck (for me) that the case took place in Nuremberg: There certainly can't be too many cities that kept this much evidence from the Nazi era. That this story occured in Nuremberg is most likely a coincidence; it could have taken place in almost any other German city. For that reason, the book is not an attack against the city of Nuremberg; instead it serves as an attempt to recreate a piece of everyday life from the Nazi era.

During my visit to Israel in October 1996 I spoke with Leo Katzenberger's two daughters, Käthe and Lilo. At the time, I inquired about letters from the 1930s, but no one knew where they were. I spoke on the phone with Joach

Freimann, Käthe's son, and he told me that there was indeed a carton full of papers that someone had saved, but he had no idea what might be included. Several months later, after he had examined the contents of the box, David Seldner intercepted an Internet call for help from Israel: did anyone know any of the relatives of the Katzenberger family? David Seldner, with whom I'd been in contact for some time, was Leo Katzenberger's great-grand-nephew and had been working on a family tree. He contacted Joach Freimann — and so, with the help of the Internet, I acquired the letters that Leo and Claire Katzenberger had written prior to 1942 to their children in Palestine. The transcript of the interrogation recorded by Attorney Richard Herz in 1942 had also been preserved in Israel, as well as the handwritten draft of Leo Katzenberger's plea during the trial in 1942.

After all my research, I am certain of one thing: it cannot be true that people in Nuremberg and elsewhere did not know about the insults, degradation, and mistreatment suffered by their Jewish neighbors or about the deportation of the Jews. Whether they were clerks at the municipal housing authority or in town hall, civil servants at state office buildings or bank tellers, insurance agents or railroad workers — by the very nature of their jobs, many thousands of Germans were involved in the annihilation of German Jews. Soon after Kristallnacht, notaries, real estate brokers, used car dealers, goldsmiths, and ordinary citizens all profited from their Jewish neighbors' distress. As early as 1936, the organizers of Nuremberg's pre-Lenten carnival reviled their city's Jews, to the amusement of the populace, with their float titled "Off to Dachau." Later, local tavern owners often rented their properties for use as collection points for the deportations; the rental costs were passed on to the Jews.

It should also be stated that no one was obliged to inform on people. No one pushed the Heilmanns to spy on their neighbor, no one put any pressure on the Mäsels to look into Irene's windows, and certainly nobody used force on Betty Kleylein to make her feel that she had to complain to the Party about the alleged goings-on in the Spittlertorgraben apartment house. The best proof of this is given by those who didn't collaborate: the chauffeur Wilhelm Fabro, the florist Rosa Haselbacher, Judge Groben, who wanted to terminate the proceedings against Katzenberger, and the civil servant Leis from the land registry, who did not participate in the Nuremberg real estate scam. The Nazis did not lay a hand on any of those people.

Often the basest motives led people: the lust for profit, mistrust, nastiness, corruption, or careerism. On the other hand, there was an obvious lack of empathy and any sense of shared responsibility for what was happening. Even in a dictatorship, however, it comes down to the individual, and the standard for behavior has to be common humanity. Whether someone was in the party or not seems less significant to me than how people behaved toward their oppressed neighbors.

The neighborhood gossip along Spittlertorgraben lacked proof; there was, and is, no single, incontrovertible piece of evidence of a love affair between Leo Katzenberger and Irene Seiler. I am firmly convinced that the most that went on between them was some heavy flirting, certainly nothing more. As Prandl maintained, if there had been a true affair there certainly would have been more evidence, given all the attention Leo and Irene received. But even if there had been something between the two of them, it does not excuse those people who spied, informed, and condemned, and who ultimately sent Leo Katzenberger to the guillotine.

CHRISTIANE KOHL
HAMBURG, 1997

GLOSSARY OF NAMES

THE KATZENBERGER FAMILY

Lehmann Katzenberger (1873) Known as Leo, he was born in Massbach, near Bad Kissingen. Together with his brothers, David and Max, Leo was owner of the wholesale shoe company D. & M. Katzenberger, at 19 Spittlertorgraben in Nuremberg, as well as the chain stores Springmann's Footwear and Comet Shoes, with some thirty stores in southern Germany. He was also for many years the deputy chairman of the Jewish congregations in Nuremberg and, after the summer of 1939, its chairman. He was executed on June 3, 1942 in the prison at Munich-Stadelheim.

Claire Jessel Katzenberger (1884) Leo's wife, known as Big Claire, was born in Schlüchtern, near Frankfurt. On March 24, 1942, she was deported to Izbica, near Lublin.

David Katzenberger (1875) Born in Massbach, David Katzenberger was deported to Theresienstadt on September 10, 1942. In the spring of 1945, he volunteered to board a train that was rumored to be going not to Auschwitz, but to Switzerland as part of a ransom effort. He was the only Katzenberger family member of his generation to survive the Holocaust.

Max Katzenberger (1878) Born in Massbach, Max Katzenberger and his family lived one floor below Leo Katzenberger in the building at 23 Praterstrasse. He was deported to Izbica, near Lublin, on March 24, 1942.

Claire Jessel Katzenberger (1892) Wife of Max Katzenberger, "Little Claire" was Big Claire's cousin, and born in Kassel. She was deported to Izbica on March 24, 1942.

Käthe (1907) *and Bernhard Freimann* (1903) Käthe is the daughter of Leo Katzenberger. The couple and their children lived in Nuremberg. In September 1934 they emigrated to Palestine.

Lilo Katzenberger (1911) Lilo is the second daughter of Leo and Claire Katzenberger. She lived in Nuremberg and Dortmund before emigrating to Palestine in 1936. She lives in Israel.

Hilde Katzenberger (1922) Daughter of Max Katzenberger and Little Claire, she emigrated to Palestine in March 1939. She has since moved back to Germany.

Leo (1895) *and Else Weglein* (1905)   The Wegleins lived in the apartment house at 19 Spittlertorgraben. Leo Weglein was the son of Leo Katzenberger's sister Klothilde. Else was a sister of Leo Katzenberger's son-in-law, Bernhard Freimann. Leo was one of D. & M. Katzenberger's business managers, in charge of bookkeeping. The Wegleins emigrated to the United States in 1939.

Sally (1898) *and Marga Weglein* (1905)   The Wegleins lived in Nuremberg. Sally, Leo Weglein's brother, also worked for D. & M. Katzenberger and was in charge of the branch stores. In the fall of 1938, the Wegleins emigrated to the United States.

Joach Freimann (1953)   Son of Käthe and Bernhard Freimann, he was born in Israel in 1953. Today he runs the shoe business founded by his parents after they left Germany in 1934.

Walter Weglein (1930)   Son of Leo and Else Weglein, he emigrated to the United States with his parents late in 1939. Today he works as a journalist.

TENANTS, NEIGHBORS, AND COWORKERS

Irene Scheffler Seiler (1910)   Irene was a professional photographer and from 1932 ran a studio in the building at 19 Spittlertorgraben. She married Hans Seiler (born 1912) in 1939. From December 1941 until June 1943, she served a prison sentence for perjury. Died 1984 in Apolda, East Germany.

Paul (1900) *and Betty Kleylein* (1905)   The Kleyleins lived in on the first floor in the building at 19 Spittlertorgraben. Trained as an orthopedic appliance maker, Paul ran a prosthesis shop on Glockendonstrasse. Betty was a homemaker. Paul died in 1980; his wife died several years later.

Wolfgang (1887) *and Margarete Östreicher* (1883)   The Östreichers lived on the fourth floor of 19 Spittlertorgraben. Wolfgang worked as a salesman; they took in boarders in their large apartment. Wolfgang died in 1961; Margarete died in 1968.

Johann Heilmann (1899)   Heilmann initially trained as a carpenter, and lived with his family in an attic apartment on the fifth floor of 19 Spittlertorgraben. Until 1937, he worked as truck driver, stockroom clerk, and janitor for D. & M. Katzenberger. After being dismissed from the company, he worked as a driver for a drafting supply company in Nuremberg. He died in 1955.

Hans Mäsel (1903)   Mäsel lived with his wife in the coachhouse facing the courtyard of 19 Spittlertorgraben and worked as a toolmaker at the United Brush Company. He died in the 1990s.

Babette Gilger   Gilger owned a tobacco shop on the Plärrer and claimed that Katzenberger often bought cigarettes for Irene.

Rosa Haselbacher   A florist who worked in the shop on Dennerstrasse, Haselbacher neither participated in the gossip about Leo and Irene nor provided the Gestapo with any testimony about the matter.

Wilhelm Fabro (1910)   Chauffeur for Leo Katzenberger, Fabro remained aloof from the gossip about Leo and Irene and did not testify against Leo. Furthermore, he brought kosher food to Leo while he was in prison and was called a "Jew's lacky" for doing so. No action was taken against Fabro by the Nazis. After the war he worked in a automobile factory in Nuremberg; he died in 1983.

Margarete Hölzel (1899)   Hölzel worked as secretary and bookkeeper's assistant in the D. & M. Katzenberger Shoe Co. She managed the rental accounts for the apartment building.

Otto Feuchtwanger (1910)   A stockroom clerk for the Katzenberger firm, Feuchtwanger emigrated to the United States in 1939.

Marga (1927) *and Fritz Söltner* (1928)   Marga, daughter of Johann Heilmann, grew up in 19 Spittlertorgraben. In 1949 she married Fritz Söltner, once a member of the Hitler Youth and the son of a Nazi party member.

REPRESENTATIVES OF THE NUREMBERG JEWISH COMMUNITY

Bernhard Kolb (1882)   Kolb became secretary of the Nuremberg congregations in 1923. He was the last chairman of the Nuremberg section of the Association of Jews in the German Reich. He and Leo Katzenberger worked together for many years on the Nuremberg congregations' affairs. Kolb and his family were deported to Theresienstadt. They returned to Nuremberg in 1945 and emigrated to the United States in 1947.

Herbert Kolb (1922)   Son of Bernhard Kolb, Herbert was born in Nuremberg. He was deported to Theresienstadt, along with his parents and sister, Erna, in 1943. After the liberation in 1945, he returned to Nuremberg, but emigrated to the United States in 1947.

Walter Berlin (1887)   Berlin was a lawyer and chairman of the Nuremberg section of the Central Organization of German Citizens of the Jewish Religion. Together with Leo Katzenberger, he supported Alia, which was responsible for resettling more than three thousand Jewish teenagers in Palestine. He emigrated from Germany at the end of 1939.

THE NUREMBERG NAZIS

Julius Streicher (1885)   Streicher, born in Fleinhausen, near Augsburg, was a public-school teacher in Nuremberg. He became founder of the Nuremberg branch of the Nazi Party in 1922, a comrade-in-arms of Adolf Hitler, and participant in the 1923 Munich Putsch. Founder and publisher of the anti-Semitic propaganda sheet *Der Stürmer*, Steicher became the Franconian Gauleiter in 1930. In spite of his good connections with Hitler, he never rose to the highest levels of the party hierarchy. Along with Göring and Dönitz, Streicher was one of twenty-one defendants at the Allied war crimes trials in Nuremberg. He was condemned to death and executed on October 16, 1946.

Benno Martin (1893)   Martin obtained a law degree and became Nuremberg's Chief of Police in 1934. A member of the Nazi Party from May 1933, he joined the SS in April 1934 and attained the rank of Waffen SS general in 1941. He signed the deportation orders at Nuremberg. After the war, Martin was incarcerated until 1949; various legal proceedings against him later ended in acquittal.

Karl Holz (1895)   A Nuremberg municipal employee, Holz was discharged in 1925 because of slander. From 1927 he was editor of *Der Stürmer;* he became Franconia's Deputy Gauleiter in January 1934 and acting Gauleiter in 1942. Holz died in April 1945 during a gun battle with American soldiers in Nuremberg's police headquarters; he may have committed suicide.

Hanns König (1904)   Initially a deliveryman for a cheese producer, König became Streicher's driver and then his adjutant. He was a member of the Nazi Party and SA from the 1920s. In April 1933 he became Nazi advisor to the city council and two years later Councilman and Overseer of the Municipal Theaters. He committed suicide on February 5, 1939.

Willy Liebel (1897)   Son of a newspaper publisher and printing firm owner,

Liebel was a brother-in-arms of Streicher. He learned the printing trade in his father's business and headed the Tannenberg Society in Franconia. In 1929 he was elected Nazi representative on the city council; from 1930 he was leader of the Nazi members on council. In March 1933, the party appointed him Mayor of Nuremberg. He shot himself in April 1945, shortly before the city surrendered.

Georg Haberkern (1899)   Nazi district inspector for Franconia, Haberkern was also chairman of the Nuremberg Nazi party and member of the city council as well as innkeeper of the Blaue Traube, a tavern in Nuremberg's Pfannenschmiedgasse. He was a friend of Judge Oswald Rothaug. Georg Haberkern took poison in a wheatfield near Georgensgemünd in 1945.

JUDGES AND OTHER JURISTS

Oswald Rothaug (1897)   Rothaug was the son of a public-school teacher. He obtained a law degree in Nuremberg. A member of the Nazi Party since 1937, he became an influential informant for the security services of the SS. Rothaug worked initially as state's attorney and judge in Schweinfurt, Hof, and Nuremberg. In 1937 he became Presiding Judge of the Nuremberg Special Court, where he became known as the Executioner. In 1943 he was transferred to the Peoples' Court in Berlin, where he functioned as state's attorney. Rothaug received a life sentence at the Judges' Trial in Nuremberg in 1947 but was released from prison in December 1956. He died in December 1967.

Karl Josef Ferber (1901)   Ferber earned a law degree and became a judge in Nuremberg. Member of the SS from 1934, he joined the Nazi Party in 1937. In addition to sitting on the bench, he worked in the office for racial-political affairs. Ferber became Presiding Judge of the Special Court after Rothaug's departure but was eventually relieved of that post. At the postwar Nuremberg Judges' Trial, Ferber appeared as the star witness against Rothaug. He went on to work in the export trade. Sentenced to three years' imprisonment in 1968 for his role the Katzenberger case, he evaded an appeal trial and possibly stiffer sentence by claiming illness.

Heinz Hugo Hoffmann (1906)   Initially of moderately liberal inclinations, Hoffmann studied in Munich and Geneva and did his thesis work for the Doctor of Law degree in England. He joined the Nazi Party in 1937. In 1968 he was sentenced to two years in prison for his involvement in the

Katzenberger case. Appeals proceedings against him were terminated because he claimed illness. Hoffmann practiced as an attorney for several years thereafter.

Hermann Markl (1908)   Markl studied at the university at Regensburg, and subsequently took a law degree. He became a member of the SA in 1934 and joined the Nazi Party one year later, the same year he became state's attorney in Nuremberg. In the 1940s he functioned as informant for the security services of the SS. After the war, Markl entered Bavarian civil service and advanced to the post of judge at the Superior State Court at Munich. Proceedings against him in the Katzenberger case were suspended because it was said he had acted on orders.

Hans Groben (1907)   Investigational Judge in Nuremberg, Groben wanted to cancel the proceedings against Leo Katzenberger but was overruled by Rothaug, who took control of the case.

Hans Zeuschel (1906)   As a detective on the Nuremberg Police Department Vice Squad, he conducted the investigations into the Katzenberger case. He died in November 1996.

Roland Freisler (1893)   Freisler was secretary of the Justice Ministry of the Reich and, from 1942, president of the People's Court in Berlin. He was killed in an air raid in 1945 in Berlin.

Richard Herz (1894)   Herz was a lawyer and member of Adas Israel. He defended Leo Katzenberger in 1942. On June 18, 1943, Herz and his wife were deported to Auschwitz.

Ludwig Prandl (1920)   A state's attorney in Nuremberg following the war, Prandl dedicated himself to the punishment of those responsible for the murder of Leo Katzenberger. Prandl died in 1987.

Robert Kempner (1899)   Legal advisor to the police in the Prussian Ministry of the Interior, Kempner was discharged from his position by the Nazis. He emigrated to the United States in 1939, worked for the Roosevelt administration, and after the war became the Deputy Chief Prosecutor at the Nuremberg war crimes trials. In later years he sought restitution for Nazi victims in numerous legal proceedings. In the 1973 trial concerning the murder of Leo Katzenberger, Kempner represented Katzenberger's daughters, who were co-plaintiffs. He died in 1993.

NOTES AND SOURCES

To RECONSTRUCT THE LAST YEARS of the life of Leo Katzenberger it was necessary to travel extensively throughout Germany, Israel, and the United States. I have conducted interviews with approximately fifty contemporary witnesses or descendants of people who had been involved in the events of that time, as well as having studied the files and transcripts of nearly all of the investigations and trials connected to the case of Leo Katzenberger.

Among those interviewed were Lilo and Käthe Katzenberger in Israel; and Marga and Walter Weglein, Otto Feuchtwanger, Herbert Kolb, and Baroness Elisabeth Kalnoky in the United States. Colleagues of mine who work in the United States interviewed Abby Mann, the author of the screenplay for *The Judgment at Nuremberg*. In Germany I met with Hilde Katzenberger, Robert Kempner, Jane Lester, Irene Seiler's sister-in-law Vera Seiler, and the neighbor from the Gubener days, Dorothea Tappert. I also spoke with Geo Müller, the buyer of the Spittlertorgraben apartment house, who is now ninety years old; Otto Kranzbühler, the lawyer from the time of the Nuremberg trials; and many others. I was too late, however, to interview detective Hans Zeuschel, who had led the investigations against Katzenberger: He had died ten years before my 1996 visit.

There were many papers to go through: the investigation files and trial transcripts of the postwar years alone spanned eighteen volumes; the transcripts and investigations of the Nuremberg trials of 1947 that pertained to the Katzenberger case come to nearly a thousand pages. After the war the district court in Nuremberg handled the case in several arbitration board procedures against Nazi judges as well as in two trials in 1968 and 1973.

Furthermore I looked into personal and prison files, legal documents and transcripts from restitution trials, old letters and notes from the Katzenberger family, and many maps that contained general source notes on the Nazis, Nuremberg, and the Jewish congregations.

Documents were obtained from the following offices and archives:

Staatsanwaltschaft beim Landgericht Nürnberg; Staatsanwaltschaft beim Landgericht Frankfurt; Amtsgericht Nürnberg; Stadtarchiv Nürnberg; Staatsarchiv Nürnberg; Staatsarchiv München; Bayerisches Hauptstaatsarchiv München; Hessisches Hauptstaatsarchiv Wiesbaden; Thüringisches Hauptstaatsarchiv Weimar; Stadtarchiv Apolda; Bayerisches Landesentschädigungsamt München; Wiedergutmachungsbehörde in Ansbach; KZ-Gedenkstätte Dachau; Bundesarchiv Berlin; Der Bundesbeauftragte für die Unterlagen des Staatssicherheitsdienstes der ehemaligen Deutschen Demokratischen Republik, Berlin; Leo Baeck Institute, New York; YIVO-Institute for Jewish Research, New York; National Archives Washington; Yad Washem Archives, Jerusalem; Archives for the History of the Jewish People, Jerusalem.

I made use of a whole series of records that are for the most part unpublished:
Kolb, Bernhard. "Bericht über die Vorkommnisse bei dem Pogrom der sogenannten »Kristallnacht« am 9./10. November 1938, 1946," manuscript, Leo Baeck Institute, New York.
———. "Betrifft Nürnberg, undatiert," manuscript, Leo Baeck Institute, New York.
———. "Die Juden in Nürnberg, 1946," manuscript, Stadtarchiv Nürnberg.
———. "Geschichte der Familie Kolb, 1947," manuscript, Leo Baeck Institute, New York.
Dr. Blum, Fred. "Über seine Zeit in Nürnberg," manuscript, Stadtarchiv Nürnberg.
Bing, Rudolf. "Mein Leben in Deutschland vor und nach dem 30. Januar 1933," manuscript, Leo Baeck Institute, New York.
Goldstein, Kurt. "Retrospect and Reflections," manuscript, Leo Baeck Institute, New York.
Seldner, David. "Reise in die jüdische Vergangenheit," unpublished manuscript, 1997.
Bal, Kurt. "Aus der Zionistischen Vereinigung Berlin, 1945," manuscript, Yad Washem Archives, Jerusalem.

I also drew information from the following old publications:
"Nürnberg-Fürther Israelitisches Gemeindeblatt, Jahrgänge 1930 bis 1938," Leo Baeck Institute, New York.
"Wichtige Mitteilungen der Israelitischen Kultusgemeinde Nürnberg, 1938 bis 1943," Yad Washem Archives, Jerusalem.

Der Stürmer. Various issue years, Stadtarchiv Nürnberg.

"Jüdische Verbrecher — Zur Strecke gebracht von der Nürnberger Polizei,
»dem Führer im Kampf gegen den Weltfeind Juda«." Commemorative
publication by the chief of police of Nürnberg-Fürth, delivered on
February 12, 1938 on the occasion of Julius Streicher's birthday, Yad
Washem Research Center, Jerusalem.

"Geheime Reichssache: Bericht der von Göring eingesetzten
Prüfungskommission über die im Gau Franken zwischen dem 9.
November 1938 und dem 9. Februar 1939 vorgenommenen Arisierungen
jüdischer Betriebe, 1939," Nürnberger Stadtchronik während des Dritten
Reiches.

The following published sources were helpful.

Regarding Nuremberg

Fritzsch, Robert. *Nürnberg unterm Hakenkreuz, Fotografierte Zeitgeschichte.*
Düsseldorf: Droste-Verlag, 1983.

———. *Nürnberg im Krieg, Fotografierte Zeitgeschichte.* Düsseldorf: Droste-
Verlag, 1984.

Grieser, Utho. "Himmlers Mann in Nürnberg, Der Fall Benno Martin: Eine
Studie zur Struktur des Dritten Reiches in der »Stadt der
Reichsparteitage«" Nürnberger Werkstücke zur Stadt- und
Landesgeschichte. Schriftenreihe des Stadtarchivs Nürnberg, 1974.

Hambrecht, Rainer. "Der Aufstieg der NSDAP in Mittel- und Oberfranken
(1925–1933)" Nürnberger Werkstücke zur Stadt- und Landesgeschichte.
Schriftenreihe des Stadtarchivs Nürnberg Band 17.

"Konzentrationslager. Lebenswelt und Umfeld." Dachauer Hefte, Studien
und Dokumente zur Geschichte der nationalsozialistischen
Konzentrationslager, Heft 12, 1996

Müller, Arnd. *Geschichte der Juden in Nürnberg 1146–1945, Beiträge zur
Geschichte und Kultur der Stadt Nürnberg.* Selbstverlag der
Stadtbibliothek Nürnberg, 1968.

Ralf Rossmeissl. *Jüdische Heimat Roth,* Roth, 1997.

Schicksal jüdischer Mitbürger in Nürnberg 1933–1945, Dokumentation bear-
beitet vom Stadtarchiv Nürnberg, Selbstverlag des Stadtrats zu
Nürnberg, 1985.

Schultheis, Herbert and Isaac E. Wahler. *Bilder und Akten der Gestapo
Würzburg über die Judendeportationen 1941–1943.* Bad Neustädter
Beiträge zur Geschichte und Heimatkunde Frankens, Band 5. Bad
Neustadt a. d. Saale: Rötter Druck und Verlag GmbH, 1988.

Schwarz, Klaus-Dieter. *Weltkrieg und Revolution in Nürnberg, Ein Beitrag zur Geschichte der Arbeiterbewegung.* Stuttgart: Klett-Verlag, 1971.

Centrum Industriekultur Nürnberg. *Unterm Hakenkreuz, Alltag in Nürnberg 1933–1945.* München: Heinrich Hugendubel Verlag, 1993.

General

Adam, Uwe Friedrich. "Zur Entstehung und Auswirkung des Reichsbürgergesetzes." Aus Politik und Zeitgeschichte. Beilage zur Wochenzeitung *Das Parlament,* November 1985.

Battenberg, Friedrich. *Das europäische Zeitalter der Juden, Band II: Von 1650 bis 1945.* Darmstadt: Wissenschaftliche Buchgesellschaft, 1990.

Benz, Wolfgang. *Die Juden in Deutschland 1933–1945, Leben unter national-sozialistischer Herrschaft.* München: Verlag C. H. Beck, 1996.

Beuys, Barbara. *Heimat und Hölle, Jüdisches Leben in Europa durch zwei Jahrtausende.* Reinbek: Rowohlt Verlag, 1996.

"Deutschlandberichte der Sozialdemokratischen Partei Deutschlands (SOPADE) 1934–1940." Frankfurt am Main, 1980.

Jäckel, Eberhard, Peter Longerich, and Julius H. Schoeps, *Enzyklopädie des Holocaust, Die Verfolgung und Ermordung der europäischen Juden.* München: Piper, 1998.

Friedländer, Saul. *Nazi Germany and the Jews, The Years of Persecution, 1933–1939.* New York: HarperCollins Publishers, 1997.

Friedrich, Jörg. *Freispruch für die Nazi-Justiz, Die Urteile gegen NS-Richter seit 1948—eine Dokumentation.* Reinbek: Rowohlt, 1983.

———. *Kalte Amnestie, NS-Täter in der Bundesrepublik.* Frankfurt am Main: Fischer-Taschenbuch-Verlag, 1984.

Gebhard, Paul and Klaus Michael Mallmann. *Die Gestapo im Zweiten Weltkrieg. `Heimatfront` und besetztes Europa.* Darmstadt: Wissenschaftliche Buchgesellschaft, 2000.

Genschel, Helmut. *Die Verdrängung der Juden aus der Wirtschaft im Dritten Reich.* Göttingen: Musterschmidt Verlag, 1966.

Goldhagen, Daniel Jonah. *Hitlers willige Vollstrecker.* Berlin: Siedler Verlag, 1996. (First published in the U.S. as *Hitler's Willing Executioners: Ordinary Germans and the Holocaust.* New York: Knopf, 1996.)

Gruchmann, Lothar. "»Blutschutzgesetz« und Justiz, Entstehung und Anwendung des Nürnberger Gesetzes vom 15. September 1935" Aus Politik und Zeitgeschichte, Beilage zur Wochenzeitung *Das Parlament,* November 1985.

Haffner, Sebastian. *Germany: Jekyll & Hyde, 1939—Deutschland von innen betrachtet.* Berlin: Verlag 1900, 1996.

Hamann, Brigitte. *Hitlers Wien, Lehrjahre eines Diktators*. München: Piper Verlag, 1996. (Published in the UK as *Hitler's Vienna: A Dictator's Apprenticeship*. Oxford: University Press, 2000.)

Hilberg, Raul. *Täter, Opfer, Zuschauer, Die Vernichtung der Juden 1933–1945*. Frankfurt am Main: Fischer Taschenbuch Verlag, 1992. (Published in the United States as *Perpetrators, Victims, Bystanders: Jewish Catastrophe 1933–1945*. New York: Perennial, 1993.)

Kempner, Robert M. W. *Ankläger einer Epoche, Lebenserinnerungen*. Berlin: Ullstein Verlag, 1986.

Klemperer, Viktor. *Ich will Zeugnis ablegen bis zum letzten, Tagebücher 1933–1941, Tagebücher 1942–1945*. Berlin: Aufbau-Verlag, 1995. (Published in the United States as *I Will Bear Witness: A Diary of the Nazi Years: 1942–1945*. New York: Modern Library, 1999.)

Knopp, Guido. *Hitlers Helfer*. München: C. Bertelsmann, 1996. (Published in the United Kingdom as *Hitler's Henchmen*. Gloucestershire: Sutton Publishing, 2000.)

Kropat, Wolf-Arno. *Kristallnacht in Hessen, Der Judenpogrom vom November 1938*. Wiesbaden: Kommission für die Geschichte der Juden in Hessen, 1988.

Müller, Ingo. *Furchtbare Juristen*. München: Kindler-Verlag, 1987.

Das Nürnberger Juristenurteil (Allgemeiner Teil). Sonderveröffentlichungen des Zentral-Justizblattes für die Britische Zone. Hamburg: Rechts- und Staatswissenschaftlicher Verlag, 1948.

Robinsohn, Hans. *Justiz als politische Verfolgung, Die Rechtssprechung in »Rassenschandefällen« beim Landgericht Hamburg 1936–1943*. Stuttgart: Deutsche Verlagsanstalt, 1977.

Rossel, Seymour. *The Holocaust, The World and the Jews, 1933–1945*. Springfield, NJ: Behrman House Inc., 1992.

Schoeps, Julius H. *Antisemitismus, Vorurteile und Mythen*. München: Piper, 1995.

———. *Ein Volk von Mördern?* Hamburg: Hoffmann und Campe, 1996.

Walk, Joseph. *Das Sonderrecht für die Juden im NS-Staat*. Heidelberg: C. F. Müller Verlag, 1996.

Wollenberg, Jörg. *"Niemand war dabei und keiner hat's gewußt," Die deutsche Öffentlichkeit und die Judenverfolgung 1933–1945*. München: Piper, 1989.

Wyden, Peter. *Stella*. Göttingen: Steidl Verlag, 1993.

The household community at 19 Spittlertorgra

1 Irene Scheffler, later Seiler   **5** Ös

2 Kleylein family   **6** He

3 Weglein family   **7** Mä

4 Travel agency   **8** Bu

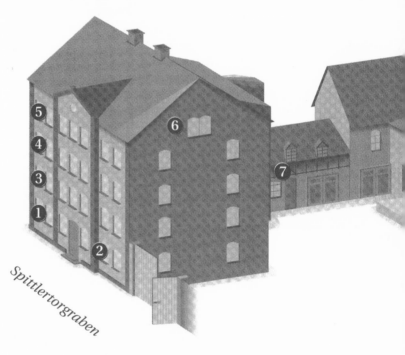